Integrating Performance and Budgets: The Budget Office of Tomorrow

IBM Center for
**The Business
of Government**

THE IBM CENTER FOR THE BUSINESS OF GOVERNMENT BOOK SERIES

Series Editors: Mark A. Abramson and Albert Morales

The IBM Center Series on The Business of Government explores new approaches to improving the effectiveness of government at the federal, state, and local levels. The Series is aimed at providing cutting-edge knowledge to government leaders, academics, and students about the management of government in the 21st century.

Publications in the series include:

Integrating Performance and Budgets: The Budget Office of Tomorrow

EDITED BY

JONATHAN D. BREUL
IBM GLOBAL BUSINESS SERVICES
AND
CARL MORAVITZ
IBM GLOBAL BUSINESS SERVICES

ROWMAN & LITTLEFIELD PUBLISHERS, INC.
Lanham • Boulder • New York • Toronto • Plymouth, UK

ROWMAN & LITTLEFIELD PUBLISHERS, INC.

Published in the United States of America
by Rowman & Littlefield Publishers, Inc.
A wholly owned subsidary of The Rowman & Littlefield Publishing Group, Inc.
4501 Forbes Boulevard, Suite 200, Lanham, Maryland 20706
www.rowmanlittlefield.com

Estover Road
Plymouth PL6 7PY
United Kingdom

British Library Cataloguing in Publication Information Available

Library of Congress Cataloging-in-Publication Data:
Integrating performance and budgets : the budget office of tomorrow / edited by Jonathan
D. Breul, Carl Moravitz.
    p. cm.
Includes bibliographical references.
ISBN-13: 978-0-7425-5831-1 (cloth : alk. paper)
ISBN-13: 978-0-7425-5832-8 (pbk. : alk. paper)
ISBN-10: 0-7425-5831-2 (cloth : alk. paper)
ISBN-10: 0-7425-5832-0 (pbk. : alk. paper)
1. Government productivity. 2. Budget. 3. Administrative agencies—Management. 4.
Customer services. 5. Expenditures, Public. I. Breul, Jonathan D. II. Moravitz, Carl,
1945– JF1525.P67I53 2006
    352.4'8—dc22
                            2006036675
Printed in the United States of America

To Hannah and Sarah Breul

and

Carla and Jason Martin

TABLE OF CONTENTS

CHAPTER ONE

The Budget Office of Tomorrow

Jonathan D. Breul
Partner, IBM Global Business Services,
and Senior Fellow, IBM Center for The Business of Government

Carl Moravitz
Managing Consultant, IBM Global Business Services

Introduction

Governments are under increasing pressure to produce—and to demonstrate—results in terms of their mission. Over the last decade, countries around the world have undertaken reforms with the aim of improving the relevance and effectiveness of public services and the quality of public sector management. A key aspect of most reform strategies has been a focus on mission results and outcomes.

A focus on results and outcomes can help enhance government's capacity to assess competing claims for budgetary resources by arming decision makers with better information both on the results of individual programs as well as on entire portfolios of policies and programs addressing common goals. The use of performance information is not an end in itself, but rather a means to support better decision making, leading to improved performance and accountability. While performance budgeting will never answer the vexing resource trade-off questions involving political choice, it does hold the promise of modifying and informing policy decisions and resource allocation by shifting the focus of debate from inputs to the program outcomes and results that are crucial to an organization's success and to the nation's security.

This book showcases attempts by federal and state governments, as well as a mix of developed and developing countries, to introduce performance or results-oriented budgeting and performance management. In this chapter, we describe how these developments are changing and reshaping the budget office of tomorrow. This is followed by a collection of four reports for the IBM Center for The Business of Government that explores the use of budgeting, performance, and cost information at different levels of government.

In Chapter Two, Philip G. Joyce focuses on the U.S. federal government. Beginning with an overview and history of performance budgeting, Professor Joyce presents a comprehensive view of how performance information can be used at the various stages of the budget process, including preparation, approval, execution, and audit and evaluation. Joyce finds that previous studies of the use of performance information in the federal budget process have tended to focus almost exclusively on uses by the U.S. Office of Management and Budget (OMB) and Congress. He argues that this is an incomplete view, because it fails to recognize the opportunities to use performance information at other important stages of the budget process. He also describes how performance-based information is used at departmental and agency levels.

In Chapter Three, Julia Melkers and Katherine Willoughby explore how many of the same issues face state governments. Their research examines the extent to which states are effectively integrating planning and budgets, as well as assessing progress made in that area. Melkers and Willoughby describe why performance initiatives continue to be touted by both legislatures and central leadership in the states. They describe which components of performance measurement and performance-related initiatives have been most useful in the states. They also identify key trends. First, the integration of performance-based budgeting efforts has occurred along with other public management initiatives such as strategic planning. Second, states now appear prepared to stay the course and continue to enhance their performance management systems for broader application.

In Chapter Four, Burt Perrin looks at the issues of performance measurement on a global basis. Perrin provides substantial evidence that internationally, national governments are moving toward a results-oriented approach in a wide variety of contexts. Until recently, the process and performance of governments has been judged largely on inputs, activities, and outputs. Based on a two-day forum sponsored by the World Bank and the IBM Center involving officials from six developed and six developing countries, Perrin identifies state-of-the-art practices and thinking that go beyond the current literature. He identifies what needs to be done in terms of both small steps and large steps that have had success in reorienting government systems to an outcome approach. Perrin makes it clear that there is not one "correct" or best model that could or should apply to all countries. Indeed, the political and social context, past history, and other factors require an approach tailored to the situation in each country. Both developed and developing countries have demonstrated that it is possible to move toward an outcome orientation that places emphasis on results that count to citizens.

In the fifth and final chapter, Lloyd Blanchard takes a different tact, looking in detail at how two federal agencies have successfully linked performance, full cost, and efficiency information. Blanchard begins with a description of the statutory and conceptual foundations of costing requirements. He follows with a framework for integrating costs and performance. Then, drawing upon published reports and articles, as well as his own experience leading reform efforts at the National Aeronautics and Space Administration (NASA) and the Small Business Administration (SBA), he tells how these two very different federal agencies successfully implemented performance costing methodologies. According to Blanchard, NASA's full cost initiative relies on a statistical-based approach to allocating indirect costs that cannot be directly attributed to program outputs. SBA's survey-based approach uses an activity-based costing model. Blanchard concludes his report with practical recommendations based on the advantages and disadvantages of the two approaches and specific steps that agencies can take to improve existing procedures and policies.

Budgeting Today

Until recently, the performance of most public programs, and of their managers, has been judged largely on inputs and activities—particularly on how their allocated budget has been spent, and, perhaps, on the types of activites undertaken and outputs produced. Government too often is preoccupied with *process* and with following the rules, without adequate focus on the *benefits* that actually arise from public sector expenditure and activities. Measures of effectiveness across organizations and functions remain a major challenge.

Integrating performance and results with decision making for budget resources has long been a goal in the U.S. federal government. During the past decade, Congress and the executive branch have increased their emphasis on improving management across all departments and agencies. A series of legislative proposals and changes to the federal budget guidance have highlighted the presentation of performance and results information for the annual investment of public dollars. The Government Performance and Results Act (GPRA) of 1993 was first implemented on a government-wide basis in 1997 with the fiscal year 1999 budget. GPRA fundamentally changes the focus of federal management and accountability from a preoccupation with inputs and processes to a greater emphasis on the outcomes and results that programs should be achieving. It brings together managers, workers, and stakeholders to focus on (1) the purpose of programs, (2) the means to achieve it, and (3) progress toward achievement.

More recently, the George W. Bush administration has made a focus on performance the centerpiece of the President's Management Agenda. OMB has been pushing agencies to integrate budget and performance, using the Program Assessment Rating Tool, or PART, to assess program performance and consider that information during the annual budget review process.

Performance Budgeting

Performance budgeting seeks to increase decision makers' understanding of the links between requested resources and expected performance results. Such integration is critical to sustain and institutionalize performance and management reforms. Figure 1.1 illustrates some of the many activities that can support performance in the budget process and play a role in overall performance management of the organization.

Performance information can inform the policy debate and help determine the agenda. In this way, questions of outcomes, and what forms or approaches are likely to be effective or not, can be taken into consideration in the allocation of resources. Performance budgeting can help enhance

Figure 1.1: Overview of Performance Budgeting in Government

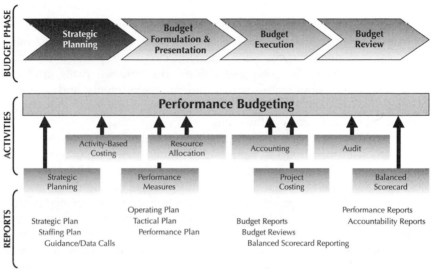

Source: IBM Center for The Business of Government.

the government's capacity to assess competing claims for taxpayer dollars by arming decision makers with better information both on the results of individual programs as well as on entire portfolios of policies, programs, and other tools designed to address common goals. At a minimum, linking performance to budgets can illustrate what benefits arise from expenditures. However, a mechanistic link between performance outcomes and budget alloactions is neither possible nor desirable. Nonetheless, information about performance can play a significant role in the overall budget process. Goals, objectives, outputs, and outcomes can be tracked at every level to allow for continual assessment and reassessment of the allocation of resources in relation to those elements in as close to real time as possible.

Linking budget formulation and budget execution has many benefits for organizational improvement. First, it helps the budgeting process become a major decision-making vehicle, supporting an organization's development, presentation, and execution of budget and performance requests at all levels of review. Second, it connects assessments of agency resource requirements and performance results, providing valuable linkages to the execution results of available funding. Last, it provides more valued analyses and associations of results in budget-process decision making and in the linkages between formulation and execution phases. It can bring additional meaning to an organization's internal financial plan development processes as approved funding is distributed to program managers.

Aligning Budget, Performance, and Cost 'Silos'

Implementation of performance budgeting is proving to be deceptively difficult. One important reason is that budgeting, performance planning, and cost accounting systems often operate in separate, parallel "silos." As Figure 1.2 illustrates, budget presentations, performance plans, and cost accounting vary considerably across federal departments and agencies, depending on the missions, organizational arrangements, and other specific operational characteristics of the entity.

Federal departments and agencies have developed many methods to link their plans with their budgets. Figure 1.3 illustrates how some agencies link budget information with performance goals and objectives. Looking at the illustration (with performance on the left and budget on the right), one can see how agencies can connect strategic objectives and performance goals to agency budget accounts and program activities. For instance, a general goal may be broad and large in scope, composed of smaller strategic objectives. These more focused objectives rely on the accomplishment of even more specific performance goals. As one moves to the budget side of the illustration, the tactical program activities are tied to larger agency accounts. This is the structure that needs to be in place prior to beginning a performance-based budgeting initiative.

Most federal agencies have not yet linked all three components of performance planning (budget, performance, and costs) to form a complete picture of their performance and their budget. Some only have links for performance goals to program activities, while others are linking performance goals to budget accounts. Most are connecting their performance plans with lower or more specific levels of their budget structures, such as their accounts.

Figure 1.2: Budget, Performance, and Cost 'Silos'

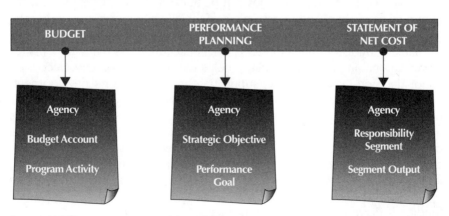

Source: *U.S. Government Accountability Office.*[1]

Figure 1.3: Agencies Use Multiple Approaches to Link Performance Planning and Budget

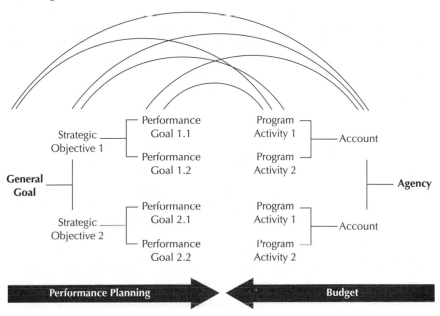

Source: *U.S. Government Accountability Office.*[2]

Similarly, departments and agencies use multiple approaches to link plans and net cost. The approaches vary significantly, with most agencies linking costs primarily to the highest levels of their goal structure.

It is unlikely that a single approach of relating performance and financial reporting will fit the variety of organizational contexts, missions, performance planning, and financial management structures. Indeed, the concept of performance budgeting will continue to evolve, and no single definition or approach can be expected to encompass the range of needs and changing interests of federal decision makers.

Agencies will continue to develop their own approaches to linking resources and results within their unique environments to meet their performance management challenges. Ultimately, the need to translate the planned and actual use of resources into concrete and measurable results remains an essential step in achieving a more results-oriented government. Moreover, the heterogeneity of the government suggests that sustained efforts and attention will be the hallmark of long-term success. Long-term connectivity of planning and budget ensures careful monitoring of strategic planning, performance management, and budget management processes—and the appropriate handoffs of information and results.

'Stuck' in Electronic Spreadsheets

How then do budget offices contend with these various and sometimes competing sets of data? In the past they depended on electronic spreadsheets and homemade budget models. Even today, electronic spreadsheets remain the de facto standard for day-to-day quantitative analysis. They are easy to understand and use; nearly all staff have some proficiency in their use.

If electronic spreadsheets have worked so well in the past, what has changed? One significant development is that most public sector organizations now have enterprise resource planning (ERP) systems, which provide copious quantities of transactional accounting data. Increasingly, budget offices are developing "dashboards" and "scorecards" to obtain budgetary and financial analysis of their organization's programs. Frequently, they are able to track key performance indicators on desktop, web-based portals. Many of these new tools provide more than a "flat file" capability of electronic spreadsheets. Software capable of collecting and manipulating "relational databases" is giving new impetus to change.

One particularly popular development in the federal government is the use of red, yellow, and green scorecards. Shortly after President George W. Bush issued his President's Management Agenda, OMB developed a quarterly "traffic light" scorecard to track the status and progress of each department and major agency. A red dot on this color-coded report signaled that an organization was failing to meet government-wide standards and needed to develop an aggressive corrective action plan. Not surprisingly, most departments have begun issuing their scorecards for their own components, to track how they are making progress.

At the same time, department executives, policy officials at OMB, and program managers themselves are pressuring budget offices to produce more detailed budgets, capital investment business cases, and performance data in the form of program outputs and outcomes. Web-enabled or portal-accessed performance scoreboards and dashboards are becoming a standard feature in budget offices. These techniques have eliminated many ad hoc data calls and the back-and-forth-exchange of electronic spreadsheets to populate congressional, OMB, and departmental data calls. Properly configured, these new systems not only collect the requested historical data, but permit forecasting and re-forecasting under various planning assumptions. This capability permits budget offices to model and test the impact of policy changes or assumptions on the fly, based on a continuous inflow of financial and non-financial performance data, without having to go back to program offices with a new data call.

A number of further new developments in ERP and business intelligence (BI) software are opening up new possibilities to link cost, performance, and budget information in ways that support policy decision makers and program managers. Executive information and decision support systems have been around for years. What is different now is that both ERP and BI software are beginning to offer the integration necessary to grab data from various software programs and databases. Leading software firms such as SAS Institute, Armstrong-Laing, Cognos, and Hyperion have developed or acquired planning and budgeting capabilities. Likewise, ERP firms such as SAP and Oracle have added budget formulation to their existing capabilities. Oracle, for example, has announced a new suite of tools and applications that will include query and analysis, enterprise reporting, dashboards, work flow, business activity monitoring, and integration with traditional electronic spreadsheets. At the same time, SAS has announced new customer data integration tools designed to synchronize, consolidate, and manage information from across an enterprise.

Budget offices can now support fuller implementations of performance-based budgeting, including consolidating information sources and improving analytical capacities. The business process changes that have the potential to yield the most immediate benefits come in the areas of simplification and standardization. Figure 1.4 illustrates how highly effective organizations are moving to improve their operations.

Figure 1.4: Improved Processes Enable Performance Budgeting

Budget Offices Today

- Offices focused on a larger set of operational and transactional activities, limiting the investment in decision support and analytics
- Control often too centralized, with offices shouldering program office accountability
- Uneven criteria and standards in application of formulation and execution processes
- Information resides in multiple locations, requiring manual entries in separate analytical tools
- Systems and software for expanded analysis not available to support organization
- Routine documents consume excessive time and interrupt other processes
- Significant staff energy investment in effectively tracking and managing document productions

Tomorrow

- Programs empowered with spending autonomy and accountability
- Barriers and roadblocks removed from agency operations
- Improved budget office management of existing resources
- Budget office's focus shifted from day-to-day transactions to broader oversight
- Budget capacities redirected to analytics, exception reporting reviews, and strong budget development decision support
- Criteria and standards implemented to meet and ensure its accountability responsibilities for oversight of statewide resources and assets
- Budget office maintains a process of continuous improvement to monitor all systems and processes
- Budget office makes available modern tools and equipment to support organization's ongoing business requirements

Source: IBM Global Business Services.

Research findings in the 2005 IBM Global CFO Survey[3] indicate that highly effective finance organizations implement standard policies, common processes, process simplification, and functional best practices enterprise-wide at a higher rate than organizations that are less effective at driving insights across the enterprise. The adoption rate of process simplifications among highly effective finance organizations is twice as high, and their adoption rate for functional best practices is almost three times as high, as that of less effective organizations.

The need for and benefits of these sorts of changes are every bit as applicable to budget offices as they are to finance organizations. The important end state is to tie together the total process of developing, securing, and managing budget resources in total support of decision making and resource management capacities over time. Assessing program performance is a key element to successful financial management and effective decision making for an organization. The challenge of translating this objective into policy and practice proves to be more difficult and time-consuming than some might assume, particularly when organizations define their mission as merely the conduct of activities and the development of reports. Success in setting out the vision often depends on an organization's ability to connect its key activities and processes to the overall management, performance, and results associated with the mission entrusted to them.

The Way Forward—Shaping the Budget Office of Tomorrow

Resources are scarce, and the way in which they are allocated is crucial to an organization's overall effectiveness. According to Comptroller General of the United States David Walker, "Credible outcome-based performance information is absolutely critical to foster the kind of debate that is needed. Linking performance information to budgeting can greatly improve the budget debate by changing the kinds of questions asked and information made available to decision makers."[4]

The demands placed on budget offices continue to expand. Budget officials are increasingly being asked to deliver insight across the three top areas of importance for their organization: budget, performance, and costs. In the past, practical limitations forced them to focus primarily on the budget, but process and technology improvements now make it possible to do more. To stand still in today's complex world is to go backward. The well-known cliché of *"promises made, promises kept"* can now be embraced as governments move beyond traditional ways of doing business and provide new levels of accountability.

Gaps Between the Importance of Performance Information and the Ability of Budget Offices to Deliver It

The IBM 2005 Global CFO Study[5] surveyed 889 private and public sector chief financial officers and senior finance professionals in 74 countries. The study shows that finance organizations that are highly effective can attribute their achievements to moving to a more predictive role of providing dynamic business insight to decision makers. It underscores a transition from primarily stewarding information to leveraging that information to deliver predictive business insight to decision makers across the organization.

The IBM Global CFO Study confirms that finance organizations are shifting from transactional activities to stronger decision support and analytics. Figure 1.5 illustrates this trend.

The IBM CFO Study is instructive for public sector budget offices, because they too are undergoing similar changes. Like finance offices, many budget organizations have gaps between the growing importance placed on delivering "insight" on performance and their ability to deliver it. Such gaps are often driven by a lack of standardization, fragmented performance information, and inconsistent tools/applications. According to the IBM CFO Study, highly effective finance and budget organizations are optimizing decision support to enhance performance insight. These organizations integrate transparent performance metrics consistently throughout the organization. In addition, they define quantifiable relationships between business drivers and scorecard/dashboard metrics to enable predictive analysis and improve the accuracy of performance outcome forecasts.

Figure 1.5: Finance's Workload Distribution

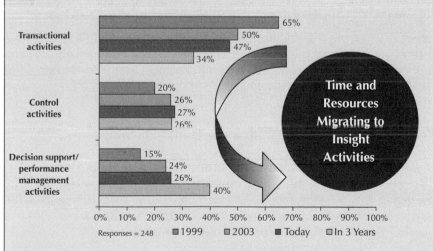

Source: IBM Global Business Services, The Global CFO Study 2005.

Recommendation 1: Get the Process Right, Then Automate

There is compelling evidence from the private sector that the order in which new technology is deployed and the alteration of business processes is undertaken is critical. In 2003, Cisco conducted a study[6] to measure the impact of technology on 300 diverse organizations across a number of industries. The Cisco study showed that network-enabled applications, when coupled with appropriate changes in business processes, resulted in four to five times greater improvement in productivity than just using Internet business applications. Deploying network-enabled applications first, however, sometimes resulted in increases in costs of up to 9 percent. Modifying business processes first and then deploying the new applications reduces costs by up to 30 percent. The key lesson for agencies intent on transformation is that throwing money at leading-edge equipment and software without first defining the necessary associated changes in business processes will fail to deliver desired productivity improvements and could significantly increase costs.

An important lesson is that organizations must first re-engineer business processes to enhance productivity and efficiency. Finance and budget officials who have developed new performance management systems have learned that it is best to first make changes to their budget process before trying to install a new system.

Technology can play a significant role in organizational improvements. If a new or improved process is to be implemented, technology can be a significant change driver. Technology, however, is not a complete answer in and of itself. Technology should be viewed as a process enabler, leading to better performance by all levels of an organization. Business users should lead the effort to develop the specifications needed to use technology in their functional roles. Only then can individuals truly benefit to the fullest extent from the addition of technology in the workplace. Unfortunately, organizations often turn first to technology before fixing broken processes, which in the long run may sub-optimize the ultimate benefit of technology investments.

Recommendation 2: Integrate Budgets into Planning

A robust planning process is critical to public sector organizations in their efforts to direct the total stewardship of dollars entrusted to them. Integrating this into the fuller and more time-consuming elements of the budget process is an important next step. The box on page 13 identifies five tips for integrating budgets into the planning process.

Five Tips for Integrating Budgets into the Planning Process

1. Develop a strategic plan that clearly links an agency's mission to each activity and program.
2. Create a performance plan with objectives that support the strategic goals.
3. Make budget decisions that support the performance plan to the extent that resources can be made available and, in the process, program priorities set.
4. Construct budgets and related justifications that address the strategic context and support the performance plan.
5. Periodically assess progress against the plan, analyzing how various inputs influenced performance.

The key to making these tips a reality and to more effectively implementing an organization's performance management goals hinges on the use of more robust analytical tools, which will permit:

- Expanded sensitivity analysis
- Simplification and standardization of processes
- Standardization of data across accounting and budgeting systems

Such tools provide budget offices with the expanded potential for smoother movement not only from planning to budget development, but also to financial planning oversight and, *ultimately*, to assessments of the results.

Budget offices can also pursue strong standards on data and systems to position themselves for effective implementation of such performance management and budgeting enhancements at a future time. Maximum effectiveness of strategic planning initiatives—and, potentially, future performance management processes—requires *full engagement of frontline staff as well as senior management* to ensure full rollout of policies and priorities and full realization of the potential that performance-based budgeting can offer. New tools and technology could allow an organization to better:

- Move smoothly between formulation and execution during internal financial plan development and distribute approved funding to agencies/ program managers
- Integrate with other financial processes
- Increase the ability to receive financial and performance results for use in developing budget proposals and analyzing choices
- Support spreadsheet capabilities vital to budget offices while providing automated and integrated capabilities

The potential rewards for making this vision real include:

- *Resources focused* on the most critical and important policy, decision making, and analysis

- *Improved analytics* and decision making about the most effective way to use limited resources
- *Improved operations* by linking budget, financial planning, and results over time
- *Increased understanding* and communication about critical issues and priorities on statewide management of resources
- *Strengthened accountability* for program decisions that affect budget priorities and the delivery of results during execution
- *Connected* budget decisions, financial planning, and results to create a management-focused organization that drives decisions and priorities and directs and monitors delivery of those priorities
- *Improved systems and processes* in support of the budget process, allowing for better targeting of decision making, priority needs, and key decision support capabilities in the management and oversight of available funds

Recommendation 3: Adopt Best Practices

According to the IBM Global CFO Survey, most public and private sector finance organizations continue to shift work from transactional to analytical and decision support activities. Recognizing the need to maintain strong internal controls, organizational investments in control activities have remained almost constant over the last few years, with a major shift between transactional and decision support/analysis.

High-Performing Organizations

High-performing organizations realize the importance of focusing on the contribution of their activities and reports to their overall performance management objectives. Focusing too heavily on transactional and operational activities detracts from the overall vision of mapping initial strategic planning processes to the ultimate management and review of invested resources.

High-performing finance organizations are moving from a role of static reporting and data stewardship to a more predictive role of providing dynamic business insight to decision makers. In the past, practical limitations forced finance organizations to focus primarily on operating and control activities, but process and technology improvements now make it possible to do more. In fact, experience is showing that ensuring strong financial management discipline in operational responsibilities allows organizations to invest more of their resources to provide high-value decision support and strengthen their role as trusted advisers.

Over the long term, high-performing finance organizations leverage change and improvement in four broad ways. First, high-performing organizations simplify, standardize, and optimize policies and business rules. Second, they integrate information across the enterprise. Third, they expand overall oversight. Fourth, and finally, they optimize decision support. These focus areas (see Figure 1.6) provide strong insight into the process improvements possible over time.

Just as finance organizations are changing, budget offices need to change, too. The important theme that runs through all four areas is the process of constantly updating strategies to reflect changes to business goals and adopting executive ownership of processes and data. Without developing an overall strategy for streamlining transactions and operations with the goal of strengthening decision support, organizations will struggle constantly to provide insights, primarily relying on time-consuming manual consolidation of static spreadsheets. A common result is time wasted discussing the veracity of the data instead of focusing on the information provided and analyzing it to provide predictive insights. Increasing the use of common processes and pursuing simplification can have positive effects throughout the organization.

Figure 1.6: Leveraging Change and Improvement—Key Best Practices

Simplify, Standardize, and Optimize

- Standardize policies and business rules
- Move to common processes and simplify processes
- Use functional best practices, where appropriate
- Utilize enhanced finance and budgeting tools
- Optimize delivery methods of products and information
- Seek common finance platforms and data standards
- Utilize data warehouses for management of data

Integrate Information

- Create a governance structure to ensure common information standards
- Consolidate and integrate actual, budget, and forecast data
- Drive ownership and mapping of processes
- Manage external data sources

Expand Overall Oversight

- Drive understanding of control points
- Automate processes to improve controls
- Provide business activity monitoring through use of operational dashboards
- Use analytical tools to support actual work flow activities and processes

Optimize Decision Support

- Use streamlined, integrated budgeting process
- Utilize collaborative planning and decision-making process
- Employ rolling forecasts, based on relevant business events
- Focus on exception-based reporting and analytics
- Create enterprise-wide reporting/access procedures
- Use linked and aligned scorecard metrics cascaded down
- Identify and assess business opportunities and synergies
- Implement sound costing and analytical methods
- Create centers of excellence around client needs

Source: IBM Global Business Services, The Global CFO Study 2005.

Reviews of highly effective finance organizations show that these organizations use key best practice activities, which include:

- Simplifying and standardizing processes
- Optimizing decision support activities using integrated and role-based metrics and exception reporting
- Driving organizational activities from compliance/control functions in the direction of analytics/business intelligence (while ensuring appropriate balance between the two)
- Expanding the use of dashboards and analytics to focus risk/reward planning and decision support

Organizations are directing work in the areas of:

- Integrating information and related analysis, recognizing the need for process improvement and common information standards and tools
- Adopting business performance processes, focusing on exception-based reporting and analytics, and freeing up time and resources for budget development and analysis as well as planning and monitoring
- Adopting business performance tools in an effort to drive greater value from current business processes
- Automating processes and acquiring automated tools to enable risk analysis—supporting the development of real-time dashboards/portals and alerts to support risk assessment and decision making

This overall shift in direction and capacity from transactional activities to stronger management and oversight and increased analytical capacities is the primary direction for strengthening budget office capabilities. Such a shift supports not only improved operations but, more importantly, improved capabilities to measure performance, align resources with strategic objectives, and monitor performance through increased analytical capacities.

Endnotes

1. Based on a similar chart in U.S. General Accounting Office. *Managing for Results: Agency Progress in Linking Performance Plans with Budgets and Financial Statements.* GAO-02-236, January 2002. http://www.gao.gov/new.items/d02236.pdf.

2. Based on a similar chart in U.S. General Accounting Office. *Managing for Results: Agency Progress in Linking Performance Plans with Budgets and Financial Statements.* GAO-02-236, January 2002. http://www.gao.gov/new.items/d02236.pdf.

3. "The Agile CFO: Acting on Business Insight," (2005), IBM Global Services, Somers, NY.

4. Comptroller General David Walker, GAO-02-1106T, Performance Budgeting: Opportunities and Challenges, September 19, 2002.

5. "The Agile CFO: Acting on Business Insight," (2005), IBM Global Services, Somers, NY.

6. "Net Impact: United States Private Sector, First Edition," Cisco Executive Thought Leadership Research Studies.

CHAPTER TWO

Linking Performance and Budgeting: Opportunities in the Federal Budget Process

Philip G. Joyce
Associate Professor of Public Policy and Public Administration
School of Public Policy and Public Administration
The George Washington University

This report was originally published in 2003.

Introduction

Government reformers have been trying to increase the use of performance information in budget processes for more than 50 years. In the federal government, these types of reforms have been exemplified by such past efforts as performance budgeting (in the 1950s), the Planning-Programming-Budgeting System (PPBS) in the 1960s, and zero-based budgeting (ZBB) in the 1970s. Further, one of the major goals of the Government Performance and Results Act (GPRA) of 1993 was the introduction of more performance information into the federal budget process. Consistent with this trend, the George W. Bush administration has made the use of performance information in the budget process one of its key management priorities. First, the administration is using a Program Assessment Rating Tool (PART) in the executive budget process. Second, the centerpiece of the President's Management Agenda (PMA) is the "budget and performance integration" (BPI) initiative, which attempts to further the use of performance information for budgeting.

Why does this recurring reform have such currency? In short, because budget processes allocate scarce resources among competing purposes. This is always true—it does not depend on whether the given budget is projected to be in surplus or deficit. If resources were not scarce, we would neither need a budget process nor require performance information. Since resources are limited, however, understanding the effects of resources on the objectives of government action is important. In fact, the more scarce the resources, the more important it is that they be allocated wisely. In such an environment, it becomes even more vital that resource allocation decisions be focused on the effectiveness of spending and tax policies.

The use of performance information in the budget process (what this chapter calls "performance-informed budgeting"), while it can pay dividends in terms of the efficient use of resources, is difficult to carry out in practice. It can contribute to efficient resource use because it involves focusing government allocation processes at all levels on relationships between dollars and results. It is hard to do well because it involves a number of different and related subcomponents (including strategic planning, performance measurement, and cost measurement) and because logical connections between funding and results are often difficult to make.

The reporting of performance information in government budgets is nothing new. Governments have consistently reported performance information as a part of budget documents for many years. Unquestionably, the supply of performance information, at all levels of government, has increased over the past 20 years. For example, research on U.S. state government reporting of performance information in their budget documents demonstrates a steady increase in the number that report that they present information on performance.[1] Recent research on state governments also reports that 47 out of 50 have either legislative or administrative requirements for performance measurement.[2] There is less evidence of the use of performance information by these governments—that is, of performance information having widespread influence on government funding decisions.

In part, this chapter argues, this lack of evidence occurs because observers have not looked in the right places. That is, the assumption that is implicitly used most frequently is that resource allocation is something that occurs only (or at least mostly) in the central budget office or in the legislature. This chapter embraces a more comprehensive definition of performance-informed budgeting and attempts to demonstrate that there is ample opportunity to use performance information at each stage of the budget process—that is, not only in the Office of Management and Budget (OMB) and the Congress but in the agencies and by the audit community as well. Further, high-quality performance measurement can be the key to effective management of resources, even if that performance information did not affect the initial allocation of those resources.

For example, a May 2003 report supported by the IBM Center for The Business of Government in conjunction with the National Academy of Public Administration provided several examples in which agencies used performance information to allocate and manage resources after budgets had been approved by the Congress and the President. For example, the U.S. Department of Housing and Urban Development's Public and Indian Housing program uses information on results to prioritize the allocation of resources among field offices in four states based on data collected through the Public Housing Assessment Systems (PHAS).[3] The Veterans Health Administration, which in the early 1990s reorganized so that much decision-making authority resided in 22 Veterans Integrated Service Networks (VISNs), uses performance data to allocate and reallocate resources among VISNs and to different facilities within VISNs during budget execution.[4]

At this point, the renewal of the effort to introduce more performance information into the federal budget process, which began in the George H. W. Bush administration, has now been sustained through the Clinton and George W. Bush administrations, and it is fair to say that (in some form) it now seems inevitable that connections between performance information and the budget will be sustained. The important next step involves moving from making the necessary information available to having it used. And as much as federal agencies have struggled with the production of performance information under GPRA, the challenges of producing performance data pale in comparison to the difficulties involved in using those data in the budget process.

The remainder of this chapter is organized into five main parts:

- A brief history of legislative and administrative efforts to bring more performance information into the federal budget process, including both early governmentwide initiatives, such as PPBS and ZBB, as well as more recent efforts, such as GPRA.

- The Bush administration's current attempt to integrate the budget with performance, including the role of such integration in both the President's Management Agenda and the Program Assessment Rating Tool.
- A comprehensive framework for considering the budget and performance simultaneously, in an effort to clarify that performance-informed budgeting can (and does) occur at each stage of the traditional budget process: budget preparation, budget approval, budget execution, and audit and evaluation.
- For each of these stages of the budget process, a discussion of the specific manner in which performance information could be used by decision makers at that stage.
- Finally, a series of findings and recommendations intended to provide helpful guidance to policy makers and federal managers in an effort to sustain the progress that has been made to date and to assist in taking performance-informed budgeting to the next level.

The Federal Budget and Performance—
Historical Antecedents

Current efforts to better integrate performance information into the budget process occur in the context of many reforms that have been attempted in the past. While the past decade has seen a renewal of efforts to make the budget process more informed by performance, the trend toward making budget processes more focused on performance has been ongoing for at least the last century, and reforms that were implemented in the past laid the groundwork for these more recent 1990s reforms. (See "Performance and the Budget: 1921–1980" on page 24 for a brief summary of these historical antecedents.)

Beginning in 1990, the federal government saw a more explicit focus on bringing performance information into the budget process. This new emphasis is differentiated from past reforms primarily by a focus on legislation rather than solely on executive action. Perhaps the first indicator of this revival came with the passage of the Chief Financial Officers Act of 1990 (CFO Act).[5] This law, which grew primarily out of the financial management scandals that had plagued the federal government in the 1980s, created chief financial officers (CFOs) in 24 cabinet departments and other governmental entities. The CFO Act had as its main focus the improvement of federal financial management. But the bill also included a provision that requires agency CFOs to develop "systematic measures of performance" for programs in their agencies. It also instructs CFOs "to prepare and submit to the agency head timely reports" and requires that financial statements "shall reflect results of operations."[6]

The CFO Act is less significant for what it was able to accomplish in terms of improved government performance and more important for laying the legislative groundwork for the Government Performance and Results Act (GPRA). GPRA was introduced in the Congress initially during the George H. W. Bush administration; was redrafted in the early 1990s by staff from the Office of Management and Budget (OMB), the General Accounting Office (GAO), and the Senate Committee on Governmental Affairs; and ultimately was signed into law by President Clinton in August of 1993.[7] GPRA directs all federal agencies to engage in strategic planning, objective setting, and performance measurement. Beginning with fiscal year (FY) 1999, the budget for the U.S. government was required to include a performance plan. Agency strategic plans show performance goals and indicators (quantitative, where possible) enabling the Congress and the public to gauge whether agencies have complied with the goals. Each agency submits a specific performance plan covering the major activities for which it is responsible. Program performance reports are also required to be submitted on an annual basis to the Congress. These reports include information comparing actual with planned performance, a discussion of the success in meeting goals, and remedial action if goals are not met.[8]

The CFO Act and GPRA were followed by a number of other laws that focused on management reform in the federal government, each of which had a significant results orientation. (For a discussion of statutory management reform, see the General Accounting Office's report, "Managing for Results: The Statutory Framework for Performance-Based Management and Accountability," GAO/GGD/ AIMD-98-52, January 1998.) These include the following:

- The 1994 Federal Acquisition Streamlining Act, which requires major capital purchases to be justified on the basis of cost, schedule, and performance. Specific benchmarks are developed for each of these criteria, and projects must meet at least 90 percent of these baseline goals or be terminated.[9]
- The Federal Financial Management Improvement Act (FFMIA) of 1996, which imposed standard general ledger and accounting principles on federal agencies as they produce financial statements and maintain financial management systems. FFMIA also provided for a closer working relationship between federal financial management professionals, including CFOs, the Office of Federal Financial Management within OMB, and agency inspectors general.[10]
- The Information Technology Management Reform Act of 1996 (also known as Clinger-Cohen), which requires agencies to take a more performance-based approach to procuring information technology (IT) investments. This includes a specific requirement to select and manage

Performance and the Budget: 1921–1980

The 20th century saw many efforts designed to promote a more effective allocation and management of federal budgetary resources, and many of these focused in whole or in part on the budget process. Here is a brief listing:

Date	Reform	Brief Description
1921	Budget and Accounting Act of 1921	Created the executive budget and the Bureau of the Budget (BOB); consistent with a control orientation for budgeting
1937	President's Committee on Administrative Management (Brownlow Committee)	Created the Executive Office of the President (EOP) with expanded White House staff, including moving BOB from the Department of the Treasury to EOP
1940s–1950s	Hoover Commission	Focused on "performance budgeting" consisting of establishing closer relationships between resources (inputs) and activities (outputs)
1960s	Planning-Programming-Budgeting System (PPBS)	An effort to more consciously connect resources with results, first in the Department of Defense (successfully) and then with less success in civilian agencies
1970s	Management by Objectives (MBO)	Nixon-era strategic planning effort
1970s	Zero-Based Budgeting (ZBB)	Carter administration's attempt to more systematically review existing programs in the budget process

These efforts were characterized by Allen Schick in the classic article "The Road to PPB: The Stages of Budget Reform" as demonstrating the evolution of budget systems from control (the executive budget movement in the early part of the 20th century) to management (the late 1930s through the 1950s, as typified by the recommendations of the Brownlow Committee and the Hoover Commissions) to planning (the program budgeting movement of the 1960s, embodied in the federal government by the PPBS system and later by ZBB).[11] It has become fashionable to view these reforms as "failures." This is in part because past postmortems were not conducted at enough distance (in terms of time or perspective) from the "reform" to permit a real evaluation of effects (which would include effects on capacity of the federal government to engage in the necessary activities, such as strategic planning, performance measurement, and cost accounting). Viewed through the lens of history, these reforms can be seen as part of a general upward trend in attention to performance concerns throughout the entire 20th century—each reform developed capacity and made it more likely that future reforms would progress beyond the accomplishment of the previous initiative.

investments with a specific focus on the extent to which they assist the agency in fulfilling its mission, to establish measures for IT performance, and to report the results of these measures to OMB.[12]

In addition to these legislative initiatives, the Clinton administration undertook a high-profile effort to focus on performance issues during its eight years in office embodied by Vice President Gore's National Performance Review (NPR), later renamed the National Partnership for Reinventing Government. The NPR, using federal agency career staff as a primary resource, focused on promoting government performance, customer service, and managerial flexibility, and claimed success in not only improving the performance of many federal programs and agencies but saving billions of dollars as well.[13] As a part of this overall strategy, the NPR advocated a conversion from a budgeting system that focuses on inputs to a system that focuses on results.[14] The NPR report also embraced the goals of the CFO Act and GPRA, although GPRA and NPR were running on somewhat parallel but separate tracks during most of the Clinton administration.

Early evaluations of these efforts suggest that a culture of performance does seem to be infiltrating federal agencies, albeit somewhat slowly and unevenly. Consider the following as specific evidence:

- At least three different major initiatives were focused on performance during the 1990s: the CFO Act, GPRA, and NPR.
- Significant movement has occurred on the part of some federal agencies toward developing more (and better) measures of results. While by no means alone, the U.S. Coast Guard has been engaged in a particularly sustained and impressive effort here, developing a much clearer sense of mission and measures to evaluate performance, initially as part of the GPRA pilot effort.[15]
- Agency financial management now focuses on demonstrating consistency with GPRA, and cost accounting has been emphasized consistently throughout the federal government as a necessary part of developing more performance-focused management.

Taken together, these 1990s reforms laid the groundwork that was present when George W. Bush took office, and they are demonstrative of the increasing commitment of the federal government to performance measurement. These reforms have, as of yet, been less successful in integrating the use of performance information into government decision processes. They have tended to focus on the supply of information, rather than on its use. Against this backdrop, the Bush administration desired to take the next step—attempting to make judgments about performance and then attaching consequence to those judgments. This effort to move beyond "supply" to "use" is central to the Bush administration's management and budgeting initiatives, which are outlined in the next section.[16]

Bush Administration Efforts Designed to Better Integrate Budget and Performance Information

The Bush administration took office in early 2001 with its own set of management priorities, articulated in the President's Management Agenda (PMA), which was published in September 2001.[17] This agenda included five governmentwide management reforms, which the administration identified as the areas of greatest management concern in the federal government.[18] For each of these areas, agencies are evaluated on a management "scorecard" that gives them scores (in the form of "traffic lights"—green, yellow, and red) on the basis of criteria established to define success in each of the five areas and also to assess progress made by agencies in achieving the goals articulated by the criteria. Of the five, budget and performance integration (BPI) is the one most central to the theme of this chapter, but the other four have in common a desire to improve the operational performance of federal programs and agencies.

- **Strategic investment in human capital:** Federal agencies face a substantial workforce challenge over the next several decades. By some estimates, more than 70 percent of today's federal workforce will be eligible for retirement by 2010, and 40 percent of those are expected to retire.[19] For this reason, and because of abiding concerns that skill imbalances in some federal agencies impede the achievement of mission success, the Bush administration is pushing federal agencies to focus more intently on human capital issues such as recruitment, compensation, discipline, and succession planning.

- **Competitive sourcing:** The administration believes that federal agencies will perform their work better and more cheaply if a greater number of commercial-type jobs are competed with private sector firms. Therefore, the PMA established a goal (which has since been scaled back) of 50 percent of these roughly 850,000 commercial-type jobs being competed with private sector firms. An effective competitive sourcing effort would demand valid cost and performance comparisons across public and private sector service providers.

- **Improved financial performance:** Federal financial management systems have historically not provided accurate financial information in a timely fashion. Further, federal agencies have not been able to generate unqualified audit opinions, and some programs, such as Medicare and Social Security, have had chronic problems with fraudulent or erroneous payments. Upgrading the financial systems is essential to providing program managers with the information that they need to better manage programs, as well as preventing waste and mismanagement.

- **E-government:** Using technological resources to maximum effect is crucial to the ability of the government to meet public demands for service delivery. This means ensuring that a good "business case" is made for technology investments, that agencies use technology to make goods and services widely and easily available to the citizens, and that agencies do not duplicate efforts by developing similar systems designed to serve common purposes.

As noted previously, the fifth item—budget and performance integration—is the linchpin of the PMA, largely because agencies cannot effectively carry out any of these reforms outside the context of managing for results. The Bush administration believes that GPRA has to date involved little more than the production of data, with virtually no evidence that this information has been used to guide decisions.[20] Accordingly, the PMA set the bar high for agencies that expect to receive a "green" light for budget and performance integration by establishing the following standards:

- Senior agency managers meet at least quarterly to examine reports that integrate financial and performance information that covers all major responsibilities of the department. This information is used to make decisions regarding the management of agency programs.
- Strategic plans contain a limited number of outcome-oriented goals and objectives. Annual budget and performance documents incorporate all measures identified in the PART and focus on the information used in the senior management report described in the first criterion.
- Performance appraisal plans for 60 percent of agency positions link to agency mission, goals, and outcomes; effectively differentiate between various levels of performance; and provide consequences based on performance.
- The full cost of achieving performance goals is accurately (+/- 10 percent) reported in budget and performance documents, and the marginal cost of changing performance goals can be accurately estimated (+/- 10 percent).
- All agency programs have at least one efficiency measure.
- The agency uses PART evaluations to direct program improvements, and PART ratings are used consistently to justify funding requests, management actions, and legislative proposals. Less than 10 percent of agency programs receive a Results Not Demonstrated rating for more than two years in a row.[21]

In order to "get to green," an agency must fully comply with each one of these standards. Even with the stringency of the standards, however, there is some evidence of progress. While in the FY 2003 budget, only three agencies (the Environmental Protection Agency, Department of Transportation, and Small Business Administration) even achieved "yellow" status (suggesting compliance with some but not all standards), that number had increased to nine by the time that the FY 2004 budget was presented. The Departments of Commerce, Defense, Labor, and Veterans Affairs, along with the National Aeronautics and Space Administration (NASA) and the Social Security Administration, had joined these other agencies by upgrading from "red" to "yellow." Agencies fared even better on "progress" scores, with 17 of 26 agencies rated as "green," nine as "yellow," and none as "red." This level of achievement—nine yellows and 17 greens—was maintained in the report accompanying the Midsession Review issued in July 2003.

The Bush administration's other governmentwide performance-based initiative, the Program Assessment Rating Tool (PART), was first unveiled for use in the FY 2004 budget process. The PART takes the "program" as the unit of analysis and attempts to determine whether programs are successful in meeting their stated objectives. Significantly, one of the characteristics of "programs" is that they must have funding associated with them at a level where budget decisions are actually made.[22] OMB has defined approximately 1,000 programs throughout the federal government. For the FY 2004 budget process, OMB reviewed 234 programs in an effort to determine their effectiveness, and it seeks to evaluate an additional 20 percent of agency programs each year, over five years, until ultimately (presumably by FY 2008) 100 percent of programs are reviewed annually.

The PART is a menu-driven device that attempts to evaluate all programs according to a consistent set of criteria. The programs are evaluated according to program purpose and design, strategic planning, program management, and program results and accountability. This fourth area is the most crucial, as it accounts for fully 50 percent of the PART "score." In general, programs with a clear purpose, solid planning, strong management, and demonstrable results will score highly on the PART. The PART reviews are to inform budget decisions not only by the director of OMB but also by agency officials during

---

Comptroller General David M. Walker on "Linking Performance and Budgeting"

A key objective of GPRA is to help the Congress, OMB, and other executive agencies develop a clearer understanding of what is being achieved in relation to what is being spent. Linking planned performance with budget requests and financial reports is an essential step in building a culture of performance management. Such an alignment infuses performance concerns into budgetary deliberations, prompting agencies to reassess their performance goals and strategies and to more clearly understand the cost of performance. For the fiscal year 2005 budget process, OMB called for agencies to prepare a performance budget that can be used for the annual performance plan required by GPRA.

Source: *Statement of David M. Walker, Comptroller General of the United States, before the Committee on Government Reform, House of Representatives, September 18, 2003.*

budget formulations, and they are intended to feed into actions and proposals designed to improve performance.

Perhaps the most significant finding in the first round of PART evaluations was that more than half of the programs reviewed could not demonstrate results, at least according to the PART criteria. It is important to note that this does not mean that these programs were ineffective; rather, it means that they could not prove their effectiveness. As the PART becomes more integrated into the budget process, OMB hopes that agencies will be encouraged to develop better information on the effects of their programs in order to increase the probability of success in securing resources.

For the vast majority of programs, the relationship between funding and performance is not well understood, even where good performance data exist. Some programs received more funding in the President's FY 2004 budget because of demonstrated effectiveness; others had funding reduced because of poor performance. In many other cases, there was no direct relationship between the PART findings and budget allocations. OMB hopes to integrate PART findings even more clearly into the budget process for FY 2005. Even if PART works well, however, it is important to note that there will not—and cannot—be a direct relationship between PART scores and funding. There are many other legitimate possibilities, including that a program without adequate justification in terms of results is nonetheless a high priority for funding, that (conversely) a program that works well is a lower priority given available resources, or that there is a preference that government not carry out a given activity independent of performance considerations.

Taken together, the PMA and the PART provide tangible evidence of the commitment of the Bush administration to measure performance and to integrate performance information more specifically into the budget process. *Saying* that budgeting and performance should be "integrated," however, is not the same thing as *doing* it. In part, this is because it has not always been clear what is meant by integrating budgeting and performance. Integrating budgeting and performance could involve allocating resources in the first instance, reallocating resources after the fact, managing resources in budget execution, or holding officials accountable for the use of resources to achieve results. In other words, just as budgeting is not a narrow enterprise that happens only in discrete places at discrete times, the opportunities for integrating budgeting and performance information are also not narrow and limited. In the next section, a comprehensive framework for considering budget and performance information is presented in an effort to make the many possible linkages between the budget process and performance information more explicit.

A Comprehensive Framework for Considering Budget and Performance Integration

All past and current reforms described in previous sections have one thing in common: their attempt to more explicitly bring together performance information, on the one hand, and the budget process, on the other. Understanding what that really means, however, has been less than straightforward. Scholars and practitioners have used many different terms to describe this desired linkage, including performance budgeting, performance-based budgeting, results-based budgeting, performance funding, and budgeting for results.[23] Each of these has in common some desired linkage between the budget and performance. They also have in common the desired contrast between performance-informed budgeting and traditional budgeting. (See "Contrasts Between Traditional Views of Budgeting and Performance-Informed Budgeting.")

If the budget process is to become more informed by performance, such a transformation from traditional budgeting involves simultaneously considering two factors. The first is the availability of appropriate information—on strategic direction, results, and costs—in order to make budgeting more

---

Contrasts Between Traditional Views of Budgeting and Performance-Informed Budgeting

Performance-informed budgeting exists in a context of more traditional input-focused efforts to allocate resources. This input focus has historically been less on results and more on incremental levels of funding. The table below presents a contrast between traditional budgeting and performance-informed budgeting. It is important to keep in mind, however, that while performance-informed budgeting is probably unattainable, by the same token "traditional" budgeting, as described, is overly stylized. They are best viewed as ends on a continuum rather than discrete options.

Traditional Budgeting	Performance-Informed Budgeting
Inputs as ends in themselves	Relationship between inputs and results
Changes in inputs at the margin (for example, how many more dollars than last year)	Changes in inputs and results for the entire program (for example, how much more results for how much more money)
Divorced from planning and management in agencies	Budgeting integrated with planning and management
Budgeted resources	Costs

results focused. The second is the actual use of that information to make decisions at each stage of the budgeting cycle.

In the federal budget process, assessments of the use of performance information in the budget process traditionally focus on two (and only two) sets of decisions. The first is on decisions by OMB about what is in the President's budget. The second is on decisions by the Congress about what is in the budget. Without denying the importance of OMB and congressional decisions, the focus on only these two stages encourages an overly narrow view of the budget process. This impedes our ability to successfully study and articulate the many possible situations in which budget and performance information can and should be integrated.

Given this situation, how do we create a clearer articulation of "performance" and "the budget"? First, we should recognize that the budget process does have clear (if not always smoothly functioning) stages (see Table 2.1 on page 32).

- **Budget preparation,** where agencies develop internal budget allocations and requests that are eventually (after some give and mostly take) integrated into the President's budget
- **Budget approval,** where the Congress and the President ultimately enact the laws that will permit taxing and spending to occur
- **Budget execution,** where agencies implement the budget within the constraints established by the Congress and the administration
- **Audit and evaluation,** where agencies and auditors/evaluators decide (after the fact) what the effects (financial and performance) of budgetary activities have been

If we recognize that traditional discussions of performance-based budgeting involve discussions of a portion of the first stage (decisions by OMB and the President) and the second stage (decisions by the Congress), a further articulation of the process permits us, at a minimum, to recognize that there is ample opportunity for integrating the budget and performance at any of these stages.[24] There are two relevant questions:

1. To what extent was performance and cost information available at this stage of the process? This question implies three separate activities. First, public entities need to know what they are supposed to accomplish. Malcolm Holmes, who was an architect of the Australian budget reforms, noted that a key condition for performance management in government is "clarity of task and purpose."[25] Strategic planning (preferably government-wide), to the extent that it enables decisions to be made that establish clear direction for government programs, is crucial. This is often quite difficult to carry out in practice, particularly in countries like the United States that have a horizontal and vertical diffusion of authority, responsibility, and political decision making. It is relatively easier in parliamentary systems, where the majority party or coalition actually runs cabinet ministries.

Table 2.1: Stages of the Federal Budget Process

Stage of Budget Process	Key Actors Involved	Description of Activities	End Product
Budget Preparation—Agency	Agency budget offices, agency subunits	Agency preparation of a budget for submission to OMB	Budget request
Budget Preparation—OMB	Agency head, agency budget office, OMB, President	Analysis of agency budget request on behalf of the President; negotiation with agencies on budget allocation levels	President's budget
Budget Approval—Congress	Agencies, congressional committees	The Congress makes overall fiscal policy, authorizes programs, and appropriates funds	Budget resolution, authorization bills, appropriation bills
Budget Approval—President	President, agencies, OMB	Action on congressional legislation affecting budget	Signature or veto
Budget Execution	Agencies, OMB	Implementation of programs by federal agencies; allocation of dollars by agency subunit	Administration of programs
Audit and Evaluation	Agencies, auditors (internal and external)	Review of tax and budget actions after the fact; recommendations made for changes	Audits and evaluations

Despite this difficulty, however, strategic planning is an important focus of budget reformers, explicitly because it establishes the context in which performance and cost information is considered. In order for any organization to evaluate either its performance or its use of resources in pursuit of that performance, it must first know what it intends to do. For this reason, GPRA quite reasonably focused initially on strategic planning rather than performance measurement. Performance information established outside a planning context is not useful. On the other hand, planning that occurs without attention to resource constraints is also not meaningful. For this reason, the integration of planning and budgeting is most likely to pay dividends in terms of improved performance.

Second, valid measures of performance need to exist. It is hard to measure outcomes in the great majority of public programs, and far easier to measure outputs. Beyond conceptual challenges of defining relevant indicators, most public sector organizations reasonably resist being held accountable for outcomes, since they are influenced by so many factors that are outside of agency—or even government—control.

Third, accurate measures of cost need to be developed. Connecting resources with results implies knowing how much it costs to deliver a given level of outcome. Most public organizations cannot even track how much it costs to deliver an output, largely because of problems with allocating indirect costs. In such situations, extrapolating from output to outcome cost is simply not feasible. There are clear tradeoffs between the accuracy of cost information and the resources necessary to obtain that information, but some effort to approximate the cost of delivering services is necessary if resources consumed are to be related to results obtained.

2. To what extent was performance and cost information actually used to make decisions about the allocation, management, or monitoring of resources at this stage of the process? In short, cost and performance information need to be brought together for budgeting decisions. There is no simple decision rule for relating cost and performance in the public sector, at least at a macro level. A simple, but incorrect, approach (allegedly embraced by some members of the Congress) would be to take money from those who fail to meet performance targets and give more money to those who meet targets.[26] While this may sound good in theory, it relies on heroic assumptions, one of them about the causal link between money and results. In fact, for any program, sorting out the contribution of funding versus other factors would require a full understanding of the logical relationships among inputs, outputs, and outcomes, also taking into account other internal and external factors that influence performance. Further, budget decisions are appropriately influenced by other (nonperformance) concerns, such as relative priorities, unmet needs, and equity concerns, to name three.

Beyond the conceptual underpinnings of the relationship, however, participants in the budget process must have incentives to use performance information. If successful performance-informed budgeting occurs only when those involved in the budget process move beyond the production of information to the use of information to make decisions about resource allocation and management, then this can only occur if all budgetary actors have effective incentives (and resources) to collect and use information. In fact, the incentive question is probably the most important one to focus on in determining the possibility that performance information will actually be used as an input in the various stages of budget decision making.

The disaggregated approach that is advocated here supports a more robust understanding of the role of performance information in the budget process. Looking at the full budget process enables one to recognize that there are important questions to be asked regarding the availability and use of performance information at each stage of the traditional budget process.

The preoccupation with OMB and the Congress is consistent with a view that policy making in the formal sense involves almost exclusively the Congress and the President. It fails, however, to acknowledge the formal and informal use of discretion—which also is policy making—that occurs in federal agencies. Since performance information may be used in important ways at other stages of the process—agency budget preparation, budget

The Wye River Conference

On March 30 and 31, 2003, The George Washington University, with support from the IBM Center for The Business of Government, brought together a small group of leaders in linking performance information and budgeting for a two-day "thought leadership" conference at the Wye River Conference Center in Queenstown, Maryland. (A full listing of these leaders appears on the next page.) The purpose of this conference was threefold:

- To obtain feedback on a preliminary version of the framework for performance-informed budgeting included in this paper
- To permit these "key players" to share ideas in an effort to further progress in performance-informed budgeting in the federal government
- To assist in the development of a research agenda in performance-informed budgeting

The conference was successful on each of these fronts. First, the participants uniformly agreed that the term "performance-informed budgeting" best captured the goals of the integration of performance information and budgeting because it did not imply some mechanistic connection, but rather the insertion of performance information into what will always be a political process. Further, these participants agreed that a comprehensive framework, which focuses on the availability and use of performance information at all stages of the budget process, was helpful in communicating to various actors what specific information they might need and how they might use it.

Second, the conference provided a rare forum for key officials from OMB, GAO, the Congressional Budget Office, the Congress, federal agency staff, academics, and the private sector to share experiences. The free exchange of ideas that followed focused on several issues, including the Bush administration's implementation of the PART, constraints placed on federal agencies in their efforts to implement a performance-focused management agenda, and changes necessary to better support performance-informed budgeting.

Third, the conference participants had a number of ideas concerning the current state of performance-informed budgeting in the federal government that could further both research and practice on the topic. The participants generally agreed on the following:[27]

- One of the key potential venues for "performance budgeting" is the agency budget justification to the Congress. Where agencies are able to make connections between funding, programs, and results in budget justifications, the conversation in the congressional budget process is more likely to be—but by no means ensured to be—focused on performance.
- Nonetheless, the Congress is unlikely to transform its budget decision making anytime soon, particularly in the appropriations process. Perhaps the area of greatest potential payoff is the authorization process, where performance expectations could be made clearer.
- Current administration initiatives, such as the PART, need to be aligned with GPRA and other ongoing initiatives. Agency staff and program managers need to understand that they are all part of a single performance-focused agenda. Neither the PART nor GPRA can be permitted to degenerate into a paper exercise.

- It is important to understand what types of information—on performance and cost—are needed by different people inside the agency (agency heads, program managers, and so on) and outside the agency (OMB, the Congress, external stakeholders).
- It is important to continue to try to make connections between national goals, agency-specific objectives, and program-specific targets. This may be particularly true in cases where a number of agencies contribute to a single result or where third parties actually deliver the service.
- Agencies need to understand how all their management functions (IT, human resources, financial management) contribute to performance and take an integrated approach to management with a focus on results.
- Attention must be paid to the incentives that exist, or can be made to exist, for decision makers to demand and use performance information.

Conference Participants (Affiliations current at the time of the conference.)

Executive Branch

Lisa Araiza
Department of Justice

Mark Catlett
Department of Veterans Affairs

Phil Dame
Office of Management and Budget

Tony McCann
Smithsonian Institution

Michael McNiff
U.S. Marshals Service,
Department of Justice

Marcus Peacock
Office of Management and Budget

Justine Rodriguez
Office of Management and Budget

Mary Scala
Department of Defense

Woody Stanley
Federal Highway Administration,
Department of Transportation

Judy Tillman
Financial Management Service,
Department of the Treasury

Legislative Branch

Barry Anderson
Congressional Budget Office

Denise Fantone
General Accounting Office

Paul Posner
General Accounting Office

John Salamone
Senate Committee on Governmental Affairs

Experts

Mark Abramson
IBM Center for The Business of Government

Jonathan Breul
IBM Center for The Business of Government

Philip Joyce
The George Washington University

John Kamensky
IBM Center for The Business of Government

Lily Kim
IBM Center for The Business of Government

Kathryn Newcomer
The George Washington University

Srikant Sastry
IBM Business Consulting Services

Howard Smith
The George Washington University

Barry White
Council for Excellence in Government

Joseph Wholey
University of Southern California

execution, and audit and evaluation—such a limited scope of inquiry risks missing important opportunities for applying and capturing the benefits from performance-informed budgeting.

There are, then, many possible decision points at which performance information can be incorporated into the budget process. At each of these decision points, the twin questions of availability and use are equally relevant. A given department or agency might have or make use of performance information at one stage of the process, independent of what might happen at other stages of the process. For example, agencies might make substantial use of performance information in building the budget (an effort that can pay dividends for resource management in budget execution), even if other actors (OMB and the Congress) make little or no use of that information at subsequent stages. Conversely, the absence of performance concerns in preparation and approval would not prevent a given agency from using its discretion to execute its budget by considering the effects of different execution strategies on its goals and objectives (that is, applying outcome measures). In short, *all agency managers could use performance and cost information to manage their programs,* even if they did not receive those resources through a performance-informed process. If agency managers have timely and accurate data on cost and performance, they can use that information to direct and redirect resources and to hold the responsible staff accountable to achieving results.

The next section further articulates this argument by discussing performance-informed budgeting at each stage of the budget process. For each stage, these twin issues of availability (what kind of performance information is necessary and who needs to have that information) and use (what kind of decisions need to be made or supported) are presented.

Potential Uses of Performance-Informed Budgeting in the Federal Budget Process

The comprehensive framework outlined in the previous section permits a more robust look at performance-informed budgeting by permitting an analysis of the reform at each stage of the budget process. This section looks at each of these stages in more detail, attempting to flesh out the specific issues involved with both availability and use, and drawing some preliminary conclusions concerning the current state of budget and performance integration at each of these stages. Looking at the budget process comprehensively, it is clear that performance information has great potential to be used at all stages. While the federal government does not yet have a fully mature performance-informed budgeting system, there are parts of the system (particularly in budget preparation and budget execution) where there are important success stories. Other stages—most notably budget approval—lag behind in the use of performance information for budgeting.

Budget Preparation

The budget preparation stage of the budget process is divided into two phases: the development of the request from the agency to OMB and the analysis of the request by OMB. Performance information can be used during both of these portions of the process, either to maximize the effects of funding on performance or to better justify the budget request as it goes forward to OMB or from the President to the Congress.

Development of the Agency Budget Request

As noted, the budget preparation stage begins with the initial planning by the agency, which can start a year or more prior to the submission of the budget request to OMB. For large agencies, this process can entail a time-consuming internal process within the agency. Many cabinet departments, for example, contain a great many subunits or bureaus. The process of arriving at an OMB budget request for such an agency involves a number of different steps, each of which can be time consuming and contentious. As one illustration, the secretary of Health and Human Services, a highly decentralized agency,[28] must ultimately decide on a requested budget figure for many disparate bureaus, such as the Food and Drug Administration, the Centers for Medicare and Medicaid Services, the Centers for Disease Control, the Health Resources and Services Administration, and the Public Health Service. This situation is similar to that of other large and decentralized departments, such as the Department of Defense, the Department of Homeland Security, the Department of the Interior, the Department of the Treasury, and the Department of Transportation. The process of arriving at a budget request to OMB for the executive branch invariably involves a protracted process within the department and agencies. This process can itself be enhanced by the availability of performance and cost information, which can be used in various ways by different people throughout the process.

For federal agencies, the budget preparation stage is constrained by many factors, including political constraints imposed by interest groups and the Congress. Within those limitations, the budget request itself, and the information required to be included in the request, is dictated by OMB Circular A-11, and particularly Part 2 of that circular, entitled "Preparation and Submission of Budget Estimates." OMB Circular A-11 prescribes the specific information that must be provided with agency budget submissions.

The FY 2004 circular, for example, requested the following information related to the performance of the agency:

- Information related to progress in implementing the President's Management Agenda, including the section focusing on budget and performance integration
- Evaluation of selected programs using the Program Assessment Rating Tool (PART)
- The integration of the budget request with the annual GPRA performance plan, including the performance targets outlined in that plan (Part 6 of OMB Circular A-11 deals in its entirety with preparation of GPRA strategic plans, performance plans, and performance reports)
- A requirement that programs with similar goals report common performance measures that have been articulated by OMB
- Information indicating the unit cost of delivering various agency programs, reflecting "the full cost of producing a result including overhead and other indirect costs"[29]
- Consistency with guidelines for performance-based investments, including those in the Clinger-Cohen Act and the OMB Capital Programming Guide (which is included as Part 7 of OMB Circular A-11)
- A program evaluation schedule, including the issues to be addressed and the methodology to be employed

Further, the budget request should be informed by the "judgment of the agency head regarding the scope, content, performance and quality of programs and activities proposed to meet the agency's missions, goals and objectives."[30] While this is by no means a comprehensive list of all the information related to cost and performance that agencies are required to submit, it indicates the extent to which budget requests to OMB, and therefore budget formulation within federal agencies, are expected to be informed by performance considerations (see Table 2.2).

Most agencies (particularly decentralized ones) have begun their internal budget process far in advance of the receipt of the circular. Upon receipt of the circular, agencies review the requirements to ensure that the information desired by OMB will be included in the request and continue (or begin in earnest) the process of developing the budget request, which (as noted previously) may involve a number of separate stages within a given cabinet department. The "traditional" budget request to OMB in many agencies has not been focused on the effects of funding on performance. Rather, it has been dominated by anecdotal information justifying additional expenditures by the agency, coupled with "current services" and "new initiative" requests from the agency. The process has been heavily focused on funding changes at the margin, asking questions such as, "How much more will it cost us to maintain current staff?"

During this first stage of the budget process, agencies can use a variety of tools and measures to make their budget request more focused on performance.

Table 2.2: Performance-Informed Budgeting in Agency Budget Preparation

Possible Measures Available	Potential Use of Measures	Who Uses the Measures
• Agency strategic planning and performance planning • Cost information • Outcome measures • Output measures • Productivity measures	• To build budget justification for submission to central budget office • To make tradeoffs between agency subunits to allocate funds strategically • To determine productivity of components of an agency • To determine overlapping services within an agency • To determine in-house versus contractual production of services	*Agency head:* • Effectiveness of program • Appropriate distribution of staff • Cost/outcome comparisons (program to program, public to private) *Bureau head:* • Cost/output/outcome relationships *Line managers:* • Cost/output

This information is used by a number of different individuals in the agency to respond to a variety of questions necessary to build a budget request that is focused on the performance implications of funding. Making budget development more focused on performance normally requires that the agency budget office develop some framework for budget requests that clarifies the relationship between costs and performance. Such a budget request made to the agency budget office would include the following characteristics:

- **A strategic and performance context:** At least since GPRA became fully effective, departments and bureaus are expected to have articulated some strategic vision. That means that budget requests should be presented in the context of their effects on the strategic priorities of the agency, normally established in the agency strategic plan. But further, this means that "programs" (or, in the language of federal budgeting, "programs, projects, and activities") should be related to the larger strategic goals and performance targets of the agency. In other words, there should be a logical connection that is presented between what the agency "does" on a day-to-day basis and its larger strategic and performance objectives.
- **Performance information:** Agencies should have output and outcome measures related to programs that are related to the larger strategic vision of the agency. The agency should have indicators of its success

in meeting its objectives. These measures may be at several levels (output, intermediate outcome, final outcome), but ideally the agency, at all levels, could show a logical relationship between its various types of measures and its strategic objectives.

- **Cost information:** The budget request should identify the true cost of providing services, with costs charged to the appropriate bureau or program. This will not be possible without some relatively sophisticated means of allocating overhead or indirect costs. Administrative costs are now often accounted for separately and not allocated to individual services.

How can this information be used? First and foremost, it can be used to justify budget requests. Presumably most bureaus or subunits desire to be as successful as possible in the budget process (with "success" defined as achieving the largest budget possible to carry out programs within the subunit).[31] Bureaus can, therefore, present the information to make a specific linkage between costs (inputs), activities (outputs), and results (outcomes) in the context of the strategic vision of the agency. In this manner, the components can make transparent the effect of additional (or decreased) funding on performance in hopes that the agency head will find the case for funds more compelling if the performance implications are made clear. At the level of the line manager, and for the individual program, this may mean only that the relationship between inputs and outputs is clear. At the level of the bureau head, however, some linkage of these inputs and outputs to results is essential. A number of specific questions can be addressed at this level:

- How well are my programs working to achieve their goals and objectives?
- How productive is my staff, compared to past productivity or perhaps benchmarked against staff in some other agency or organization? (Productivity is normally defined as the relationship of inputs to outputs.)
- What opportunities exist to contract out particular services in order to save money while maintaining or improving performance?
- Does my organization have the right mix of skills (from staff or contractors) at the right place and at the right time in order to maximize the achievement of performance goals?
- What are the effects of different levels of funding on the performance of the bureau, given key performance measures?

The U.S. Department of Justice (DOJ) has recently revised its entire budget development system, dividing the department's budget into "decision units." These decision units include all costs related to program activities, and administrative (overhead) costs are allocated across decision units. Further, the budget request for each decision unit must identify the baseline level of performance and funding and then specify changes in performance that would result from changes in funding. This makes the relationship between dollars and results transparent and permits decision makers to better understand that relationship in the context of making budget decisions.

For example, the U.S. Marshals Service (USMS) has three decision units: Protection of the Judicial Process, Fugitive Apprehension, and Seized Assets. All funds in the budget request for the USMS are allocated to one of these three decision units. This required the existing budget, which was divided into nine decision units, to be significantly realigned to match with Department of Justice strategic objectives. Further, the budget requests for the decision units are expressed in terms of historical performance, baseline performance for the budget year, and performance changes expected from changes in funding.

It is hard to overstate the importance of agency budget preparation to the overall effort to make the budget process more informed by performance. If the agency budget request, at all levels of the agency, has not laid the groundwork for relating funding to performance, it is highly unlikely that, as changes are made at higher levels (in OMB and the Congress, for example), the agency will be able to understand the performance implications of those changes. Further, when the agency implements its budget, it will be much more difficult for individual line managers to understand how they can use the money provided to them to help the agency maximize achievement of its strategic objectives. If these relationships are not well understood, agency managers and line employees may later find themselves managing "pots of money" without any clear understanding of how their actions can contribute to—or detract from—the overall performance of the agency.

Ultimately, the central budget office within the agency, on behalf of the agency head (the cabinet secretary or similar official), must collect and analyze each of these budget requests in order to determine what should be included in the budget request to OMB. It would be possible, of course, for the agency central budget office to simply collect the information, aggregate it, and send it to OMB without change. More frequently, however, the agency head needs to trim budget requests to fit them within some perceived envelope that represents what the agency head believes to be an "acceptable" budget request (this notion of acceptability varies from agency to agency and from agency head to agency head). Given that OMB desires information on the performance effects of funding, at a minimum the agency budget office must ensure that the request going forward is fully justified in terms of presenting the best case for why the agency budget request should be fully funded to achieve the President's (or at least the agency's) strategic objectives.

A performance-informed budget at the agency level would be focused much more on outcomes than that at the bureau level. There may be a number of different bureaus that affect the same outcome, or a number of different federal agencies that affect that outcome. The department head needs to have information on how different funding levels will affect key results, especially those that are presidential priorities. For example, many federal agencies are currently involved in activities designed to enhance security," so agency heads need to understand the effect of proposed budget allocations on that goal. As another example, "reducing fraud and abuse in student loan programs" is one of the President's specific management agenda items. In that context, it would be important for the secretary of education to understand the effect that his proposed budget will have on the achievement of that objective. In the end, having appropriate performance and cost information can enable the agency head (and the agency budget office on behalf of the agency head) to analyze budget requests in the context of their performance implications, make tradeoffs in a way that maximizes performance, and build a better justified budget request to OMB.

OMB Analysis of the Agency Budget Request

Once the agency submits the budget request to OMB, the President's budget office begins the difficult job of attempting to fit too many expenditure requests into too few revenues. That is, invariably the sum of agency requests far exceeds the total amount that can (or at least will) be included in the President's budget. This means that the process of arriving at a recommendation for each agency will involve, in most cases, attempts by the budget office to reduce the agency's budget request to a number that will fit within the overall budget constraint (see Table 2.3).

The same performance, cost, and strategic planning information that is necessary at the agency level is also necessary for OMB's evaluation of the budget request, with one addition. The extent to which some overarching or governmentwide strategic or performance plan exists can assist OMB in determining the relative priority attached to different requests. Although a specific governmentwide performance plan, published in a separate volume from the overall budget, has not existed since FY 2001, a clear articulation of administration priorities may give general guidance concerning the direction of the administration. For example, the Bush administration has clearly identified homeland security, national security, and economic growth as three of its key policy priorities. Policies that might affect one or more of these priorities can clearly be evaluated from that perspective, particularly to the extent that there are performance measures that exist to evaluate progress, that there are common performance measures that may exist that cut across different programs that affect those outcomes, and that there is a clear understanding of the relationship between cost and performance. Such a statement of priorities, however, is not as comprehensive as the governmentwide plan had been; it does not provide as much direction to federal agencies and the Congress concerning the President's performance expectations.

Furthermore, frequently only a limited number of resources are actually "in play" in a given budget. That is, those expenditures that are relatively

Table 2.3: Performance-Informed Budgeting in OMB Analysis of Agency Budget Request

Possible Measures Available	Potential Use of Measures	Who Uses the Measures
• Government wide strategic plan and performance plan • Agency strategic and performance plans • Cost accounting • Performance (outcome) measures • Evaluation of programs	• To make tradeoffs between agencies to allocate funds strategically • To build budget justification for submission to legislative body • To determine overlapping services between agencies • To evaluate in-house versus contract services	*President:* • Cost of achieving national goals *OMB director:* • Marginal costs and marginal results • Cost/results comparisons across programs, or between government and the private sector *OMB examiner:* • Costs, outputs, and results • Cost of different alternatives

"uncontrollable" (interest on the debt and most entitlement expenses) account for approximately 65 percent of the current federal budget, although presidential budgets routinely propose changes that affect entitlement programs and tax laws. Even for the remaining 35 percent of discretionary (appropriated) accounts, the process is not "zero-based"; that is, decisions are almost always being made "at the margin" (how much more and how much less will the agency receive compared to last year). It is the decisions concerning how these marginal dollars are to be allocated that are most likely to be informed by performance considerations.

For example, the Bush administration's PART was designed largely to bring information on the performance of federal programs into budget decisions. In order for this process to become fully effective, it will be necessary for OMB—not only on the performance of the programs that are under review but on the relationship between federal funding and performance levels. Since these programs are affected by many factors that are outside of the control of program managers, these program managers (and OMB examiners) must understand the relationship between dollars and results in order to determine the effect of more (or less) funding on performance. For example, a program that is deemed "effective" may be effective because of factors other than funding; it might not be made more effective by giving it more money. Conversely, a program that is not effective may be an appropriate candidate for elimination; it may also be a candidate for more funds if its lack of effectiveness results from underfunding.

Clearly, these issues are difficult to address, but they are better addressed with information on performance and cost than they are without that information. Simply building a "current services" budget without paying attention to the performance effects (past, present, and future) of funding runs the risk of freezing current priorities and policies in place, rather than continually evaluating expenditures to determine which mixture of policies will best achieve the President's aims. In fact, it is crucial to remember that the President's budget is, first and foremost, a political document that reflects the President's funding priorities. Whatever information on performance that is brought into this process must be considered in the context of this political decision making.

Perhaps the greatest payoff to the use of better performance and cost information during this stage will come in the "conversation" between the agency and the OMB budget examiner(s). To the extent that cost and performance information is available and brought together, the debate between the parties can focus truly on whether the level of funding requested is justified by the results that will be achieved, as opposed to being driven solely by anecdotal evidence on one side or the other. This may prove advantageous to agencies that can build a strong case for the performance effects of their programs. It may prove advantageous to OMB in cases in which programs or agencies have continually received funding despite a general lack of evidence for the success of their programs.[32]

At higher levels of OMB and in the White House, the existence of better performance and cost information is likely to have an additional effect. While it is important for these higher level officials to have information on the effects of funding on performance in individual programs or agencies, performance and cost measures can also inform the difficult choices that must be made between agencies. Decisions, particularly toward the end of the budget process, often come down to comparing the relative effects of providing a limited amount of money to two or more agencies. For example, $500 million might be made available to divide among a teen pregnancy prevention program, a program that provides grants for higher education to poor students, and a program designed to make the air cleaner. Given such a choice, it would be useful to know, for a given level of additional resources, how many fewer teens would become pregnant, how many more low-income students would graduate from college, and how much cleaner the air would be. These projections do not tell us which of these uses of resources is most appropriate, but they may make the process of choosing among different uses of resources more informed.

Budget Approval

Once the President's budget is transmitted to the Congress, the budget approval stage begins. Budget approval is largely the province of the Congress as it approves legislation that affects both taxes and spending. It does involve the President in the sense that he must approve the bills that are passed by the Congress prior to their becoming law. In advance of this formal presidential action, the President and his advisers interact continually with the Congress, making various congressional committees and the congressional leadership aware of the President's positions on legislation moving through the Congress. The consensus is that currently the Congress makes very little systematic use of performance information for budgeting, particularly in the appropriations process. There are, nonetheless, a number of opportunities at various stages of the budget process for the Congress to make greater use of performance information if the incentives are present to do so (see Table 2.4 on page 46).

The congressional budget process consists of three primary (and related) activities:

- **Development of the budget resolution** lays out the "big picture" of fiscal and budget policy, and creates the overall framework for specific decisions on taxes and spending that must be made by congressional committees as the process goes forward.
- **The authorization process creates and extends programs**, creates the terms and conditions under which they operate, and may create performance expectations for programs and agencies. This can include creating or making changes in mandatory spending programs, such as Social Security and Medicare (where funding is provided in continuing law), or making changes to laws governing the collection of revenues.
- **The appropriations process** provides funding for the approximately 35 percent of the federal budget that receives its funding through annual appropriations (the remaining 65 percent is either interest on the debt or represents mandatory spending).

Any of these three processes can be affected by performance information, but the specific uses of that information differ among these three processes. The presidential approval processes can be affected by performance information as well.

Budget Resolution

The budget resolution does not deal with the details of the budget, but rather it creates a framework within which decisions on those details can be made by congressional committees. It is organized by type of spending (mandatory versus discretionary) and by major budget function (national security, international affairs, natural resources, health, and so on). The bud-

Table 2.4: Performance-Informed Budgeting in Budget Approval

Budget Approval	Potential Information	Potential Uses	Who Uses the Information
Legislative	• Performance measures, accurate cost estimates, and strategic/performance plans included with budget justifications • Structuring accounts by program rather than by source of inputs	*President:* • To create a congressional "performance resolution" as part of the budget resolution • To establish specific performance expectations as part of the authorization process • To compare costs to marginal effects on performance during the legislative funding process • To make performance expectations clear as part of budget allocation	*Budget committees:* "Social indicators" for setting broad fiscal policy direction *Authorizing/tax-writing committees:* Results expected for each year of tax/authorization legislation *Appropriations committees:* Cost, outputs, and results from different levels of funding; comparing marginal dollars to marginal outputs and results
Chief Executive	• Requiring agencies to assess implications of legislatively approved budget for achieving government strategic objectives	• To make decisions on signature or veto, and statements of administration policy, informed by performance implications	*President:* • Results expected through authorized programs • Relating costs to outputs and results in proposed and enacted legislation, compared to those in the President's budget

get resolution currently specifies levels of spending associated with these different functions and discusses in broad terms the assumptions behind these functional totals, but it does not specify any performance expectations. GAO has suggested that the Congress adopt a "performance resolution" as a companion to the budget resolution.[33] This performance resolution would provide information on the performance expectations that would accompany the budgeted dollars in the budget resolution. It would cover not only spending programs but taxes as well. That is, if the budget resolution anticipates a tax cut or a tax increase, for example, the performance resolution would outline the expected effect on aggregate economic variables, such as economic growth. If the budget resolution anticipates an increase in funding for health care, the performance resolution would outline the expected effect on the number of uninsured persons, on the level of health care provided, and on the overall economy.

This performance resolution might be adopted annually, but it would take on particular significance in years where *reconciliation* legislation was being considered. The reconciliation process is used by the Congress during years in which changes are anticipated above or below the baseline level for mandatory spending or revenues. If reconciliation is not used, the assumption is that *the current services level* is being funded; that is, that revenue or tax programs are provided for as under current law. Because reconciliation involves changes (sometimes substantial) in current programs, the Congress should welcome information on the effects of those changes before they are acted upon.[34] This would presumably be true whether or not there was a performance resolution, but a performance resolution would make congressional performance expectations more explicit, especially as it relates to programs or activities with common objectives.

Authorizations

Federal programs operate under laws, which create them and establish the conditions under which they operate. Some programs are authorized indefinitely, while others are authorized for a specific period of time. For example, defense programs are subject to annual authorization, while agriculture or transportation programs have authorization bills considered every few years. Authorizing legislation is under the jurisdiction of committees that have specific expertise in a particular substantive area. Thus, a "farm bill" is an authorization bill covering agriculture programs, or a "transportation bill" is one covering transportation programs. Two authorizing committees—the House Ways and Means Committee and the Senate Finance Committee—consider laws governing tax legislation, which is frequently used to further social and economic objectives. Authorization bills often include direction concerning performance expectations, but frequently are not clear or quantifiable. Further, many agencies find themselves saddled with multiple and conflicting missions, and these conflicts are normally not resolved in legislation. Thus, agencies know what they need to accomplish in general but are often not given enough direction to allow them to set meaningful performance targets (or at least ones where there is consensus between the Congress and the agency, or even within the Congress, on the performance expectations for the agency or program). This lack of specificity leads to a situation in which agencies are more likely to need to resolve conflicts between congressional committees, or between the Congress or the President, or between competing interests, when implementing federal programs.

In this context it might be very useful to federal agencies and programs if performance expectations were made clearer in authorizing legislation. This would assist agencies in developing priorities, since authorizing legislation involves reaching consensus between the Congress and the President. It would necessitate more frequent authorizations for some programs than has historically been the case, since meaningful performance expectations must be consistent with the views of the current Congress and the current President. More significantly, many programs currently do not have formal authorizations at all, often because of disagreements in the Congress or between the Congress and the executive branch concerning some details of organization or program design. Lack of authorization is a widespread problem. The Congressional Budget Office estimated that, in FY 2002, $91 billion, or almost 30 percent of all domestic appropriations, went for programs with no current authorization.[35]

The important point is that the authorization process is crucial to developing expectations about the performance of programs, and it is therefore the most logical place for performance information to gain a foothold into the congressional budget process. While certainly many see it as desirable to have performance information integrated into the appropriations process as well, the most likely payoff would come by focusing first on the authorization process, for two reasons. First, the authorization process is already set up to deal with comprehensive questions of program design, redesign, and performance. Second, while only 35 percent of federal spending goes through the appropriations process, all federal spending and all tax laws are subject to authorization (although, as noted, efforts would need to be made to subject programs to more routine and systematic authorization than currently is the case).

Appropriations

In the appropriations process, decisions are made on funding levels for the 13 regular appropriation bills that together make up the 35 percent of federal spending referenced earlier. Those agencies funded from discretionary appropriations have no legal authority to spend money without the appropriation of those funds. Thus, the appropriations process is an important (in many years, the most important) annual budgeting ritual. Among the criticisms of this process, three seem particularly connected to the potential use of performance information:

- The process is usually focused only on marginal decisions rather than on the comprehensive effects of spending.
- There is little evidence that appropriations committees consider performance information in any systematic way when making decisions on allocations, relying instead on anecdotal information on program and agency performance.
- Members of Congress use the appropriations process, in part, as a vehicle to dole out money for "member priorities" (frequently referred to as "pork barrel projects"), sometimes at the expense of program or agency performance.

In addition, many appropriation accounts are not connected to programs or specific activities of the agency. Frequently the accounts are aggregate "salary and expense" items, which commingle several programs or activities into one relatively large account. This can make it difficult or impossible to tie the costs to specific programs, let alone to performance of particular programs.[36]

How could performance and cost information be used in the appropriations process? First, accounts could be reorganized so that they tie more specifically to agency missions or programs. GAO has done extensive work on federal account structures and has found that these accounts are generally not well aligned with performance goals. A reform of account structures might allow for a more transparent illumination of costs that are associated with programs, and that reform could lay the groundwork for relating program costs to program performance. Changes in account structures are already being advocated by executive branch agencies, which have had some success in convincing the Congress to allow them to restructure accounts. For example, the U.S. Marshals Service completely restructured its accounts in the context of its FY 2004 budget request.[37]

Second, the appropriations committees could demand, and make better use of, performance information as a part of the appropriation process. To the extent that many members of the Congress attempt to focus on "member priorities" or on anecdotal information when making budget decisions, they may be less likely to demand information on the effects of overall spending. If such information became a normal part of the congressional debate, however, it is more likely that the effects of appropriation decisions on performance would become more transparent.

Third, the appropriations committees could consider agency budgets more comprehensively, instead of focusing on changes at the margin. That is, they could relate program performance to cost at different funding levels, including the baseline (current services) level, as well as at levels that deviate from the baseline level (either positively or negatively). This would allow members of the Congress to have a better idea of the performance tradeoffs inherent in providing different levels of funding to different agencies and programs.

These last two uses of performance information are much more likely to occur if the authorization process is more explicitly focused on performance, as suggested previously. But including more performance information in authorizations will not by itself translate into its use for appropriations. The major problem here is one of incentives. Simply put, it may not be in the interest of the appropriations committees or other members of the Congress to focus more explicitly on the performance implications of funding until and unless members see it as in their electoral interest to do so. Currently, there is an explicit connection—real or perceived—between money spent in the home state or district and electoral outcomes. Members of the Congress are unlikely to trade that relatively certain connection for an uncertain payoff in terms of overall program results (only some of which may affect the home state or district), unless information on paths not taken (roads not built?) becomes more transparent. The Bush administration's PART initiative could assist in making the performance implications of funding more transparent, particularly since OMB has taken the rather extraordinary step of making these PART results widely available (www.expectmore.gov).

The President

Bills cannot become law without the President's signature. So for each of the latter two types of legislation (authorizing bills and appropriation bills) the President also requires information prior to the completion of the budget approval process. Since the budget resolution does not require the President's signature, it is less directly important that the President have information on the performance implications of this resolution. But if the process is to work as designed, it is important that the President understand the performance implications of the budget resolution and how that expected performance compares to the performance that was expected in his budget proposal.[38] This will require a more explicit articulation of performance expectations in the budget resolution, since currently these performance expectations are not at all clear.

For authorization and appropriation bills, there is an even more practical reason for the President to understand the performance expected from proposed legislation, since he has the power to sign or veto the legislation. For authorizing legislation, the President could compare the performance expected under the bill as passed with that expected in the President's own proposed authorization for the agency or program (if applicable). For appropriation bills, the President could compare the congressional level of expected performance, by agency and program, with that included in his budget. Of course, in both of these cases, the President will have been following the legislation as it moves through the House and Senate and would be making his views known through statements of administration policy (SAPs). These SAPs, at present, normally focus on the level of funding (for appropriations) or on specific procedural or organizational requirements (for authorizations). They rarely focus explicitly on performance concerns. The process of presidential consideration of this legislation will become much better informed if, prior to taking a position on the legislation or deciding whether to approve it, the President understood the full performance implications of the proposed law.

Budget Execution

Without question, there are important potential applications of performance information in each of the preceding stages of the budget process. A system in which the budget and performance were fully integrated would start with agency budget preparation informed by performance and would continue with OMB and the Congress focusing on performance when making funding decisions. Even if none of these preceding applications has occurred, however, there are myriad ways in which federal agencies can use performance information for budget execution—that is, for implementing the budget after it has become law.

Put simply, agencies have discretion. Authorizing and appropriation bills do not provide all the direction agencies require in order to operate, and the law does not anticipate all the circumstances that may arise in the course of managing federal programs. In part, this discretion occurs because it is easier to pass nonspecific and vague legislation that allows agency discretion rather than spelling out these details. Further, the Congress and the President do not possess all the technical expertise necessary to resolve all the issues necessary in running federal programs. Agencies and their management, for these reasons, need to "fill in the details" during the implementation (or budget execution) stage of the process. Budget execution is, therefore, about resource allocation (see Table 2.5 on page 52).

There are many specific ways in which performance information can be brought to bear on allocating resources for the execution of the budget.

Understanding the Specific Implications of the Approved Budget for Performance

Regardless of whether the Congress and the President made clear the specific level of performance expected from the approved budget, the agency should review the budget as approved and translate the level of funding received into the expected performance that can be achieved at that level. This means evaluating how all the factors that affect performance—such as funding, legislative factors, environmental or economic conditions, or regulations—would be expected to affect performance. It is important that this analysis involve input from agency program officials concerning how these factors would affect results. After such analysis, the agency should communicate the expected performance from the approved budget to agency staff and other interested parties. If agency staff and external stakeholders are still operating under the assumption that the current expected level of performance is consistent with the level expected when the budget was formulated, that assumption will result in inaccurate signals. Therefore, these expectations should be revised based on the budget as approved. As noted previously, it is most likely that the performance expectations associated with the approved budget will be transparent if the performance implications of the budget were made clear at earlier stages, beginning with the development of the budget request from the lowest levels of the agency.

Table 2.5: Performance-Informed Budgeting in Budget Execution

Possible Information Sources	Potential Uses	Who Uses the Information
• Agency and governmentwide strategic plans • Levels of funding (through apportionments and allotments) • Performance (outcome) measures • Output (activity) measures • Cost information	• To understand legislative and other constraints and their effects on the achievement of agency performance goals • To allocate funds among agency missions, subunits, or regions/local offices • To allocate funds to third parties • To monitor cost and performance during budget execution • To evaluate other specific means that can be used to leverage performance • For congressional oversight	*Agency head:* • Allocating funds to agency subunits • Communicating performance expectations *Program managers:* • Using flexibility to spend money in line with strategic priorities • Communicating performance expectations *Individual employees:* • Managing funds/ spending money consistent with their contributions to strategic objectives *Grant recipients:* • Purchasing goods and services with an eye toward overarching program goals *Congressional committees:* • Using program goals and targets to influence oversight agenda

The ability to show the relationship between resources and results, and how that relationship has changed in the budget as approved, implies the ability to track costs by program. For many agencies, this means (as discussed previously) revisions to the account structure so that appropriation accounts do not contain multiple programs or programs are not contained within more than one budget account. If these revisions have not occurred, agencies will need to "crosswalk" between their appropriation accounts and the resources that are associated with individual programs.

GAO notes that the analysis of changes to the budget as enacted should result in written guidance issued to program officials that outline "known or anticipated changes in the agency's goals, performance issues and resource constraints since formulation."[39] If lower-than-expected resources will result in a performance gap, the agency should "begin to address the issue as part of the performance management and budget process."[40]

In the end, the analysis of differences between the proposed and enacted budget should result in operating plans that inform agency subunits how the enacted budget has affected expectations of performance for those agency subunits as well as for individual programs. For example, GAO notes that in the Nuclear Regulatory Commission "as the budget is executed, operating plans ... are used to compare actual office resources to budget estimates and actual performance to targeted performance, and to identify necessary programmatic and fiscal actions."[41]

Using the Agency's Discretion to Allocate Funds within the Agency

The approved budget from the Congress normally leaves a significant amount of discretion in the hands of the agency to allocate resources. For many agencies, this means allocating dollars toward different agency programs, or regional subunits, or both. In these cases, the agency can use information on the relationship between dollars and performance to attempt to maximize the level of performance that may be leveraged from a given budget. Several examples illustrate this point:

- The Food and Drug Administration restructured staff assignments in order to enable it to complete reviews of generic drugs in a more timely fashion.[42]
- The Internal Revenue Service allocated training resources among its toll-free customer service centers based on needs as indicated by the error rates across the different centers.[43]
- The Administration for Children and Families (ACF) often allocates Training and Technical Assistance funds and salary and expense dollars to its different programs "based on program performance and needs." For example, Dallas regional officials told GAO that their record for achieving results in tribal demonstration projects led to receiving additional funds from headquarters for FY 2001. Further, in ACF, "all regions are required to develop and operate according to work plans that link program and agency goals and objectives to expected performance."[44]

- The Department of Agriculture's Animal and Plant Health Inspection Service's Fruit Fly Exclusion and Detection program uses outcome data to "allocate field personnel, vehicles, supplies, and other resources to … problem area(s)."[45]
- The Department of Housing and Urban Development uses outcome information, in part, to prioritize its use of resources for its Public and Indian Housing program in two specific ways. First, it prioritizes site visits based on outcome information, allowing limited staff and travel resources to be targeted to areas of greatest need and focusing the site visit on the most critical performance issues. Second, it uses information on physical conditions of buildings to prioritize capital spending.[46]
- The Veterans Health Administration (VHA) allocates funds to its 22 health-care networks (or VISNs) based on the number of veterans being served. After funds are allocated to the networks, however, performance information plays an important role in the allocation of resources to different hospitals, clinics, and offices within each VISN. VISN directors are held accountable for the achievement of outcome goals within their network, giving them incentives for maximizing performance partially by using their discretion to allocate dollars where they are most needed.[47] GAO reviewed budget execution practices at two VISNs and found that "(i)ntegrating performance information into resource allocation decisions is apparent" in these networks.[48]

This is by no means a comprehensive listing of performance-informed budget execution strategies by federal agencies. It likely only scratches the surface. For example, these GAO and IBM Center for The Business of Government reports and reviews have not examined in detail budget allocation practices at the lowest managerial levels of the organization—in an individual veterans' hospital, a national park, or a local immigration office. Clearly, the payoff for performance-informed budgeting also occurs at these lower levels. A hospital administrator can allocate staff between missions or between shifts based on the implications for veterans' health, or a national park superintendent can use resources in a way that best assists the National Park Service in achieving its customer service, conservation, and maintenance objectives. The more the relationships between activities at lower levels of the organization and the achievement of the objective of the agency are made clear, the more agency employees can manage resources with a focus on the achievement of agency results.

The important point is that, in each of these cases, it is obvious that agencies are using their discretion to allocate resources in part based on performance considerations. While congressional and presidential buy-in are important to performance-informed budgeting, each of these cases demonstrates the substantial effects that can come from an agency's focus on performance during budget execution, with or without the support of the Congress and the President. And while the agencies mentioned clearly have some focus on performance in budget execution, there are just as clearly other cases in which agencies are failing to take advantage of the flexibility they have to allocate and manage resources to maximize performance. Further, there are many cases in which OMB and (in particular) congressional practices (such as earmarking, full-time equivalent (FTE) floors or ceilings, or excessive itemization) may deter an agency from achieving key objectives.

Two other characteristics of effective allocation are important to note. First, it is important to provide agency program officials with ample opportunities for dialogue and appeal about the performance implications of funding allocations. A "top-down" approach, where staff are informed of the expected level of performance but do not agree that this level of performance can be achieved with the dollars provided, is not likely to be successful. A fully mature performance-informed budgeting system will feature an ongoing dialogue between staff at all levels of the agency where the performance implications of different levels of funding are transparent to all parties. This is hard to pull off in practice, but it is far superior to a process in which such adjustments are not made and therefore the link between funding and accountability for results is severed.

Second, it is vital that funds be allocated in a timely manner. Resources that are provided late—which routinely occurs in the federal government when final appropriations are not provided until well into the fiscal year—impede effective financial and performance planning in agencies. Further, many agencies do not have adequate accounting systems, which means that managers lack timely access to information about the availability of resources, making it very difficult for these program managers to maximize the use of those funds.[49]

Allocating Funds to Third Parties

Many federal agencies do not operate programs directly but rely on third parties to operate them. These third parties can include state and local governments, which operate many large programs (Medicaid, welfare, unemployment insurance) and small programs. They also include contractors, who play a vital role in the operations of many agencies, including the Department of Defense, the Department of Energy, and NASA. Clearly performance information may be used by these agencies to attempt to allocate resources to these external parties in a way that can best leverage performance. Two specific uses are allocating and reducing funds to grant recipients, and deciding whether to contract or provide a service in-house, as well as monitoring the performance of contractors.

Allocating funds to grant recipients. An inherent problem with grants is that agencies with the grant funds do not directly control the behavior of the grant recipients. Many grants are allocated by formula. In the case of formula grants, performance considerations do not influence budget allocations during budget execution, but they can influence the design of the program and the formula itself. For discretionary awards (so-called "project grants"), however, it is crucial that granting agencies are attentive to the performance implications of grants before the fact. A recent evaluation of three programs in the Department of Education unearthed examples of this phenomenon:

- The Adult Education and Literacy program used outcome data to determine which states would receive monetary incentive awards. State performance on adult education outcomes partially determines the amount of money each state receives.[50]
- The Migrant Education program uses outcome data to determine increases or decreases in funding for grantees from year to year, and also for eligibility for funds that may be remaining at the end of the year.[51]
- The Rehabilitation Services Administration uses performance information to allocate technical assistance dollars and to take funds away from poor performers. Grantees are required to have "passing scores" on two primary outcome indicators and on two of three secondary indicators in order to be eligible for continued funding.[52]

Further, the Administration for Children and Families (ACF) uses an instrument, the Grant Application and Budget Review Instrument (GABI), along with other information to help it identify applicants that have unusually high administrative costs, teacher/classroom ratios, and the like. This assists ACF in both monitoring existing grants and deciding on future grant funding.[53]

Outsourcing decisions and contract management. Federal agencies have contracted out a great many services for some time, and this outsourcing has increased in recent years.[54] Among the services most frequently contracted out include IT, maintenance services, food services, and specialized technical services (for example, legal services). As discussed previously, federal agencies are currently under pressure to compete with the private sector to provide a larger percentage of their commercial activities. Performance and cost information can be used to inform both contracting and competition decisions. Frequently the stated justification for outsourcing is that outside vendors will be able to provide services at a lower cost. These cost comparisons themselves can be difficult to make, given the state of many federal and private sector accounting systems. Even if this problem can be overcome, however, a reasonable comparison of in-house versus contractual production of a good or service requires a thorough understanding of the performance implications of both options. Spending less money for worse performance is not necessarily a good deal; spending less money for the same or better performance, on the other hand, is a clear improvement.

Performance considerations also come into play in the contract management process. The initial contract should specify performance targets and milestones for the agency. After the contract has been awarded, it is also important that the agency monitor the contractor for compliance with its key provisions, including performance. Since many contracts are monitored by line staff at lower or regional levels of the organization, this is yet another place where it is important that the relationships between micro-level activities and macro-level results are made clear.

Monitoring the Budget and Performance during Budget Execution

It is not only important for initial allocation decisions to be informed by performance. It is also crucial that personnel in the agency engage in constant communication about the relationship between resources and performance during the budget execution phase. Priorities change, as do factors that influence performance, during the budget year. The cost of items important to service delivery may change, as may environmental factors. GAO highlights the importance of performance monitoring during budget execution so that "management has credible, up-to-date information for monitoring and decision making. Such monitoring should form the basis for decisions that address performance gaps by looking for root causes and, if necessary, adjusting funding allocations to rectify performance problems."[55] GAO, in a separate report, identified a practice in the Nuclear Regulatory Commission whereby "operating plans track performance against established targets for each planned work activity to call attention to significant performance issues needing corrective action."[56]

Sometimes performance monitoring may occasion transfers or reprogramming, where agencies spend resources for purposes other than those originally intended. In more extreme cases, they may lead to supplemental appropriations, where agencies seek additional funds to address performance gaps. In either event, it is important that the agency have a full understanding of the implications of the change, as well as the potential performance implications of the status quo.

Tracking costs during the fiscal year can have important implications for performance. If the costs of a given activity or program run substantially over or under projections, this can clearly affect performance. Further, for many programs productivity or cost measures are a significant component of performance measurement. It is particularly important that the costs captured represent the full cost of doing business, as opposed to only direct costs. As noted previously, this is a significant challenge for most federal programs, which have woefully inadequate accounting systems that cannot track full costs by program. Thus GAO notes that the ability to account for direct and indirect costs necessitates an information system that permits total costs (direct and indirect) to be associated with program goals.[57]

Evaluating Other Specific Means That Can Be Used to Leverage Performance

A number of other approaches can be used to assist agencies in meeting performance goals, particularly where incentives need to be created to leverage performance. This is particularly true where multiple agencies or levels of government need to act in order to meet performance goals. For example, the Administration for Children and Families has joined with other federal agencies to form interagency councils that attempt to bring together public and private agencies with similar missions and agendas. This potentially prevents duplication of effort and assists in the efficient use of resources. ACF also attempts to take advantage of state and local efforts that allow more targeted use of federal dollars.[58] In addition, ACF and other programs that rely on third parties for administration often must create the incentives necessary for these administrative agents to collect reliable data in a timely manner. ACF has attempted to create these incentives by making technical assistance dollars available to state and local governments to assist them in improving their capacity to collect and report information important to ACF's management and reporting needs.[59] Finally, financial incentives can be provided not only to external actors but to individuals and teams within an agency as well. Frequently agencies make use of devices such as financial bonuses, additional management flexibilities, promotions, and awards and recognition as motivators for agency staff to engage in behavior consistent with achieving the goals of the organization.

Congressional Oversight

Performance information could be used by the Congress for oversight of programs. Unlike other budget execution activities, congressional oversight is obviously not the province of the agencies. Instead, the Congress and its committees use oversight to monitor the progress of federal programs and agencies in implementing legislation, including the budget. The criticism of congressional oversight historically is that it has not been focused on the extent to which programs have achieved their objectives. Rather, oversight has been used to draw attention to politically sensitive or high-profile issues. Some political scientists have argued that the Congress engages in "fire alarm" oversight, where high-profile issues get attention, as opposed to "police patrol" oversight, where agencies or programs are looked at in detail in an effort to determine what works and what does not.[60]

If, as discussed, budget resolutions, authorizations, or appropriation bills are more explicit about specifying expected performance, it will be far more likely that oversight will also focus on these performance issues. Currently the attention that congressional committees pay to detailed oversight of programs varies substantially from committee to committee. Certainly some committees make substantial use of hearings and GAO studies, for example, to evaluate the effectiveness of programs. Other committees are less likely to focus on the performance of programs and more likely to focus on "oversight" episodically or in an effort to promote a political agenda. In these cases, while it would be desirable for oversight to focus on performance questions, there are currently limited incentives for members of committees to focus in detail on oversight of programs. More emphasis on oversight will probably not occur until some of these incentives have been changed. It is possible that changing the terms of the debate by greater specification of performance expectations in legislation would help create more incentives for detailed oversight.

Audit and Evaluation

Finally, performance information can be used in important ways in the audit and evaluation stage of the process, during which federal programs are reviewed to determine compliance with laws, management practices, and program performance. Theoretically, the results of the audit and evaluation stage should feed into the formulation of the budget during some subsequent fiscal year. This frequently occurs with a significant time lag, because by the time audit results are known from one fiscal year, the budget preparation phase may be under way for a fiscal year two or more years after the year to which the audit information applied. Still, recent years have seen significant developments in the questions that are being asked in audits and evaluations, in the capacity of the federal government to answer those questions, and in the reporting of information to the public after the fact (see Table 2.6).

Table 2.6: Performance-Informed Budgeting in Audit and Evaluation

Type of Information	Potential Uses	Who Uses the Information
• Agency strategic goals • Cost estimation • Performance reporting • Logic models • Data quality and reliability	To shift the focus of audits and evaluations to include performance questions, rather than only financial compliance	*Internal and external auditors:* • Determining success or failure of a program • Determining compliance with applicable law *Agency leadership:* • Determining areas of emphasis for management improvements *OMB and the Congress:* • Highlighting management and performance problems

The audit and evaluation stage of the budget process historically looked only at the use of inputs. It fit squarely within what Allen Schick referred to in 1966 as a "control" function of budgeting.[61] Agencies were evaluated according to whether the funds that had been appropriated had been used for the specific purposes intended, and not according to what resulted from those expenditures. Given this history, even moving to asking more "output" oriented questions, which began to occur in the 1950s, was a step forward.

Beginning in the 1960s, however, research and program evaluation offices began to be created in many federal agencies. In fact, agencies like the Department of Defense and the Department of Health, Education, and Welfare were noted for their capacity to engage in long-term planning and evaluation. These evaluations often focused on performance after-the-fact and certainly addressed resource issues as one of many factors that could affect program success. The capacity for many federal agencies to ask out-come-related questions was almost certainly enhanced by the PPBS reform, in spite of the fact that the reform is viewed overall as less than successful.

At the same time, GAO was shifting its focus from asking traditional accounting questions—which focus rather narrowly on inputs—to asking more questions about the operations and performance of federal agencies. Further, other positions—such as agency inspectors general and chief finan-cial officers—were subsequently created and charged with asking perfor-mance questions, in addition to supporting the development of the data that would be necessary to connect resources and results.

As noted previously, the last 15 years have seen substantial legislative impe-tus for performance measurement and therefore for a greater performance focus in audit and evaluation. The CFO Act, GPRA, the Clinger-Cohen Act, and other laws had in common the notion that we should better understand the relationship between resource use and results. The George W. Bush administration's initia-tives share this focus, perhaps particularly manifested in the PART, which requires after-the-fact knowledge of performance and inputs in order to succeed.

In what specific ways, then, can the audit and evaluation process be supportive of performance-informed budgeting?

- **Appropriate estimating of cost:** As noted previously, understanding the connection between resources and results requires the appropriate measurement of each. Financial audits typically focus on expenditures by budget account and on compliance with legal restrictions on spend-ing. These are important considerations. Perhaps more important for performance-informed budgeting, however, is that agencies have the capacity to establish costs by program or mission. Audits can assist by providing information on the status of cost accounting and by making recommendations on further developments.
- **Reporting on performance:** The performance reports that are required under GPRA are clearly exemplary of a performance-informed audit and evaluation process. Prior to GPRA, there was no systematic requirement

that agencies report on results. These reports, to the extent that they highlight gaps between expected and actual performance, can be useful tools for future planning.

- **Developing "logic models" concerning the relationship between resources and results:**[62] Understanding costs and understanding performance levels is not enough. A mature performance-informed budgeting system must be able to connect the two. And making connections between dollars and performance requires that we understand how the former affects the latter, meaning that the causal relationships between resources and results must be clearly understood. Since many other factors (besides the level of funding) can affect performance, tracking causal relationships is potentially a complex undertaking. It is vitally important, however, to the eventual linkage of inputs and outcomes. It also can present the relationship between inputs, outputs, intermediate outcomes, and outcomes. This enables agency and program staff to understand the relationship between "what they do" as individuals and the goals of the organization.
- **Highlighting data limitations and problems:** Audits and evaluations can present information that helps users understand the limitations and problems associated with the data necessary to develop a mature performance-informed budgeting system. This can include problems with data reliability, timeliness of collection, timeliness of reporting, or failure to understand causal relationships.

In the end, any sophisticated performance-informed budgeting system requires the ability not only to specify performance before the fact and to use performance information in allocating resources at all stages of the process, but the ability to evaluate performance after the fact and make adjustments for the future accordingly. This necessitates an investment in evaluation capacity that has been lacking recently in federal agencies.[63] It also requires that auditors and evaluators ask the right questions and that the information included in the audits be provided to agency staff and leadership, OMB, and the Congress in a timely fashion.

Findings and Recommendations

The preceding discussion has illustrated many potential uses of performance information in the federal budget process and numerous examples, particularly at the agency level, where such information is already being used. There are also significant gaps in our understanding of performance-informed budgeting, and filling these knowledge gaps can contribute to making the budget process, in all stages, informed more by performance. This concluding section summarizes the key findings of this chapter and recommends actions that may be taken if the federal government is to make further progress in performance-informed budgeting.

Finding 1

The attention of the federal government to strategic planning and the supply of performance and cost information has increased substantially in the years since the passage of the Government Performance and Results Act.

The George W. Bush administration took office at a time when much of the groundwork had been laid for performance-informed budgeting to gain more widespread acceptance. The Clinton administration could arguably not have done what the Bush administration is attempting to do now (certainly not in its first term) because this infrastructure had not been built. In that sense, GPRA is doing exactly what was expected—it has laid the foundation for the use of performance information. As difficult as it has been for the executive branch to increase the production of performance information, these challenges pale in comparison to the problems that agencies face in getting the data used for decision making. The impediments to the production of meaningful performance and cost information are largely technical ones. The impediments to the use of performance and cost information stem from a lack of incentives. Those incentives are likely to determine the fate of performance-informed budgeting.

Recommendation 1a
Current initiatives should not be replacements for the GPRA-required reports and process but should be consistent with the requirements of GPRA, in an effort to communicate a consistent message to federal managers whose cooperation is key to success.

In particular, OMB should make it clear to agencies that the current Program Assessment Rating Tool initiative and the President's Management Agenda are not "new" initiatives but are fully consistent with preexisting requirements under GPRA. An agency that is managing for results should find complying with GPRA and the PART initiative and "getting to green" on the PMA to involve a fully consistent set of management practices.

Recommendation 1b
Consistent with the requirement of OMB's "budget and performance integration" (BPI) initiative, planning and budgeting should be undertaken in concert with each other, not as disconnected processes.

The initial set of criteria provided to agencies for success in BPI explicitly stated that, in order to achieve success, agencies must coordinate strategic planning and budgeting, as opposed to conducting these two processes separately. Although the more recent criteria are less explicit concerning this coordination, it remains essential for planning to inform budgeting and for budgeting to inform planning. This means that GPRA initiatives need to be developed with an eye toward the resource implications of performance goals, and the budget needs to be developed in a way that clarifies the relationship between dollars and the achievement of desired results.

Recommendation 1c
Agencies should continue to focus on developing better performance and (particularly) cost information, and on linking these measures to the strategic goals of the agency.
Federal agencies have made substantial progress in developing better performance information, particularly on results. There are still many cases, however, where outcome information is a work in progress and where there is inadequate understanding of the relationship between agency activities and agency performance. Further, many agencies currently have even less information about costs than they do about performance, which impedes their ability to understand the relationships of cost to performance.

Finding 2

The federal government has never been in a better position to make its budget decisions more informed by considerations of performance.
The opportunities to use performance information for budgeting exist at each stage of the budget process but are particularly pronounced in budget execution. Contrary to the opinion of skeptics, there is evidence of sustained activity on multiple fronts. Presidents have not been consistently enthusiastic about performance-informed budgeting, and the Congress has given only lip service to the concept. Nonetheless, the sustained activity of many federal agencies over the past 10 years, coupled with the preexisting groundwork already laid in many agencies, have created a nurturing environment for performance-informed budgeting.

Recommendation 2a
For the most fruitful and immediate payoffs of performance-informed budgeting, attention toward further developing performance-informed budgeting should focus less on the Congress and more on how performance information can influence the management of resources within the executive branch.
A primary finding of a 1993 Congressional Budget Office report on the use of performance information for budgeting was that "the largest potential for real payoffs may be in the area of agency management of the resources once they have been provided in the budget process."[64] More than 10 years later, that remains true. There are temptations in some circles to declare that the budget cannot be more focused on performance because the Congress will not change (or at least has not changed) its behavior.

Such a criticism is ill-founded, given the substantial potential of agencies to affect performance in budget development and budget execution.

Recommendation 2b
Federal agencies should seek to understand how they can use performance information at every stage of budget development, execution, and audit and evaluation.

Consistent with the previous recommendation, agency staff at each level of every federal agency should endeavor to understand how their management of resources contributes to the achievement of the agency's mission and the improvement of performance. This starts with developing a clear understanding of the relationship between the work that is done by employees at all levels of the agency and the achievement of that agency's strategic goals. It also involves building the agency budget request to OMB and the congressional budget justification with a clear focus on the relationship between resources and results. In budget execution, agency staff at all levels of the organization need to understand the implications that their resource management decisions (such as allocating funds to agency subunits, making discretionary grant awards, and awarding and managing contracts) have on the achievement of the agency's strategic goals.

Finding 3

The Congress can contribute to the ability of the federal government to engage in performance-informed budgeting, but progress is not wholly dependent on congressional action.

Even though federal managers have significant discretion to pursue improvements in performance independent of congressional action, there are clearly ways in which the Congress could enable these agencies to use their resources more efficiently. First, it can make performance expectations clearer, which would reduce the level of ambiguity for federal managers in budget execution. Second, it can reduce or eliminate impediments to agency performance, such as FTE floors or ceilings or earmarks. Finally, it can make more systematic use of performance information to drive the congressional oversight agenda.

Recommendation 3a
The Congress should focus on ways in which reforming the authorization process could provide clearer signals to agencies regarding congressional performance expectations.

This would include a more systematic authorization of federal programs and the clear articulation of performance expectations in authorizing legislation. This could have two positive effects: better articulating performance expectations for agencies and providing a clear basis for a congressional oversight agenda.

Recommendation 3b
The Congress should investigate the ways in which the constraints that it places on agencies impede the performance of those agencies.

For example, the Congress routinely imposes detailed input restrictions on agencies that may impede agencies from relocating staff, closing facilities, or taking some other action that could provide for more cost-effective programs. While the Congress is fully within its rights to impose these restrictions, its performance implications should be better understood. Further, the Congress needs to investigate ways in which reforming the account structure of federal agencies would assist in sending better signals concerning the relationship of cost to performance.

Endnotes

1. Robert D. Lee, Jr., "A Quarter Century of State Budgeting Practices," *Public Administration Review* 57 (1997), 133-140.

2. Julia Melkers and Kathryn Willoughby, "The State of the States: Performance-Based Budgeting Requirements in 47 Out of 50," *Public Administration Review* 58(1) (1998), 66–73.

3. Harry Hatry, Elaine Morley, Shelli Rossman, and Joseph Wholey, "How Federal Programs Use Outcome Information: Opportunities for Federal Managers" (Washington, D.C.: IBM Center for The Business of Government, May 2003), 41.

4. Hatry, Morley, Rossman, and Wholey, "How Federal Programs Use Outcome Information: Opportunities for Federal Managers," 62.

5. Chief Financial Officers Act of 1990, Public Law (P.L.) 101-576.

6. A. C. Riley, "Reporting of Performance Measures for Federal Agencies: The Initial Impact of the Chief Financial Officer (sic) Act of 1990," *International Journal of Public Administration* (1995), 18 (2 and 3), 521–580.

7. Government Performance and Results Act of 1993, P.L. 103-62.

8. For more detail on how GPRA works, see Jonathan Breul, "Performance Budgeting in the United States," paper prepared for the Strategic Planning and Environmental Governance Conference, Ministry of Environment and Territorial Protection, Formez, November 28–30, 2002, Rome, Italy, 5–12

9. Suzannah Zak Figura, "Capital Considerations," *Government Executive*.com (February 1999).

10. L. R. Jones and Jerry McCaffrey, "Financial Management Reform in the Federal Government," from Roy Meyers, ed., *Handbook of Government Budgeting* (San Francisco: Jossey Bass, 1999), 76–77.

11. Allen Schick, "The Road to PPB: The Stages of Budget Reform," *Public Administration Review* 26, Number 4 (1966), 243–258.

12. Nancy Ferris, "High-Tech Hurdles," *Government Executive*.com (February 1999).

13. John Kamensky, "Role of the 'Reinventing Government' Movement in Federal Management Reform," *Public Administration Review* 56, Number 3 (May/June 1996), 247–255.

14. National Performance Review, "Mission-Driven, Results-Oriented Budgeting," (September 1993).

15. Anne Laurent, "The Curse of Can Do," *Government Executive* (March 2000).

16. While GPRA had not succeeded in bringing performance measures into the budget process, it was clear that the integration of budget and performance was a key eventual goal of GPRA. See Breul, "Performance Budgeting in the United States," 12.

17. Office of Management and Budget, *The President's Management Agenda* (September 2001).

18. Mark W. Everson, "The President's Management Agenda: An Update," *The Journal of Public Inquiry* (Fall/Winter 2002), 5–8.

19. Office of Management and Budget, *The President's Management Agenda*, 12.

20. To quote specifically from the President's Management Agenda: "In 1993, Congress enacted the Government Performance and Results Act (GPRA) to get the federal government to focus federal programs on performance. After eight years of experience, progress toward the use of performance information for program management has been discouraging." See Office of Management and Budget, *The President's Management Agenda: Fiscal Year 2002*, 27.

21. Office of Management and Budget, "Scorecard Standards for Success," Chapter 23 of *Fiscal Year 2003 Budget, Analytical Perspectives* (Washington, D.C.: U.S. Government Printing Office, 2002), 415. It is worth noting that these standards have shifted since early 2003 to tie the standards more explicitly to the administration's PART initiative, but the new standards are still largely consistent with the guidelines presented here. See http://www.results.gov/standards.pdf.

22. Diana Espinosa, Deputy Assistant Director for Management, Office of Management and Budget, presentation before the Capitol.net Workshop on White House and Congressional Relations, May 20, 2003.

23. Philip G. Joyce and Susan Tompkins, "Using Performance Information for Budgeting: Clarifying the Framework and Investigating Recent State Experience," in K. Newcomer, E. Jennings, C. Broom, and A. Lomax, eds., *Meeting the Challenges of Performance-Oriented Government* (Washington, D.C.: American Society for Public Administration, 2002).

24. This following section relies heavily on the discussion contained in Rita M. Hilton and Philip G. Joyce, "Performance Information and Budgeting in Historical and Comparative Perspective," in B. Guy Peters and Jon Pierre, eds., *Handbook of Public Administration* (Sage, 2003).

25. Malcolm Holmes, "Budget Reform: Experiences from the Past 15 Years," Notes for a presentation to the South African Conference on Expenditure Budget Reform, Pretoria, South Africa, April 1–2, 1996.

26. Paul Posner, presentation before a thought leadership conference on performance-based budgeting, Queenstown, Maryland, March 31, 2003.

27. It is inherently risky to imply consensus among such a disparate group. Therefore, this list does not imply unanimity of opinion, but rather it is meant to capture those items where there was general agreement.

28. Beryl Radin, "Managing Decentralized Departments: The Case of the U.S. Department of Health and Human Services" (Washington, D.C.: IBM Center for The Business of Government, October 1999).

29. Office of Management and Budget, Circular A-11, Part 2, Preparation and Submission of Budget Estimates, Section 30-1.

30. Office of Management and Budget, Circular A-11, Part 2, Preparation and Submission of Budget Estimates, Section 30-1.

31. This definition of success is not intended to imply that federal managers are "empire builders" but rather that most managers are advocates for their programs and believe that more resources will enable them to carry out those programs more effectively, serve more constituents, or both.

32. The preceding discussion, of course, demonstrates an important point, which is that the introduction of more performance information into the budget process is not neutral. Clearly, there are also cases in which agencies and OMB would prefer that the performance effects of funding are not known. In fact, there are probably relatively few places where both OMB and the agency would be equally enthusiastic about having more performance information brought into the budget process. To the extent that performance information is available and used uniformly, however, it is less likely to become simply a political tool.

33. Statement of David M. Walker, Comptroller General of the United States, on *Performance Budgeting: Opportunities and Challenges*, before the Subcommittee on Government Efficiency, Financial Management and Intergovernmental Relations, House Committee on Government Reform and Oversight, and Subcommittee on Legislative and Budget Process, House Committee on Rules, September 12, 2002, 18.

34. This is not to suggest that the Congress does not currently have any information on the effects of changes provided for through reconciliation. It does not, however, consider specific effects on performance in any sort of a consistent or uniform way.

35. Congressional Budget Office, *Unauthorized Appropriations and Expiring Authorizations (Appropriations Version)* (Washington, D.C.: U.S. Government Printing Office, January 2002).

36. Breul, "Performance Budgeting in the United States," 13–14.

37. Office of Management and Budget, "Budget and Performance Integration," Chapter 1 of *Budget of the United States Government, Analytical Perspectives*, Fiscal Year 2004 (Washington, D.C.: U.S. Government Printing Office, 2003).

38. Some have suggested making the budget resolution into a joint resolution, which would require the President's signature. While that would make the budget resolution more difficult to enact in a timely fashion, it would make it much more important for the President and the Congress to agree on the performance implications of the budget resolution. See Roy T. Meyers, "The Budget Resolution Should be a Law," *Public Budgeting and Finance* 10 Number 3 (Fall 1990), 103–112.

39. General Accounting Office, *Results-Oriented Budget Practices*, GAO-0101084SP (August 2001), 18.

40. General Accounting Office, *Results-Oriented Budget Practices*, 18.

41. General Accounting Office, *Managing for Results: Efforts to Strengthen the Link Between Resources and Results at the Nuclear Regulatory Commission*, GAO-03-258 (December 2002), 16.

42. For further details, see Hatry, Morley, Rossman, and Wholey, "How Federal Programs Use Outcome Information: Opportunities for Federal Managers," 35.

43. Hatry, Morley, Rossman, and Wholey, "How Federal Programs Use Outcome Information: Opportunities for Federal Managers," 58–59.

44. General Accounting Office, *Managing for Results: Efforts to Strengthen the Link Between Resources and Results at the Administration for Children and Families*, GAO-03-9 (December 2002), 18.

45. Hatry, Morley, Rossman, and Wholey, "How Federal Programs Use Outcome Information: Opportunities for Federal Managers," 19–20.

46. Hatry, Morley, Rossman, and Wholey, "How Federal Programs Use Outcome Information: Opportunities for Federal Managers," 41–42.

47. Hatry, Morley, Rossman, and Wholey, "How Federal Programs Use Outcome Information: Opportunities for Federal Managers," 61–62.

48. General Accounting Office, *Managing for Results: Efforts to Strengthen the Link Between Resources and Results at the Veterans Health Administration*, GAO-03-10 (December 2002), 3.

49. General Accounting Office, *Results-Oriented Budget Practices*, 20.

50. Hatry, Morley, Rossman, and Wholey, "How Federal Programs Use Outcome Information: Opportunities for Federal Managers," 21–22.

51. Hatry, Morley, Rossman, and Wholey, "How Federal Programs Use Outcome Information: Opportunities for Federal Managers," 23–24.

52. Hatry, Morley, Rossman, and Wholey, "How Federal Programs Use Outcome Information: Opportunities for Federal Managers," 25–30.

53. General Accounting Office, *Managing for Results: Efforts to Strengthen the Link Between Resources and Results at the Administration for Children and Families*, 18.

54. Paul C. Light, *The True Size of Government* (Brookings, 1999).

55. General Accounting Office, *Results-Oriented Budget Practices*, 20.

56. General Accounting Office, *Managing for Results: Efforts to Strengthen the Link Between Resources and Results at the Nuclear Regulatory Commission*, 20.

57. General Accounting Office, *Results-Oriented Budget Practices*, 23.

58. General Accounting Office, *Managing for Results: Efforts to Strengthen the Link Between Resources and Results at the Administration for Children and Families*, 21.

59. General Accounting Office, *Managing for Results: Efforts to Strengthen the Link Between Resources and Results at the Administration for Children and Families*, 25.

60. Matthew McCubbins and Thomas Schwartz, "Congressional Oversight Overlooked: Police Patrols Versus Fire Alarms," *American Journal of Political Science* 28 (1984), 721–748.

61. Schick, "The Road to PPB: The Stages of Budget Reform."

62. For a discussion of logic models, see Kathryn E. Newcomer and Mary Ann Scheirer, "Using Evaluation to Support Performance Management: A Guide for Federal Executives," (Washington, D.C.: IBM Center for The Business of Government, January 2001).

63. Newcomer and Scheirer.

64. U.S. Congressional Budget Office, *Using Performance Measures in the Federal Budget Process* (July 1993), xiii.

CHAPTER THREE

Staying the Course: The Use of Performance Measurement in State Governments

Julia Melkers
Associate Professor of Public Administration
Graduate Program in Public Administration
College of Urban Planning and Public Affairs
University of Illinois at Chicago

Katherine Willoughby
Professor of Public Administration and Urban Studies
Andrew Young School of Policy Studies
Georgia State University

This report was originally published in 2004.

Introduction

This chapter provides information about the use and usefulness of performance measurement for budgeting in state governments in the United States. We hope that this chapter successfully chips away at the "mystery" of performance measurement—that is, how governments use such data to inform budgetary decisions. This chapter presents results from years of research that both has assessed the foundations of performance-based budgeting systems in state governments, and—to decipher factors related to the effective use of such reform, system-wide as well as agency specific—has engaged stakeholders' perspectives on the use of performance measurement in their states. Our work complements recent work by Hatry, Morley, Rossman, and Wholey (2003) by providing detailed findings on the uses of performance measurement in public organizations.

We want to provide an avenue for those working in and for American governments to consider various approaches to the use of performance measurement that can encompass not only program results assessment and internal management practice, but also resource allocation. We hope that public managers will gain a better understanding of the factors that have led to the successful use of performance measurement for budgeting in the states.

This chapter is not meant to persuade skeptics to use performance measurement or performance-based systems for budgeting. We believe that this case has been won—the necessity of improved information from which to govern is a given. Governments at all levels in the United States are programmatically and fiscally stressed. States, especially, are squeezed between a federal government that continues to press responsibilities down to this level (with inadequate or no funding) and local governments that need money to provide services and programs to growing populations and to address challenging and stubborn problems. Efforts that engage state personnel in strategic planning, measurement development, results assessment and cost comparisons simply must be carried out. We hope to offer a window to those factors that best support such efforts.

On the other hand, we believe that governments in the United States and worldwide, for that matter, have never and will never "arrive" or "get there" in terms of finding the "one best way" to budget and manage. This is not a bad thing, just the reality of an ever-evolving process in which different systems will work at different times and for different functions. This chapter is an effort to provide the information governments need to support their "learned accommodation" regarding the effective use of performance measurement specifically for budgeting.

The State Budget Process: Contextual Influences and Where Performance Data Fits In

A typical state government budget cycle is a routine process made up of four phases:
- Budget development (executive driven)
- Budget passage (legislative driven)
- Execution (agency driven)
- Audit (legislative-executive)

As illustrated in Figure 3.1 on page 74, a state can be characterized by its political and organizational cultures, its economic and fiscal environments, and the informational requirements and systems of the budget process.

Political Culture

The political culture encompasses characterizations of party traditions in a state, specifically party breakdown in the legislature and in comparison with the chief executive. States can be classified as strongly liberal or conservative, platforms that may be somewhat reflected in budget shares by function over time. More important, party split within a legislature (a house and a senate with different majority parties) and/or a legislative party split with the governor make for more contentious budget deliberations. If deliberations become especially combative, the budget process can break down entirely—the appropriation bill is not passed and fiscal crisis ensues, is sustained, or worsens. In fact, many a governor attempts to make significant budget changes to accommodate an ambitious policy agenda only to run into an intransigent legislature, directly, or a wary public, indirectly.

Organizational Culture

Organizational culture refers to the internal organizational climate in which government employees carry out their duties and activities. A government in which the budget process is transparent, guidelines for budget preparation and reporting are clear, and communication flow is unfettered among important actors (illustrated in Figure 3.1 as between and among the governor, the executive budget office, executive departments and agencies, and the legislature and its budget support, and extending to the public in the form of program clients, constituents, and/or citizens) provides a climate that can more successfully integrate data (performance measures) into budgeting and management decisions.

Communication Flows

Free-flowing communication among various levels in the state government is influenced by the location of budget and policy support to the governor and the legislature, the capacity of such offices to conduct budget and policy analysis, and the comfortableness exhibited by the chief executive and important members of the legislature in terms of working with such support staff (Thurmaier and Willoughby, 2001). Related to this, leadership is a sustaining factor for any budget reform, and performance-based initiatives are no different. Governors and/or legislators calling upon agencies to provide performance data for budget development purposes must champion the process and illustrate to agencies that they take advantage of the information when making funding decisions. Otherwise, agencies see little use in concentrating on the collection, preparation, and reporting of such data for budgetary purposes. On the other hand, such data can be used for management decisions if championed at least by agency heads, budget officers, and others internal to the agency.

Information Requirements

Informational requirements include budget timelines, the budget format, executive preparation guidelines, and other protocols that budget actors must ascribe to when involved in a budget cycle. Such requirements and systems influence the flexibility or constraints within which these actors

Figure 3.1: Model of State Government Budget Process

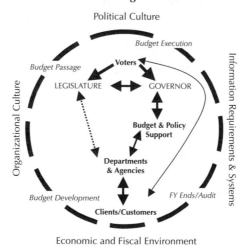

must work. Requirements and deadlines will contribute to the ease with which actors are able to gather and present information, make comparisons and analyses regarding program operations and results, and manage funds to accommodate changing workloads, economies, or other circumstances.

Budget and Accounting Systems

The integration of the budget and accounting systems (or lack thereof) will influence how data is presented and used throughout a budget process. The source of budget information requirements can also influence the credence that different actors afford to data and how they make use of data throughout a budget process. As previously noted, if agency personnel believe that performance data required by the chief executive is not considered seriously by legislators when making allocation decisions, then they will undoubtedly concentrate their use of such data internally for management purposes and perhaps budget justification when preparing their budget request. During appropriation hearings, however, agencies would be more inclined to highlight the relationships between their programs and the parochial interests of legislators rather than measures of program performance or results.

Economic and Fiscal Climate

The economic and fiscal climate is closely linked to a state's political culture. The revenue capability of a state serves as the foundation for its program operations. Politics influence a state's revenue structure, which may or may not accommodate economic fluctuations easily. Unfortunately, traditional financing capabilities at this level of government in the United States are difficult to change and often hogtie states, in the short term, regarding budget balancing capabilities. Table 3.1 shows that state tax receipts, as a proportion of total receipts, remained virtually unchanged in the last decade. Individual income tax and general sales and gross receipts remain the largest proportions of tax receipts at the state level. Motor fuel sales tax receipts decreased slightly in the past decade as a proportion of total receipts.

Corporate income taxes also declined as a proportion of total receipts. The "All other taxes" category is a conglomeration of taxes that individually compose less than two percent each of total tax receipts in the states. None has increased significantly as a proportion of the total tax receipts pie at the state level, although collectively the data illustrates some attempt in the states to tweak typically antiquated tax structures.

Total state balances as a percent of expenditures have actually stabilized in 2004 (estimated 3.2 percent; in 2000 this ratio was 10.4 percent) (NASBO

Table 3.1: State Tax Collections by Type of Tax, 1994 and 2003

Type of Tax	3rd Quarter 1994	3rd Quarter 2003
General sales and gross receipts	34.6%	31.4%
Individual income tax	31.5%	33.1%
Motor fuel sales	7.1%	6.3%
Corporate net income	6.6%	5.0%
Motor vehicles	3.3%	3.0%
Other sales and gross receipts	2.3%	2.5%
Tobacco products	2.0%	2.1%
Insurance	2.0%	1.9%
All other taxes Including: property tax, public utilities, pari-mutuels, amusements, beverage and other licenses, taxes on document and stock transactions, and death, gift, and severance taxes	10.4%	14.7%

Source: *Table 3: State Tax Collections by State and Type of Tax. Data available in Excel files qtx033t3 and qtx943t3 at http://www.census.gov/govs/www/qtax.html. Accessed on March 4, 2004.*

and NGA, 2003). However, in order to reach balance, most states exhausted their reserves and other contingency type funds and/or took advantage of all "one time only" financial management strategies, such as advancing tax due dates. Further, states cannot expect much relief from the feds in the future. In budget year 2004, the federal government provided $20 billion to the states, but for 2005, President Bush's budget calls for a decrease of 4 percent in mandatory and entitlement spending (~$10 billion) and a decrease of 3 percent in selected grants-in-aid (~$11.6 billion) (NASBO, 2004).

Gubernatorial Politics

In 2004, most governors (60 percent) were new to their job and nervous about future budget balancing. In their 2004 state-of-the-state addresses, many advocated economic development and/or encouraged government collaborations with private and nonprofit sectors, including faith-based organizations, as well as pooling federal and private dollars with state funds to advance investment in industry and capital ventures.[1] Chief executives also mentioned initiatives that require public input, such as constitutional amendments regarding balanced budgets or the creation of new funding strategies (like a lottery) or funds.

Governors suggested tax reform, with cigarette and alcohol taxes common targets for increases. A recent survey of legislators found that elected officials in this branch of state government, like governors, "are only willing to consider the least painful kinds of tax increases to balance their state budget. The most popular options are raising 'sin' taxes on alcohol and tobacco (71 percent) and increasing tolls or user fees (66 percent). Various broad-based tax hikes are found acceptable by less than half of state legislators, including raising state taxes on gasoline (43 percent), state corporate income taxes (40 percent), and state sales taxes (39 percent)" (The Pew Center on the States, 2003).

Few chief executives were more zealous regarding their tax structures. One governor specifically called for a more equitable tax system by increasing the sales tax, lowering the income tax for all except ~8 percent of upper-income state citizens, and cutting taxes on cars, food, and those related to farms and small businesses. According to Virginia's governor, "It just doesn't make any sense that someone earning only $17,000 a year should pay the same tax rate as someone earning $500,000 a year."

Performance and Accountability Initiatives

It is not surprising, then, that state governors continue to hawk performance and accountability reforms to help balance state budgets. In their 2004 addresses, they emphasized reorganizations and performance and accountability measures. Vermont's chief executive talked of a significant reorganization of that state's human services department. South Carolina's governor mapped out a detailed reorganization plan in addition to changes that already have occurred in some of that state's departments. He also suggested advancing accountability in the state "through attitudinal change." Governors of Maryland, Rhode Island, Virginia, and Wisconsin also called for new restructuring or accountability measures.

The governor of Kansas utilized "efficiency savings teams" to save "tens of millions of dollars" in the state (Greenblatt, 2004, p. 30). Oklahoma's governor asked for the application of a zero-based budgeting approach to improve productivity and reduce costs, while Vermont's governor established an institute to conduct "a top to bottom review of government operations to root out waste and inefficiencies that cost taxpayer dollars." Georgia's governor appointed the state's first "director of implementation" to ferret out waste in government. "I'm serious about transforming the culture of state government from top to bottom. I'm just as serious about giving Georgians the value for their tax resources," stated this chief executive (Badertscher, 2004).

The continued attraction of performance-related initiatives in state governments attests to the lasting quality of this latest budget reform trend. Different from previous attempts in the mid-20th century to inculcate "rationality" into an otherwise political process, states' more recent ventures into performance-related reforms have "stuck." Given increased political divisiveness in the states and sustained fiscal malaise—and coupled with advancements in technological capacity and considered attention by elected leaders in both branches to data collection and reporting—state employees should expect a continuing focus on performance measurement and use in the future. In the next section, we review specific performance-based requirements in the states, illustrating the longevity of this recent trend.

Performance-Based Budgeting Initiatives in the States: 1990s and Today

In the late 1990s, we asked executive and legislative budget officers about performance-based budgeting initiatives in their state governments. Responses were received from all 50 states—usually from the budget director or deputy director of the budget office in either or both branches of government. We defined performance-based budgeting as "requiring strategic planning regarding agency missions, goals, and objectives, and a process that requests quantifiable data that provides meaningful information about program outcomes" (Melkers and Willoughby, 1998, p. 66).

We focused our analyses on state law or administrative requirements that indicated heavy emphasis on strategic planning and a focus on measuring the results of government activity, not just a dictum to report performance measures somewhere in the budget process. Strategic planning, the development of performance measures, and consistent application and reporting of measures throughout the budget process support integrating measurement with management and budgeting decisions.

A multiyear perspective that is part of any strategic planning process provides historical (albeit usually brief) perspective on agency program/service, as well as the possibility of benchmarking against chosen standards of practice—processes that help advance efficiency and effectiveness in government operations. In this research, we asked about state law, pending legislation, and administrative guidelines or executive mandates with performance-based requirements (as defined above). For every state indicating such legislation, guidelines, or mandates, we secured hard copy.

Findings in 1998 Study

Our findings in 1998 indicated widespread existence of performance-based budgeting requirements across the United States. Thirty-one states (62 percent) had legal requirements in place by 1997, 16 states (32 percent) had administrative requirements, and just one state, Missouri, had a performance- based initiative in the form of an executive order. At the time, most of the performance-based legislation was just five years old or less; most had been passed in the early to mid-1990s. Also, three states—Arkansas, Massachusetts, and New York—had no formal performance-based budgeting initiative.

This is not to say, however, that these states did not engage in developing performance measures for budgeting and management application. For example, from 1993 to 1997, "Massachusetts provided that performance requirements be renewed annually in the appropriations bill" (Melkers and Willoughby, 1998, p. 67). In the end, our study found no significant differences between legislated and administratively driven performance requirements in the states.

The explicitness of state performance-related initiatives certainly varied substantially, however. States exhibited distinctive levels of detail related to prescriptions for the developing and reporting of measures, and particularly any directly stated relationship between the provision of measures and program funding outcomes. Many states required that performance data be developed and published somewhere, but few provided specifics regarding the relationship between performance measures, program results, and state funding. At that time, Texas was one of the few states with well-defined integration of performance measurement into its budgeting system. Performance measurement guidelines in this state required agencies to include six-year strategic plans with budget requests. These plans outlined agency goals, objectives, output, and outcome and efficiency measures, as well as strategies for meeting targets (Melkers and Willoughby, 1998, p. 68).

Washington's performance initiatives in the 1990s provided a somewhat unusual example of a focus on government service quality. That state's Government Performance and Accountability Act of 1994 (ESSB 6601) did call for "clear measures of performance that will result in quality customer service, accountability for cost-effective services, and improved productivity." Other legislation (ESHB 6680) stated that "agency budget proposals must include integration of performance measures that allow objective determination of a program's success in achieving goals" (Melkers and Willoughby, 1998, p. 68).

Mention of benchmarking was sporadic throughout state performance requirements in 1998. This finding is of interest given that subsequent research supports this "sometime" use of benchmarking in the states and use mostly for comparing performance in individual agencies against prior periods (Willoughby, 2004b, p. 32).

Most prescriptions for implementing performance-based budgeting in our 1998 survey were less than comprehensive, incomplete, or pilot-based, and they laid predominant responsibility with agencies for performance measurement identification, development, and reporting. Just 14 percent of states in 1998 provided incentives and penalties related to applying performance measurement. Some states did create new oversight capacity to monitor the developing and applying of performance measurement. Generally, such capacity was created in the form of a council, commission, or external board or was added to an existing office within state government. Very few called for direct citizen oversight of the performance initiative.

At the time, finding that the majority of "new" performance-related initiatives arose from the legislative branch of state governments, we concluded that this was positive in supporting the applicability of performance measurement to state budgeting and management practices. If legislators were interested in the program results and data about performance, then, having a vested interest, agencies would take seriously the process of measuring and reporting development. In fact, what distinguished this performance-related trend in states in the 1990s from those promoted earlier in the century was evidence of the acceptability of, and even requirements for, the ongoing development of measurement, a willingness to revise measurement, integration of measurement with strategic planning, some mention of benchmarking, and an incremental approach to assigning responsibility in terms of oversight capabilities.

Performance Measurement and System Maturation: 2004

When we reanalyzed state performance-related requirements in 2004, much legislation remained in place. In fact, proportions of states that have either legislative or administrative performance-based budgeting requirements are almost identical to those identified in 1998. Table 3.2 illustrates the breakdown between states with a legislative requirement related to performance-based budgeting (as defined on page 78) and those indicating an administrative policy or executive mandate for the performance initiative.

By 2004, 33 states (66 percent) had maintained, amended, or added legislation that prescribes a performance-based application, while 17 states (34 percent) had an administrative requirement or executive mandate for such application. Notably changed from the last survey, Arkansas, New Mexico, and Missouri passed performance-related legislation and moved into a new category regarding type of performance initiative.

Table 3.2: Performance-Based Budgeting (PBB) Requirements in the States: 2004

Legislated PBB Requirement		Administrative PBB Requirement
Alabama	Missouri	California
Alaska	Montana	Illinois
Arizona	Nevada	Indiana
Arkansas	New Mexico	Kansas
Colorado	Oklahoma	Maryland
Connecticut	Oregon	Massachusetts
Delaware	Rhode Island	Michigan
Florida	South Carolina	Nebraska
Georgia	South Dakota	New Hampshire
Hawaii	Tennessee	New Jersey
Idaho	Texas	New York
Iowa	Utah	North Carolina
Kentucky	Vermont	North Dakota
Louisiana	Virginia	Ohio
Maine	Wisconsin	Pennsylvania
Minnesota	Wyoming	Washington
Mississippi		West Virginia

It remains, too, that neither the legislated nor the administrative requirement necessarily calls for comprehensive application. For example, Alabama does not have a statutory requirement for the conduct of performance-based budgeting statewide. A pilot application was legislated, given that the state does not have the funds or the staff to implement performance-based budgeting across all agencies. Each agency must list performance goals, although they are not tied to the funding process.

Several agencies do use a performance-based budgeting approach internally, however, including the Department of Mental Health and Rehabilitation. Kentucky's performance-based budgeting law also prescribes a pilot approach to implementation.

Other initiatives can be found in a compendium of laws that point to measurement production and a performance approach in specific agencies. Utah's performance-based budgeting legislation encompasses State Code Title 36, which concerns a Strategic Planning Committee, and Title 62A, which concerns measures for human welfare services. Tennessee's Governmental Accountability Act of 2002 requires a staggered, phased-in approach to implementing performance-based budgeting across all state agencies. Although in New Hampshire the performance-based budgeting experiment was repealed in 2003, under Chapter 319: 41, Laws of New Hampshire, it is conducted in some agencies. Recent examples include the Bureau of Turnpikes in 2001 and the Department of Environmental Services in 2002 (accessible online at www.gencourt.state.nh.us/lba and at the Audit Reports and Performance Audits links).

On the other hand, some states have systems that have evolved since legislation was first implemented in the 1990s. For example, Wisconsin implemented pilot performance measurement in the 1999–2001 biennium through a 1997 law requiring that the Department of Transportation and Technology for Educational Achievement Board (TEACH Board) prepare budget requests using performance-based budgeting practices. Budget instructions to agencies for the 2001–2003 biennium require agencies to include performance measures, dictate the number of measures by size of agency (small agencies must include at least two measures for their activities; large agencies must include at least four measures), and require that budget requests include actual outcome data for selected measures for fiscal year 2000.

Other states have changed their approach to, if not the focus of, their performance initiative. Previous law in North Carolina (Ch. 18 HB 53 passed in 1996 at the second special session), notwithstanding the provisions of G.S. 143-16.3, Section 10(b) of Chapter 324 of the 1995 Session Laws, stipulated:

> [The] Director of the Budget may expend funds to continue to develop performance/program budget analysis for the 10 program areas of North Carolina State government that were identified by the Governmental Performance Audit Commission. The Office of State Budget and Management shall report to the Joint Legislative Commission on Governmental Operations by December 1, 1996, regarding the development of performance/program budget analysis of State departments and institutions, its effectiveness, whether it should be continued, and any modifications that should be made.

The most current budget manual, however, does not mention perfor-mance-measurement requirements specifically, although it does point agen-cies to the Executive Budget Act §143.8-10.1A regarding information and reporting requirements to the State Budget Office (see http://www.osbm. state.nc.us/files/pdf_files/2003_budget_manual.pdf). Assessment of Wash-ington's budget process by 2004 indicates that the state "recently adopted a statewide results-based approach that complements the traditional focus on expected changes to the current expenditure base. This process starts by identifying the key results that citizens expect from government and the most effective strategies for achieving those results. Agency activities were reviewed in this statewide context and prioritized in terms of their contribu-tion to achieving these statewide results" (Washington State's Budget Pro-cess, available at http://www.ofm.wa.gov/reports/budgetprocess.pdf).

It is clear in reading current state government performance-based budget-ing requirements that, just as in 1998, few have statewide, uniform standards with which to measure every agency's performance and that movement contin-ues to be slow in the use of benchmarking for budgeting purposes. According to Chi, Arnold and Perkins (2003, pp. 441–442), just 11 states indicate some sort of statewide application: Arizona, Delaware, Louisiana, Maryland, Minne-sota, Missouri, New Mexico, Oregon, South Dakota, Virginia, and Wyoming. Maryland's "managing for results" administrative performance initiative has comprehensive standards for measuring agency performance. In Missouri, that state's Strategic Planning Model and Guidelines establishes a common strategic planning model that includes measures of agency performance.

Performance measurement requirements in the states certainly reflect a national trend toward performance *management*. In our view, state require-ments are not dramatically different in purpose from what exists in either the 1993 Government Performance and Results Act (GPRA), at the federal level, or what is found in many local government requirements regarding perfor-mance measurement. At all levels, reforms related to performance measure-ment have sought to focus attention on outcomes rather than outputs and to link to budget and managerial decision processes.

GPRA, like many state performance reforms, requested the linkage of performance requirements with strategic plans and provided for a staggered implementation process with pilot application. GPRA is probably more comprehensive than many state initiatives—folding together strategic planning, performance measurement, management improvements, benchmarking, performance budgeting, and results oversight as well as a section that considers protocol for exceptions or waivers to requested reforms. GPRA also provided definitions to agencies along with reporting and other guidelines.

Changing Expectations

Performance-based budgeting requirements of the last decade or so are not that dissimilar to prior initiatives intended to rationalize decision making in the public policy process. While not always successful, integrating performance goals into budgetary decision making has been attempted in numerous prior reform efforts.

The efforts we witnessed throughout the 1990s and those of today include several important changes from earlier ones. First and foremost, the integration of efforts like performance-based budgeting has occurred with other public management initiatives. Today, it is more common for performance-budgeting efforts to be linked to other public management initiatives, most notably strategic planning. This integration creates momentum within organizations that can lead to a greater understanding of and support for the use of performance measures.

Related to this integration with other public management initiatives is a change in philosophy about the role that performance data plays in the decision-making process. In earlier efforts, the policy decision process was viewed as a more linear process. Today's reforms, however, acknowledge the complexity of not only public programs but also the budget process and its relationship to program performance. For example, in Washington the budget guidelines are clear that performance data inform, but do not drive, budgetary decision making. As shown in Figure 3.2, the actual budget or policy decision involves performance measures but also is affected by a variety of other factors, such as financial realities and public sentiment. This squares with our state budget process model presented earlier. In the operating budget instructions, the State of Washington, in fact, points to improved communication as one goal of advancing the use of performance measures:

> The budget is one of the most important tools for implementing policy and achieving results. In order to leverage this tool as much as possible, we use performance budgeting to ensure that financial decisions support ever-improving organizational performance by:
> 1. Targeting resources to the most important results and targeting resources to the most effective strategies;
> 2. To make performance information readily available to those who make resource decisions; and
> 3. To communicate performance accomplishments associated with the agency's enacted budget.

Also, the technological advances of the last two decades have dramatically changed the way performance data can be maintained and examined over time. User-friendly spreadsheets and databases have revolutionized our

Figure 3.2: Budget or Policy Decisions as Described in Washington State Operating Budget Instructions (Washington State, 2001)

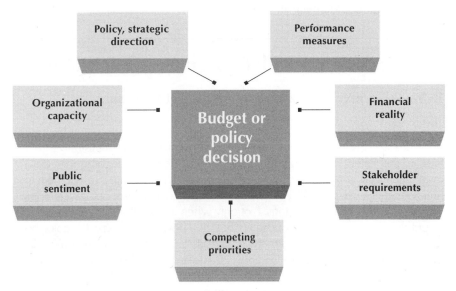

ability not only to maintain and track performance data, but also to integrate it with budget data and communicate it to stakeholders. This added capacity has enhanced expectations of what can be accomplished regarding measurement development and data manipulation.

Ultimately, the current trend in performance-based budgeting has embraced a more holistic view of performance measurement rather than simply an emphasis on changing appropriation levels. This orientation is evident in the language of requirements as well as in the attitudes of working practitioners. To integrate performance measurement across an organization and other management processes, information may be gleaned that is of use to management and stakeholders. In the language of performance measurement, information gained from the process and changes in communication patterns and relationships become somewhat of an interim outcome of using performance measurement. Measures and their supporting systems are developed concurrently with new and changing communication patterns and channels.

Other research (Joyce, 1993) finds that performance measurement in the budgeting process has had its greatest success as *a management* and *not a budgeting* tool. Joyce notes that performance budgeting and the information that results from its application help managers of public programs understand the activities carried out under their purview, thereby contributing to their ability to make more successful changes to programs. Compared to past reforms, modern technology supports these initiatives better, providing practitioners more choices in developing, massaging, tracking, and analyzing measures, more effectively and efficiently.

State Experience with Performance Measurement

Using Performance Measures in the Budget Process

The expectation that performance data plays an important role in budgeting decisions is consistent with the tone set by legislative and administrative guidelines in the states. And as performance measurement has become increasingly institutionalized at all levels of government in the United States, researchers and practitioners have looked for evidence of active use of performance data in appropriation and other fiscal decisions. Not only when information becomes available to public administrators and budgeters but also how they interpret it color how they make decisions and perform their duties throughout the government budgeting process (Thurmaier and Willoughby, 2001). Further, individuals' orientation to work is influenced by the organizational culture within which they function. The acceptance and institutionalization of performance legislation or requirements in a government naturally have some effect on the working culture.

Research shows that performance measurement use is considered advantageous to communication flow among budget actors—to increase awareness of the results of government activities, to highlight improved quality of service, and for managers to more easily discern and change strategies for realizing program results (Melkers and Willoughby, 2001 and forthcoming). On the down side, the use of performance information has not been found as effective (if at all) in changing spending levels of agencies. That is, while governments continue to strongly emphasize integrating budgeting with performance assessment, there is little recognition of how performance measurement applies to budget balancing.

In fact, research has demonstrated few active uses of performance data specifically for quantitative, fiscal decisions. Instead, such work has uncovered a range of other managerial and organizational uses of performance measures and data that is consistent with the overall goals of "performance management" and with "strategic management" philosophies (Melkers and Willoughby, 2001).

For example, at the local government level, recent research has found that performance measurement remains most essential for managerial decisions and communication purposes, while its impact on appropriation outcomes is quite limited (Willoughby and Melkers, 2000; Willoughby, 2004B, and Melkers and Willoughby, forthcoming). These expanded managerial uses of performance measurement are important to our understanding of the full impact of these requirements and activities on public organizations. And, while public administrators have attributed few budget allocation decisions directly to performance measurement input, they do report important managerial, communication, and long-term organizational effects and benefits.

Considering these findings, are there distinguishing characteristics of the performance measurement systems in state governments that could allow for greater integration of performance measurement into budgeting processes and decisions? Does the nature of a state government itself contribute in any way to the applicability of performance measurement? We present models in the "Thinking Broadly" section that move beyond purely descriptive context to a more complete picture of the relationship among various governmental, organizational, and individual characteristics with performance measurement use. We find that, contrary to sustained expectations and budgetary difference over the long term, uses of performance measurement for budgeting purposes have been limited though dramatically superseded by communication and other effects.

Expanded Understanding of the Use of Performance Measurement

An important objective of the institution of performance measurement at all levels of government in the United States is to enhance the nature and quality of decision making in the policy and budget environments. As previously noted, with the institutionalization of performance measurement in government, we can expect to witness important changes in the use of such information.

Our recent research points to strongly expanded uses of performance measurement in American governments. Although performance measurement is instituted in these governments to inform the budget process, we have learned that many of its most dramatic uses are relevant to but do not determine specific budget allocation decisions. Our 2000 survey data found performance measures to be used most prevalently for advancing communication among budget actors and for integration with other public management tools, as shown in Figure 3.3 on page 88. We find this to be true for state budgeters as well as agency administrators and staff. Importantly, measurement applicability goes well beyond its use for "cutting the budget."

We also see in Figure 3.3 some fairly substantive activities for which performance measurement use is rather lackluster. Personnel and staffing decisions, benchmarking program results against other entities, and targeting or holding local governments and contractors more accountable are activities which both state budgeters and agency staff indicate are a less frequent use of performance measurement.

Figure 3.3: How Performance Measurement Is Used in the States

	State Budgeters	State Agency Staff
More Frequent ↓ **Less Frequent**	• Strategic planning (more than one-year time horizon) • Reporting results to management and staff • Reporting or accountability to elected officials • Assessment of program results • Program planning/annual business planning/oversight activities/programmatic changes • Budgeting, including resource allocation or discussion about resources changes • Establishing or changing of policies • Reporting or accountability to citizens, citizen groups, or media • Managing operations or daily decisions • Specific performance improvement initiatives • In establishing contracts for services • Personnel decisions, including staffing levels and evaluations • Evaluation to determine underlying reasons for results • Benchmarking, or comparison of program results with other entities • Holding local jurisdictions accountable for agency-funded or agency-regulated programs • Determining which programs, local jurisdictions, or contractors to target for special studies	• Strategic planning (more than one-year time horizon) • Reporting or accountability to elected officials • Reporting results to management and staff • Reporting or accountability to citizens, citizen groups, or media • Program planning/annual business planning/oversight activities/programmatic changes • Assessment of program results • Budgeting, including resource allocation or discussion about resources changes • Establishing or changing of policies • Managing operations or daily decisions • Evaluation to determine underlying reasons for results • In establishing contracts for services • Specific performance improvement initiatives • Personnel decisions, including staffing levels and evaluations • Determining which programs, local jurisdictions, or contractors to target for special studies • Benchmarking, or comparison of program results with other entities • Holding local jurisdictions accountable for agency-funded or agency-regulated programs

Performance Measurement's Role in Enhancing Communication Among Important Budget Actors

One enduring goal of the performance-related reforms evidenced in the states is to improve budgetary decision making. What does this mean? Most might consider this to mean reducing appropriations, cutting expenditures or debt, or, at the very least, indicating the means of operating government programs more efficiently and effectively. Undoubtedly, these goals have been prominent in innumerable previous budget reforms in American governments—reforms often tossed in part or totally holding to unrealistic objectives. Part of the lasting quality of performance measurement applications in the states today, however, is a refocusing of goals that consider reform for the purposes of advancing communication and understanding among budget actors in the decision-making process.

We recognize that public budget decisions are fraught with politics and other factors that will not change immediately with the introduction of new processes. Yet, in spite of the cynicism about (or lack of) these effects on the budget process, administrators today have acknowledged that developing and implementing performance measurement have resulted in some "spillover effects" on communication during the budgeting process. Again, considering the implementation of a performance measurement system through its own lens, communication and information effects may be viewed as "interim" or "initial" (positive) outcomes of the process itself.

Our 2000 survey of state budgeters and agency staff addressed a range of questions about how developing and using performance measurement affects specific communication and information needs. Specifically, respondents were asked the questions presented in Table 3.3 on page 90. Respondents were also asked how effective the development and use of performance measures had been in their agency.

As seen in Table 3.3, some differences exist between groups of respondents. State agency practitioners are slightly more positive in their views about the effects of performance measurement on communication issues. They are also slightly more positive than state budgeters about whether performance measurement has resulted in any real appropriation changes. This is particularly true when asked whether performance measurement has "increased awareness of and focus on results." State agency practitioners also note more changes in the substance or tone of discussion among policy makers as a result of performance measurement.

Overall, state budgeters are less enthusiastic about communication effects. At the state level, budget officers generally agree about effects on communication and understanding of program activities that result from implementing performance measurement. On the other hand, budgeters willingly admit that communication has improved between agency

Table 3.3: Perspectives of State Budgeters and State Agency Practitioners on the Effects of Performance Measurement: Mean Responses

	State Budgeters (n=60)	State Agency Practitioners (n=152)
To what extent do you agree with the following? (scale: 1=strongly disagree 4=strongly agree)		
Communication between agency personnel and the executive budget office has improved with the implementation of performance measures.	2.62	2.69
Communication between agency personnel and legislators has improved with the implementation of performance measures.	2.54	2.69
Because of the implementation of performance measures, the substance or tone of budget discussions among legislators has changed to focus more on results.	2.53	2.47
Overall, program staff is aware of the desired program/service results.	2.89	2.92
Using performance measures has enhanced the management of the programs in our agency.	2.76	2.87
In your opinion, how effective has the development and use of performance measures been in your agency regarding: (scale: 1=not effective 4=very effective)		
Improving communication between departments and programs?	2.19	2.39
Improving communication with the executive budget office?	2.38	2.41
Improving communication with the legislature and legislative staff?	2.29	2.38
Changing the substance or tone of discussion among legislators about agency budgets?	1.98	2.17
Changing the substance or tone of discussion among legislators about oversight of agencies?	1.92	2.10
Changing the questions legislators or their staff ask government managers or executives?	2.04	2.06
Changing appropriation levels?	1.55	1.94
Communicating with the public about performance?	1.98	2.21
Increasing awareness of, and focus on, results?	2.38	2.74

personnel and budget officers through the implementation of performance-based systems. Slightly more than half the respondents "strongly agreed" or "agreed" when asked whether the implementation of performance measures had improved communication between agency personnel and the budget office and between agency personnel and legislators. Budget officers from states where performance budgeting is legislated tended to feel more strongly about improvements in communication efficacy (Willoughby and Melkers, 2001a). They also note a change in substance or tone of budget discussions as legislators focus more strongly on results.

Thinking Broadly: Managerial Uses of Performance Measurement

An important aspect of current performance measurement initiatives in the United States is the consideration of these reforms as a *public management tool*. If current performance measurement efforts are part of larger public management strategies intended to not only inform budget decisions but also enhance managerial processes, we should expect to see other effects on organizational processes. The intention of many public management efforts, such as strategic planning and its integration with measurement processes, is intended to improve the operations, outputs, and results of public agencies. Therefore, we might expect to see more comprehensive, long-lasting, positive effects of performance measurement as a result of the adoption of these management tools.

While performance measurement has certainly *informed* budget decision processes and has significantly enhanced communication between budget and policy actors in the public environment, what effects might it have in the long run? Will there be changes in the effectiveness of agency programs? Is measurement data used to change strategies to achieve desired results? Have agencies witnessed changes in programs/service quality and responsiveness to customers? And, through implementing the performance measurement process itself, are there cultural changes that reflect an improved understanding of the relationship between processes and results?

Our results are encouraging as regards the sustained influence of performance measurement use. When asked about performance measurement effects, executive branch budget officers in the states indicate that performance budgeting has been most effective in 1) improving effectiveness of agency programs, and 2) improving decision making in government. Legislative budget officers indicate that performance budgeting had been about equally effective in each of these variables. It is interesting to note, however, that budgeters from states in which performance-based budgeting is legislatively rather than administratively required are slightly more positive regarding its effectiveness in improving decision making in government. Perhaps the (self-imposed) legal stimulus to conduct performance-based budgeting adds weight to expected outcomes of the process. A more optimistic explanation may be that the improved information produced by a such a system is more strongly incorporated into the naturally political decisions of this branch of government.

What Makes a Difference?

In order to peer into the black box of performance measurement use, we propose a series of models that may be used to move us beyond purely descriptive assessment of critical factors in the implementation process. This analysis provides us with a more complete picture of the relationship among various governmental, organizational, and personal characteristics and performance measurement use.

No doubt, understanding the factors for successfully applying performance measurement to state government operations and budgets is extremely important to these officials right now, particularly given current political and fiscal environments. And, agency staff require continued encouragement from important budget actors that the information they are required to provide is filtered into decisions about agency budgets. In order to explore the relationship among various characteristics of performance use in these governments, we constructed a series of multiple regression models. Multiple regression is an important statistical tool for identifying relationships between variables as well as the relative strength of influence of certain variables.

From our 2000 survey, we found that use of performance measurement results in three primary categories of effects—budgetary effects, communication effects, and management effects. In developing an explanatory model that would identify the factors that influence each of these types of use, we derived three distinct dependent variables from these different effects. Overall, multiple regression analysis allowed us to identify the factors that are most important in predicting *budgetary, communication,* and *management effects* related to the use of performance measurement in state governments. Figure 3.4 illustrates the variables and the relationships of these models.

The dependent variable of each of three core models is a continuous variable created as a summative index of items by type of effect. In the first model, the dependent variable is a *budgetary effects index;* in the second model, *communication effects index;* and in the final model, *management effects index.* The budgetary effects index reflects respondents' ratings of budgetary uses for performance measures, such as affecting cost savings and reducing duplicative services. The communication effects index reflects variables such as enhanced communication with legislators, executive budget

Figure 3.4: Developing a Model of Performance Measurement Use and Effects

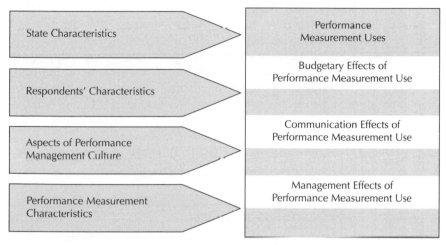

officers, and other stakeholders. The management effects index reflects measurement of long-term organizational variables, such as enhanced efficiency, effectiveness, and program management, and encompasses the administrative activities of both planning and management.

Factors That Influence Performance Measurement Use

In any policy analysis, addressing questions of influencing factors is useful, yet knowing what is not influential is also important. Our regression analysis allowed us to identify the factors that significantly (positively or negatively) affect budgetary, communication, or management effects related to the use of performance measurement (see Table 3.4 on page 94 and Table 3.5 on page 95) and also allowed us to answer this important question: Which factors are *not* significantly related to these outcomes or effects?

It is interesting to find that neither respondents' government experience nor the number of years respondents were employed in their state government is significant for agency staff for the communication effects and management effects models. However, respondents' experience with performance measures is significant in explaining budgetary effects for state budgeters. Both for years of government experience and for reported years of working with performance measures, the reported effects decreased.

While at first this may be perplexing, anecdotal evidence suggests that practitioners become jaded regarding the value of performance measurement and view new efforts through a lens of prior, often unsuccessful, experiences. This is particularly striking in the relationship between performance measurement experience and budgetary effects. These results do point out that various budget actors interpret such systems differently—that is, organizational perspective influences consideration of a budget process requirement.

Regarding organizational culture influences, leadership support is important in realizing the benefits of performance measurement, but only for agency staff. For this group, leadership support—although significant for each of the three dependent variables—was most significant to and had the

Table 3.4: Factors That Have a Significant Effect on Performance Measurement Use

Uses/Effects	Effect on Use	Factors
Budgetary Uses		**State Budget Staff**
	−	Respondents' experience with performance measurement
	+	Measurement density
		State Agency Practitioners
	−	Lack of leadership support
	+	Measurement maturity
Communication Uses		State Budget Staff
	+	Measurement density
	+	Measurement maturity
		State Agency Practitioners
	−	Respondents' years of experience in own government
	−	Lack of leadership support
	+	Inclusion of other government entities in measurement process
Management Effects		**State Budget Staff**
		None are significant
		State Agency Practitioners
	−	Respondents' years of experience in own government
	−	Lack of leadership support
	+	Formalized managing for results process
	+	Measurement maturity

Table 3.5: Factors That Have No Significantly Statistical Relationship with Performance Measurement Use

---

State Government Characteristics
- State general revenues
- Government size (population)
- Whether or not state has performance measurement legislation
- Managing for results grade

Respondents' Characteristics
- Years employed in current office

Performance Management Culture
- Performance measurement-related technology problems
- Current or prior use of program evaluations

---

strongest relationship in regard to budgetary effects, followed by management effects and, finally, communication effects. For budgeters, only measurement density and individual experience with performance measurement were useful in predicting the extent of budgetary effects, while measurement density and maturity were significant in predicting communication effects. No performance measurement culture variables were significant in the budgeter models, although cultural factors did emerge as significant for agency staff, including:

- Inclusion of other state units in the performance measurement process
- Formalization of a managing-for-results process

In terms of participation in the measurement process, state governments are not paying as much heed to client responses in the delivery of state services as has been found to be the case for local governments. The inclusion of citizens only showed itself as significant in predicting the management effects of performance measurement when all state respondents were grouped together, while the inclusion of other state organizations was significant in predicting communication effects of performance measurement for state agency staff. An explicit managing-for-results policy does seem to influence the management effects of performance measurement use for state agency staff. This supports the view that a participatory process yields more productive and longer-lasting reform.

The extent to which performance measures are shown in the budget process has some effects on use. Here, we find that measurement density (which we define as evidence of the use of performance measures in budget processes) is significant for both the budgetary and communication effects among state budgeters; however, measurement transparency (which we define as the presence of performance measures in budget documents) is not. These results seem to confirm that the institutionalization of performance measures may have some effect at the state level. In addition, measurement maturity—the extent to which performance measures are used in a range of management applications, such as benchmarking and planning—is significant for the budgetary and management effects for state agency staff, as well as for the communication effects model for budgeters.

We find little relationship between state characteristics and performance measurement effects. While it may not be surprising that the size or budget of a state may not help explain the effects of performance measures, it is somewhat surprising that a state's managing for results grade, as reported by Syracuse University, is not found to be significant for any of the models in predicting effects from using performance measurement.[2] We know that all states have either administrative or legislative requirements to conduct performance measurement. Yet, the source for this requirement has no significant relationship to the budgetary, communication, or management effects of performance measurement use.

Finally, our results illustrate distinctive perspectives of state budgeters and agency staff regarding performance measurement use. Findings show that the respondent's office was significant in predicting both the budgetary and management effects of performance measurement use. Agency staff are more likely to witness budgetary and management effects from measurement use. Examination of all responses points to the importance of leadership, the inclusion of other organizational units within state government in the measurement development process, and the extent to which measures have been integrated with other public management efforts. It is hopeful that including citizens in developing performance measures emerges as significant in predicting the management effects of performance measurement use. Although this is not a strong relationship, it does highlight the importance of external inclusion in the long-term viability of performance measurement systems.

Problems Implementing Performance Measurement Systems

While our research has pointed to important and expansive uses of performance measurement, our analyses have also teased out some problems with implementation. We know that instituting significant changes such as performance measurement applications can be a difficult and bumpy road. Table 3.6 on pages 98–99 illustrates aspects of the use of performance measurement that budget officers and agency staff perceive as significantly problematic in their state. For this analysis, budget officers and agency staff were grouped by state and office to identify any bias that might result from

multiple responses from one office or agency.[3] Significant problems for budgeters, in particular, include:
- Lack of weight in both management and budget decisions
- Lack of use by managers and elected officials
- Database incompatibilities
- Lack of interest by leadership
- Accuracy of performance measures

Overall, smaller proportions of agency staff consider any of these items to be problematic to measurement use. Database incompatibility is a significant problem for agency staff, followed by too many outside factors affecting results.

Comparison of the budget and agency perspectives yields interesting distinctions. For example, budget officers and agency staff have significantly different perceptions regarding the problems of the lack of regular use of performance measures by top management and elected officials, and the lack of interest in leadership in using performance measures. For both these problems, budget officers seem to recognize the necessity of having strong and sustained leadership to support performance measurement application for effective *budgeting* results. On the other hand, agency staff are significantly more likely than these budgeters to consider that too many outside factors affect the results trying to be achieved.

These results illustrate the differing perspectives. Whereas agency staff consider the problems related to performance measurement use to be more managerial (database linkage issues, collection of data, lack of training), the budget officers seem to consider the problems to be more related to politics—lackluster leadership and the weight that measurement carries in budget and management decisions.

It should be somewhat gratifying to consider the items that are not considered very problematic, if at all, by either group:

Budgeters do not see reporting of measures to executive leadership, legislators, citizens, or the media as much of a problem. Again, budgeters are in the business of preparing materials for reporting purposes, and with the advent of the Internet, much reporting has become fairly automatic, or at least tremendously more accessible to all these groups. Somewhat similarly, agency staff relegate some reporting to the bottom of the list of problems related to performance measurement. On the other hand, considering budget role and orientation, agency staff do not consider that performance measures are not reflective of what their programs are trying to accomplish. Given their role in the collection of data and formal reporting requirements, even if not chiefly responsible for measurement choice, agency staff do have strong influence on the evolution of measures over time. Lack of cost information about programs is not considered a

Table 3.6: Budgeter and Agency Staff Perceptions of Significant Problems Related to Performance Measurement Use

Percent of states in which budgeters consider the following as a *significant problem* to successful performance measurement application	
57%	Lack of regular use of performance measures by top management and elected officials (35)*
44%	Performance measures do not carry enough weight in budget decisions (34)
43%	Inadequate link between performance measurement database and accounting/budgeting database (35)
43%	Performance measures do not carry enough weight in management decisions (35)
43%	Lack of interest of leadership in using performance measures (35)*
40%	Development of performance measures that accurately reflect program activities (35)
39%	Lack of understanding of how to use performance measures (36)
34%	Lack of apparent link of performance measures to higher-level benchmarks (35)
31%	Collection of performance data (35)
27%	Maintenance of performance data (34)
27%	Lack of cost information about programs (34)
26%	Lack of adequate technology to support performance measurement effort (35)
26%	Performance measures are not reflective of what programs are trying to accomplish (35)
20%	Lack of training of staff responsible for collection and maintenance of performance data (35)
14%	Too many outside factors affect the results trying to be achieved (35)*
14%	Effectively reporting performance data to the legislature (35)
12%	Effectively reporting performance data to citizens (34)
9%	Effectively reporting performance data to the media (34)
9%	Effectively reporting performance data to executive leadership (35)

	Percent of states in which agency staff consider the following as a *significant problem* to successful performance measurement application
43%	Inadequate link between performance measurement database and accounting/budgeting database (47)
40%	Too many outside factors affect the results trying to be achieved (48)*
33%	Collection of performance data (48)
30%	Development of performance measures that accurately reflect program activities (48)
30%	Lack of understanding of how to use performance measures (48)
25%	Performance measures do not carry enough weight in budget decisions (48)
25%	Lack of training of staff responsible for collection and maintenance of performance data (48)
25%	Maintenance of performance data (48)
23%	Lack of regular use of performance measures by top management and elected officials (48)*
21%	Lack of apparent link of performance measures to higher-level benchmarks (47)
21%	Performance measures do not carry enough weight in management decisions (48)
21%	Lack of adequate technology to support performance measurement effort (47)
21%	Effectively reporting performance data to the media (47)
21%	Effectively reporting performance data to citizens (47)
17%	Effectively reporting performance data to the legislature (47)
13%	Lack of interest of leadership in using performance measures (48)*
11%	Effectively reporting performance data to executive leadership (47)
10%	Performance measures are not reflective of what programs are trying to accomplish (48)
9%	Lack of cost information about programs (47)

*Items are statistically significant at the 0.05 p-value or less. **Note:** The number in parentheses indicates the number of respondents.

Source: Willoughby (2004). "Performance Measurement and Budget Balancing: State Government Perspective." Public Budgeting and Finance *(Summer) 24, 2: p. 36.*

significant problem to this group either (just nine percent consider this a significant problem compared to a quarter of budgeters who view such information lacking) (Willoughby, 2004, 37).

Conclusions for Public Managers

The assessment of a decade's worth of research yields encouraging results. That is, evidence shows that performance measurement can have important and influential effects on the management of public programs as it changes the focus of discussions and even the nature of communication and relationships among budget actors in state governments. As one administrator from Texas noted:

> Performance measures have helped communication with the state government by focusing on relevant issues. On the other hand, without communicating priorities, it would have been impossible to formulate meaningful performance measures that would improve the government. Communication is also a component of the leadership factor. Communication about the vision, purpose, and objectives occurs from the top of the government and must be clear and follow up on the objectives.

Our results show real and positive effects of performance measurement application in state governments—specifically regarding the management of agency programs, and a bit less so regarding budgeting for them. We summarize these findings as follows:

Finding 1: The use of performance measurement is pervasive across the states. Whether legislatively or administratively instituted, performance measurement systems in the states have evolved rather than withered in the last decade. Use of performance measurement is now entrenched in state management practices.

Finding 2: State performance measurement systems are continually being enhanced. State elected officials, budgeters, and agency staff remain interested in making improvements to their systems to broaden applications across agencies and to develop better measures that more accurately reflect program accomplishments. Research results illustrate a commitment to performance-based decision making as well as a continuing quest to advance performance measurement applications in the states.

Finding 3: The use of performance measurement in the states has improved communication among state government budget actors. Our findings show that performance measurement use has advanced communication between and among executive agencies, as well as between and among agencies, the executive budget office, and legislators and their staff (Willoughby and Melkers, 2001b). Although we cannot definitively point to the use of performance measurement as changing state appropriations, we can say that the *substance* and *quality* of discussion about government budgets and programs among many working within these governments has been improved because of such use.

Finding 4: The communication effects from using performance measures are not just internal to state governments. Rather, our findings indicate that communication with external stakeholders is often considered "effective" or at least "somewhat effective" by state budgeters, administrators, and staff. Specifically, communication with the public about government performance has improved in the states, albeit not as markedly as it has amongst those "inside" state government. Further, reporting to external stakeholders about government performance is not considered by state budgeters or administrators to be problematic. As those in government become even more adept at measuring and explaining program performance, we can expect that communication to those outside of government will continue to improve—both in the understandability of reported material, as well as the extent to which information is disseminated. This bodes well for advancing citizen input to budget and management processes in the states.

Finding 5: Concentrating on outcomes rather than outputs advances state management and budget practices. We should expect that the more substantive the measure, and the more entrenched the performance measurement system in the state budget process, then state managers and budgeters would realize greater understanding about government operations and the results of those operations. In fact, we found that respondents from governments that report more developed systems of performance measurement, where measures reflect more outcomes than activity-based measures, also indicate stronger, improved communication effects. This suggests that, although challenging to develop, sound outcome measures add value to the deliberations about government activities and programs.

Finding 6: The use of performance measures for benchmarking is still in its infancy. This is a bit surprising, though understandable. Our past research findings indicate that the most prevalent type of benchmarking conducted in states by both budgeters and agency staff is a comparison of agency performance with prior periods—97 percent of budgeters and 98 percent of agency staff noted to us that they "sometimes" or "always" conduct this type of benchmarking activity. The next most popular forms of benchmarking conducted are comparisons of agency performance with other similar agencies in other governments, and then with national standards or professional guidelines. However, the proportions of budgeters and agencies applying this type of benchmarking (~80–88 percent for both groups) indicate just "sometimes" and not "always" concerning the use of performance data (Willoughby 2004b). This is an area in which most states can do better, and probably will with time. Somewhat related to our fifth finding, as states become even more sophisticated in measuring agency performance, as more reliable and valid measures are developed, it will become easier to make comparisons across time periods, across agencies within the same government, with agencies in other governments, and with national, professional, and other established standards.

Finding 7: Measurement systems in the states are not comprehensive or comprehensively applied. Most states have applied a stepped or staggered approach to performance measurement implementation—not all agencies are brought on board at the same time and not all agencies must provide the same amount of information within the same time frame. This is to be expected and is no doubt recognition on the part of state administrators (and legislators) that real change, especially in government, occurs slowly rather than all at once. Pilot applications are laudable as long as the effort is sustained.

Finding 8: The use of performance measurement is improving, albeit slowly. This finding actually brings us back to our second finding (state performance measurement systems continue to evolve): They are progressing, but slowly. Given the multitude of budget and management reforms evidenced, attempted, and often discarded by American governments in the last century, the evolution of performance measurement use in state governments suggests a needed permanency.

The past decade of research about performance measurement in the states has been fruitful. As well, the current effort to present explanatory models of performance measurement use in the states provides greater specificity of the factors that influence successful use. We are able to point to much progress in the states in terms of advancing discussions and deliberations about the performance of government agencies and programs. Perhaps most importantly, we have found that the problems noted by state practitioners regarding performance measurement use are *not* insurmountable. That is, we conclude that focused, sustained, and visible organizational and leadership commitment to a performance-based management system is one avenue to institutionalizing performance measurement use for management and budgeting purposes.

Endnotes

1. State government chief executives report annually or biennially to their legislatures regarding the fiscal condition of their state, commonwealth, or territory. Governors often use their address to lay out their policy and budget agendas for their upcoming or continuing administration. The 2004 state-of-the-state addresses were accessed from January through March 5, 2004, at the National Governors Association website: http://www.nga. org/nga/legislativeUpdate/1,1169,C_ISSUE_BRIEF^D_6252.00.html. Five states did not have state-of-the-state addresses noted on this website during this time, including Arkansas, Montana, Nevada, North Carolina, and Texas. All quotes and data presented in this section are from the addresses accessed through this website or from Willoughby (2004A).

2. The managing for results grade is based on research by the Government Performance Project, conducted by the Maxwell School of Citizenship and Public Affairs at Syracuse University, which analyzes state government management capacities. This examination, conducted every several years, collects data about state government financial management, human resources, infrastructure, and information management traditions and capacities. States are then compared to each other and to various accepted standards of performance regarding these processes. An overall grade regarding states' abilities to "manage for results" is used here and can be found at http://www.maxwell. syr.edu/gpp/grade/state_2001/stategrades2001.asp.

3. These results were first presented in Willoughby (2004b).

Bibliography

Badertscher, Nancy, 2004. "Perdue Tackles Waste," *The Atlanta Journal Constitution* (July 23, 2004): D9.

Chi, Keon S., Kelley A. Arnold and Heather M. Perkins, 2003. "Trends in State Government Management: Budget Reduction, Restructuring, Privatization and Performance Budgeting," *The Book of the States* (Lexington, KY: The Council of State Governments): 419–427, 441–443.

Greenblatt, Alan, 2004. "States of Frustration," *Governing* (January 2004) 17, no. 4, p. 30.

Hatry, Harry, Elaine Morley, Shelli Rossman and Joseph Wholey, 2003. "How Federal Programs Use Outcome Information: Opportunities for Federal Managers." Washington, D.C.: IBM Center for The Business of Government.

Jenny, Nicholas W., 2003. "State Tax Revenue Grows Slightly," *State Revenue Report* (December 2003) 54, p. 3. Fiscal Studies Program, The Nelson A. Rockefeller Institute of Government.

Joyce, Philip, 2003. "Linking Performance and Budgeting Opportunities in the Federal Budget Process." Washington, D.C.: IBM Center for The Business of Government.

Joyce, Philip G., 1993, "Using Performance Measures for Federal Budgeting: Proposals and Prospects." *Public Budgeting and Finance*, vol. 13, no. 4: 3–17.

Melkers, Julia and Katherine Willoughby (forthcoming). "Models of Performance Measurement Use in Local Governments: Understanding Budgeting, Communication and Lasting Effects," *Public Administration Review*.

Melkers, Julia and Katherine Willoughby, 2001. "Budgeters Views of State Performance Budgeting Systems," *Public Administration Review* (January/February) vol. 61, no. 1: 54–64.

Melkers, Julia and Katherine Willoughby, 1998. "The State of the States: Performance-Based Budgeting Requirements in 47 Out of 50," *Public Administration Review* (January/February) vol. 58, no. 1: 66–73.

NASBO, 2004. "Federal Budget Update: Administration's Budget Lean for States; Cracks Down on Intergovernmental Transfers" (February 5), Table 1. Major Discretionary and Mandatory Program Funding.

NASBO and NGA, 2003. *The Fiscal Survey of the States*, December 2003, p. 1.

The Pew Center on the States, 2003. "State Legislators Survey: A Report on the Findings," (Princeton Survey Research Associates, Inc.): 2.

State of Washington, Office of Financial Management, 2001–03 Operating Budget Instructions, Part I. (Olympia, Washington, 2001.) Also available at: http://www.ofm.wa.gov/budinst01-03/budinst01-03part1/budinst01-03part1.htm#section2.

Thurmaier, Kurt and Katherine Willoughby, 2001. *Policy and Politics in State Budgeting* (New York: M.E. Sharpe Publishers).

Willoughby, Katherine G., 2004a. "State Revenues 2004: Governors Looking Inward?" *Spectrum: The Journal of State Government* (Spring) 77, 2: 15–18.

Willoughby, Katherine G., 2004b. "Performance Measurement and Budget Balancing: State Government Perspective," *Public Budgeting and Finance* (Summer) 24, 2: 21–39.

Willoughby, Katherine G. and Julia E. Melkers, 2001a. "Assessing the Impact of Performance Budgeting: A Survey of American States," *Government Finance Review* (April) vol. 17, no. 2: 25–30.

Willoughby, Katherine G. and Julia E. Melkers, 2001b. "Performance Budgeting in the States," in *Quicker, Better, Cheaper? Managing Performance in American Government,* edited by Richard Nathan and Dall Forsythe (The Rockefeller Institute).

Willoughby, Katherine G. and Julia Melkers, 2000. "Implementing PBB: Conflicting Views of Success," *Public Budgeting and Finance* (Spring) vol. 20, no. 1: 105–120.

CHAPTER FOUR

Moving from Outputs to Outcomes: Practical Advice from Governments Around the World

Burt Perrin

Based upon the Roundtable
"Moving from Outputs to Outcomes:
Implications for Public Sector Management"
December 15–16, 2004
Sponsored by The World Bank and the
IBM Center for The Business of Government

This report was originally published in January 2006.

Introduction

Purpose of This Report: Practical Ideas About How to Move Toward an Outcome Orientation

All governments are under increasing pressure to produce—and to demonstrate—results. The importance of an outcome focus for effective and responsive public management is generally recognized. Yet implementing an outcome-oriented approach has proved deceptively difficult. There often has been more attention in practice to activities and outputs rather than to outcomes.

What can help facilitate moving from a traditional input-activities-output model to a results-based approach that is focused on outcomes and impacts? While a number of countries have at least started to reorient their public sectors toward a focus on outcomes, there have been few evaluations of such efforts. There is limited knowledge about how to deal with some of the key challenges, such as how to generate the necessary senior-level support at both the political and administrative levels to focus on outcomes, and how to change the culture so that there is commitment and buy-in to an outcome-oriented approach across all levels within the public sector.

To address this situation, 12 present and former senior government officials, equally divided between developing and developed countries, came together under the auspices of the World Bank for a Roundtable Discussion on the ways in which their respective countries are moving toward an outcome focus in the public sector. These are not the only countries in the world that have been doing this with some success, but they are considered among the most notable. As Gregory Ingram, former director general of the World Bank's Operations Evaluation Department, observed in his opening remarks: "Each of these countries are considered leaders in this area, though they have not all taken the same path nor focused on the same framework." Pages 110–111 provide further information about the Roundtable process and format and its participants.

The purpose of the Roundtable, and the purpose of this report, was to identify state-of-the-art practices and thinking that go beyond the present literature. The emphasis was on the practical, indicating what needs to be done and identifying both small and large steps that have had at least some degree of success in reorienting government systems toward an outcome orientation. This includes good practices, learnings, and practical steps that could be of use to other governments in further developing an outcome-oriented approach to public sector management. Perhaps just as importantly, the discussion—and this report—also identifies some cautions and challenges, including past and current hindrances and how these are being addressed.

This report is not intended as a prescriptive guide for the development or implementation of an outcome focus. It is apparent that there is not just one right way. Context is very important. What works in one country may not be appropriate in another, given differing political systems, administrative cultures, and levels of development. In fact, each of the countries represented at the Roundtable has taken a somewhat different approach in the development of an outcome orientation. All countries, to some extent or another, are in transition. Nevertheless, despite these differences, many common basic principles and considerations regarding the implementation of an outcome focus have emerged, along with numerous insights and ideas about how this can be done.

Sources of Information

This report is based upon the following sources of information:
- The experiences and insights of the participants shared during the discussions at the Roundtable, which served as the primary source of information for this report.
- Short background papers prepared in advance by each of the participants. Each of these papers provided short responses to the following: the political context in each country, steps taken to change the culture and incentives in the public sector, hindrances and obstacles currently being faced, and key lessons learned from experiences to date in moving toward an outcome focus.
- The Discussion Note "Moving from Outputs to Outcomes: Implications for Public Sector Management," prepared in advance by the author of this report, to help set the stage for the discussion at the Roundtable.
- The experiences of the author, for example as Rapporteur for an Organization for Economic Cooperation and Development (OECD) experts meeting considering challenges to results-focused management and budgeting.

The Discussion Note and country background papers are available at the following website: www.worldbank.org/oed/outcomesroundtable.

"We hope that this report will be a useful tool to other countries either in the early stages of beginning this reform or those who are considering beginning such reforms. It should also help countries that are trying to move forward and finding little traction in doing so."

— Gregory Ingram, former Director General,
Operations Evaluation Department,
The World Bank

"Moving from Outputs to Outcomes: Implications for Public Sector Management" Roundtable Discussion, December 15–16, 2004

On December 15 and 16, 2004, 12 present and former senior government officials came together under the auspices of the World Bank in Washington, D.C., to discuss the ways in which their respective countries are moving forward in designing and implementing a results focus for their public sector management.

The 12 Roundtable participants, equally divided between developed and developing countries, addressed a number of key issues central to the establishment of a results orientation. The conversations over the two days focused on the political context, linking outcomes to national and sectoral strategies, linking outcomes to budget decisions, evaluating and reporting on outcomes, and the pressures of moving forward or sliding backward.

Why this Roundtable? All governments are under increasing pressure to produce results. There is general recognition concerning an outcome focus for effective public sector management. Yet implementing an outcome-oriented approach has proved deceptively difficult. As the title of the Roundtable suggests, often more attention has been paid in practice to activities and outputs than to outcomes.

What can help facilitate moving from a focus on outputs to a focus on outcomes? While a number of countries (both developed and developing) have moved their public sectors toward a focus on outcomes, few evaluations of such efforts have been undertaken. Consequently, there is limited knowledge on how to deal with some of the key challenges in public sector reform of this magnitude. For example, questions such as how to generate the necessary senior-level support at both the political and administrative levels, how to change the culture so that there is commitment and acceptance to an outcome-oriented approach across all levels within the public sector, and how to effectively establish results-based monitoring and evaluation systems that bind all levels of government together are all in need of further understanding.

This Roundtable provided an opportunity to learn from champions who have helped lead this change in their respective countries. There was frank and candid discussion of personal experiences, of what facilitated or hindered their efforts at reform, and of the challenges they faced in generating both the political will as well as institutional capacity to move forward. The discussions brought into sharp relief the need for understanding the context in the respective countries as to how to lead such change efforts.

Context is critical. It is clear that there is no magic formula or "cookbook" that can be applied everywhere. The political and cultural contexts, as well as history (such as experience with democracy) represent important factors that can influence the choice of a particular approach in moving toward outcomes. Nevertheless, as this report makes clear, there is considerable agreement among the 12 on many principles and factors that need to be in place to facilitate such a fundamental change in approach and philosophy to public sector governance.

The Roundtable produced a number of insights and suggestions on good practices, the preconditions for undertaking such an effort, and how similar/dissimilar the 12 countries are on different dimensions of building a results-based approach. What was clear was that no country would claim to have all the answers; no system is working perfectly. But what was also clear was that all 12 of these countries are moving in the same direction—they are all interested in achieving (and being able to document) results from government action.

The Format
The Roundtable format itself was different in nature from more conventional formal exchanges. It was kept very informal, with no prepared talks or presentations, in order to provide an environment facilitating honest and open discussion among a small group of some of the most knowledgeable people on this topic from around the world. To help provide some focus on the issues to be discussed, a short "Discussion Note" was prepared in advance of the meeting and shared with the participants. In addition, each of the 12 participants prepared a short three- to four-page note on the present situation in their respective countries. These notes were also shared in advance.

Roundtable Participants
(Affiliations current at the time of the Roundtable)
- Canada: Maria Barrados, Public Service Commission
- Chile: Francisco Meneses, General Secretary of the Presidency
- Colombia: Manuel Fernando Castro, National Department of Planning
- Egypt: Medhat Hassanein, American University of Cairo
- Ireland: Richard Boyle, Institute of Public Administration
- Mexico: Mohammad Azarang, Monterrey University
- Netherlands: Peter Van Der Knaap, Netherlands Court of Audit
- Spain: Eduardo Zapico-Goni, Ministry of Finance
- Tanzania: Paschal Assey, Office of the Vice-President
- Uganda: Mary Muduuli, Ministry of Finance, Planning, and Economic Development
- United Kingdom: Alex Hill, HM Treasury
- United States: Jonathan D. Breul, IBM Center for The Business of Government
- World Bank: R. Pablo Guerrero O., Ray C. Rist
- Rapporteur: Burt Perrin, France

Why Is a Strategic Focus on Outcomes Considered So Important?

Over the last decade, countries around the world have undertaken reforms with the aim of improving the relevance and effectiveness of public services and the quality of public sector management. A key aspect of most reform processes is a focus on results and, in particular, on outcomes.

Until recently, the performance of public sector programs, and of their managers, has been judged largely on inputs, activities, and outputs. This approach, however, has come into question. One of the major factors behind many reform initiatives is a concern that government too often is preoccupied with *process* and following rules, and it is not clear what *benefits* are actually arising from public sector expenditures and activities.

The importance of outcomes was reinforced by the experiences of the countries represented at the Roundtable. The exact rationale and sources of pressure varied considerably from country to country, but in all cases was driven by a *political imperative* to produce—and to be able to demonstrate—results of importance to the political leadership and to the citizenry. Following are some examples of this:

- As their background papers highlight, the major driving force in Uganda and Tanzania was a desire to achieve tangible reductions in poverty in their countries.
- The Mexico background paper indicates that the reform effort is directly connected to the goals of the new president, who was elected after 71 years of rule by a single party. The outcome focus is seen as a central element of aligning the entire government to the president's promises.
- Similarly in Colombia, the new outcome orientation was also tied to the vision of the new president, who realized that people want to see results from what the government does.
- The recent return to democracy in Chile sets the context for government needing to demonstrate its responsiveness in providing services to citizens.

"Nothing that we have advanced as a country in the last 15 years could have been done before getting democracy back. So it's very interesting how these two different levels of topics come together when the government has to show the people what it is doing and why, and why it is prioritizing one thing over others."

— Participant from Chile

- In the Netherlands, the main driving force for reform was Parliament, which felt that it was getting hardly any information on policy results.
- In some other countries in both the north and the south, such as in Egypt and Spain—and to some extent in many countries—the imperative for reform is linked to comprehensive administrative and political reforms and modernization with respect to the nature of public services, sometimes connected to a move to greater democratization. For example, in Spain:

> There was a huge increase with the change of regime from autocracy to democracy, a huge increase in 20 years on spending. At the same time, there was a huge decentralization from central government to autonomous governments, which means in fact a completely turbulent change in those years. That means a huge change. Spain has been in a huge quantitative and qualitative change in the administrative and political context without the corresponding effective public management capacity development.

- In some other countries, such as Canada and the United Kingdom, a principal driving force has been the increased pressure to demonstrate the value of public expenditures and their resulting benefits. In the United States, a main driving force is the widespread distrust of government. Unlike in some other countries, various reform efforts have taken place over a period of time and have been largely bipartisan in nature.
- Ireland may be different from some other countries, where as its background paper indicates, the primary initiative for reform came from the administrative rather than the political level. This was partly out of a recognition of the need to deliver outcomes important to citizens, and partly due to an awareness that: "If we don't do something to put our own house in order, the politicians are likely to come along and maybe impose a system on us that we like even less."

External influences also have played a role in stimulating movement toward a results orientation. An outcome focus increasingly is a prerequisite for financial and other forms of support. For example, as both Ireland and Spain have indicated, one pressure for a results orientation came from

---

"[The president of Colombia] introduced to the whole government this vision of let's show results, and people want to see results from what the government does.... This in the political context is very important because what it really expresses is that this focus on results has political gains, not only costs, and it happens very often that governments tend just to see the costs associated with this kind of focus on results."

— Participant from Colombia

Linking Outcomes to Citizens

"We are supposed to be in the business of improving services to citizens, and outcomes are what are important to them."

"Managing for results and the focus on results has been tied to administrative and political reforms and modernization processes of the state."

"There was pressure from the civil society, from the political parties, demanding real tangible results on the ground."

"Focus on what matters to people."

"A driving concern throughout is to make the public sector work better. And the second part of that is, are we really getting value for our money."

"A focus on results is a means to achieve some ends, not an end in itself."

"Outcomes reflect the intended and unintended results from government actions and provide the rationale for government interventions."

"That is what the public sector is all about—producing benefits, or results, for its citizens."

the European Union (EU). Leadership from the EU has influenced the administrative systems of the 10 new Member States, mainly from Eastern Europe, and is a major factor influencing reform in other countries that are interested in future membership or closer relations with the EU. Both Spain and Ireland touch upon the role the EU has played in influencing directions in their countries. The World Bank and other development banks, along with many multilateral and bilateral donors, are increasingly demanding an outcome orientation, along with appropriate monitoring and evaluation systems, as a condition of financial and other forms of support.

External pressure can come as well from the other direction, such as from civil society. A number of countries emphasized the importance of the demands of civil society for tangible results that helped lead to their outcome approach. Civil society attention has also been cited as an important factor in sustaining the efforts and in providing a democratic basis for reform efforts linked to the needs and desires of the citizenry.

External factors also can have a more subtle influence. For example, one of the factors influencing reform that participants (including the United States) at the Roundtable, as well as at other forums such as OECD gatherings, acknowledged is a realization that "they may be behind other countries who have made greater progress in measuring performance and putting it to some direct application in national programs."

Perhaps the single most important finding arising from these experiences is the importance of the outcome focus being *central to the raison d'être of government*, such as poverty reduction in Uganda and Tanzania or presidential reform in Mexico, and directly connected to *"something that matters"* both to the political leadership and to the citizenry. As the Tanzania background paper put it: "People wanted to know the real change that has happened as a result of the policies and strategies." Otherwise, it is likely to remain a technical exercise that is unlikely to be accepted or to result in real, positive differences.

As suggested above, a number of benefits to an outcome-oriented approach have been identified. For example, it can serve as a frame of reference to ensure that inputs, activities, and outputs are appropriate. It represents a means of demonstrating the value and benefits of public services to citizens and to the legislature. At least as important, an outcome focus is an essential component of a learning approach that can identify how policies and program approaches may need to be adjusted, improved, or replaced with alternatives. It is essential not only to demonstrate that outcomes have occurred, but that the interventions in question have contributed to these in some way.

Yet implementing an outcome-oriented approach has proved deceptively difficult. Countries that have moved in this direction indicated that it has proved to be more challenging than they had anticipated, with actual implementation uneven, at least initially. No one seems to have gotten everything right at the beginning. Even the leaders would not claim their efforts to be more than work in progress at this stage.

Why has an outcome focus proved to be so difficult? Following are some of the reasons for this:

- An outcome orientation represents a fundamentally different way of thinking and of managing, across all aspects of government and how it relates to its citizens and major stakeholders. To be effective, this means of thinking needs to be incorporated into the organizational culture at all levels. Organizational change of this nature is rarely easy. The experience in just about every country that has tried is that it always takes time to put into place and to sustain, it is certain to encounter at least some initial resistance, and it requires an array of approaches and supports.
- Outcomes are longer term in nature than outputs and typically are influenced by a variety of factors in addition to the program intervention in question. They tend to be more difficult to quantify than activities

---

"Results-oriented management clearly is both good economics and good politics, because the politicians who understand the use of focusing on the results really can ride on this and prosper in their own positions."

— Roundtable participant

---

or outputs. Given that achievement of outcomes may depend in part upon factors beyond the direct control of a program or its manager, a different approach to attribution may be required than with inputs or outputs. This can imply the need for changes to existing accountability and reward mechanisms.

Nevertheless, an outcome orientation is considered essential when the role of public services is viewed not as engaging in activities and producing outputs for their own sake and demonstrating how busy they are, but in achieving "big picture" outcomes that result in real, positive differences. Substantial evidence from many different countries shows that it *is* possible to provide for a focus on outcomes. It *is* possible to assess the extent to which outcomes have been achieved. The balance of this report identifies some of the major considerations that various countries have had to deal with in order to result in a true outcome-oriented approach to public sector management.

How Outcomes Are Being Linked to Strategy

The Use of Both Top-Down and Bottom-Up Support

It was clear from the experiences of countries with an outcome approach that both support from the top political and administrative levels, as well as from middle management and staff within government, are *both* essential for the approach to work. We consider each of these below.

The Role of Political and Senior Management Commitment and Direction

A common theme reinforced by experiences in many different jurisdictions is the necessity of top-level support for an outcome orientation. As the previous section indicated, a political imperative to produce and to be able to demonstrate results that are of central importance to government is a prerequisite for any reform effort.

"It is important to stay with the approach; it will not be perfect immediately. It takes about five to six years of continuous effort for a department to become comfortable with the results-based approach, and there will always be roadblocks in the way that the departments will need support to get around."

— Canada background paper

"It is necessary to have higher political commitment in the government, the prime minister, or even higher up. Yet, commitment is two pronged. Without eliciting the support of middle management and senior management, the results-oriented budgeting program won't fly."

— Egypt background paper

In Uganda, strong political commitment for the reform effort came from the very top, from the president himself. But "that was the beginning. What happened thereafter was that everybody was mobilized; we not only mobilized the public sector, we mobilized the private and civil society as well to become involved."

— Participant from Uganda

Thus, support from the top is essential to provide legitimacy and priority to an outcome orientation. This requires an expressed and ongoing commitment from senior-level officials as well as from the political level. Such commitment can provide direction and coordination to the reform effort as well as the necessary clout and profile to ensure attention and action. Top-level support can aid in garnering the necessary resources and system-wide supports and in providing overall coordination. As with any other major organizational change effort, senior-level commitment is required to address the inevitable challenges that are sure to come up, to continue the momentum, and to make adjustments and changes to the approach as needed.

This commitment needs to be backed by actions as well as words. Otherwise, it is not likely to be taken seriously. For example, how much attention is given to an outcome approach vis à vis other priorities? How is it resourced and supported? How much recognition is given to those who undertake an outcome approach? And perhaps most important of all, how is it used? Does it represent an actual shift in how management and policy are carried out, or is it perceived as just a paper exercise?

In addition to political support, a prominently located central unit, close to the center of power, was identified as essential to set expectations and to drive an outcome-oriented approach across government. Above all, a central unit is needed to provide overall leadership, direction, and coordination. Some type of unit, whose form varies from country to country, has served in establishing overall policy, in reviewing and adjusting the approach as needed, and in identifying how results-oriented information can be used in government-wide policy and decision making. A central unit also has served to marshal the necessary resources and to arrange for the necessary guidance, assistance, and support.

"In Colombia, the president himself is in charge of being the first communicator; so that everywhere he goes, he talks about results—everywhere. When the journalists and the media come to him to ask him questions, he always talks about results, giving figures, so the people and the media get used to that kind of information."

— Participant from Colombia

Outcome information is different in kind from financial information and can be used in somewhat different ways. This suggests staffing the central unit with experts in policy or evaluation, as well as in finance or economics, who understand the nature of outcome information and what this implies. As the Discussion Note indicates, input and participation from across government to policies and requirements developed by a central unit can help ensure that the approaches it mandates or advises are realistic and relevant, and can help with communications and enhancing the credibility of the overall approach.

Senior-level support and commitment to an outcome focus has been provided in a number of different ways. For example, in Egypt the process was led personally by the minister of finance, who met directly with those most closely involved on a bimonthly basis. In Colombia, the president himself provides the leadership, talking about results wherever he goes. The outcome approach in Mexico is closely related to the president's political agenda. But in other countries, such as the United States, support comes from across the political spectrum. In some countries, legislative or even constitutional changes may be needed to facilitate the new outcome focus, whereas this is not necessary in other jurisdictions.

Perhaps the most common placement for the central unit with lead responsibility for the outcome approach is within the Ministry of Finance or equivalent. But there can be many other arrangements. For example, in some countries, such as Chile, the office responsible for coordination of the outcome focus is located directly in the President's Office. The Ministry of Planning or equivalent is another common placement. In some places, the central unit is independent—but with close links to the President's Office or equivalent to give it the necessary authority.

The Role of Bottom-Up Support and Engagement

Bottom-Up Commitment as a Prerequisite

There was a strong consensus that while the role of the center is to provide direction and act as an enabler, actual implementation of a results orientation needs to happen at the line ministry and program level. And for

"The Ministry of Finance doesn't deliver the outcomes. It empowers departments to do so."

— Participant from Egypt

this to happen, there needs to be buy-in, commitment, and ownership to an outcome approach down the line.

Senior management sets the broad vision and provides leadership. But it is the people working in the departments, closer to the ground, who need to take responsibility for identifying how to get there.

The management literature also highlights the importance of *leadership* in facilitating culture change, and in motivating knowledge workers in particular. For example, Robert Behn[1] in a report for the IBM Center for The Business of Government argues: "Good performance cannot be compelled, commanded, or coerced." He indicates that performance systems created in law or by central management agencies representing attempts to compel good performance basically do not work. He says that what is needed is leadership.

This was reinforced by the experiences of the participating countries. Numerous presenters emphasized that it is the line ministries and not the Ministry of Finance (or other central agency) in their government that delivers outcomes and is responsiblefor results on the ground. While it is the role of the center to make it possible, middle management and staff must believe in it for an outcome approach to work in practice. The Roundtable heard

---

Involving Middle Managers

"I am fascinated with the number of different people who are addressing the issue of involving the middle in this process. We have the clear push from senior political levels, but to make it really happen, it has to involve the middle levels."

"What we are hearing is that we certainly need strong commitment from the top, be it the top levels of the bureaucracy or at a political level, but at the same time, we are hearing very strongly that we need commitment at the lower levels as well, down to those who are really delivering the services to the public."

"The trick is to subtly and incrementally fuse the performance information into those ongoing ways of doing business, not to force-fit it to the point of rejection, but to make it available and to adjust it, taking those processes into consideration."

about a series of previous results efforts in the United States (for example, Planning, Programming, and Budgeting System [PPBS], zero-based budgeting) that did not work, in large part because they were not seen as relevant or useful to those at the program level.

Many of the countries provided numerous examples of the importance of involving the middle in the process. This point perhaps was made most forcefully by Medhat Hassanein, former minister of finance in Egypt, who consistently emphasized the need to get middle managers brought into the process if it is to work. As he observed:

> We should not at all forget that bottom-up is better than top-down.
>
> I'm more interested in the middle managers than the senior managers. Senior management will remain in office for maybe the next two or three years, and this program is a long-term program in the sense that you have to address all that you have in terms of intensive training, in terms of commitment, in terms of interest for the middle management, who will still be around maybe for 10 to 15 years.

A Supportive Results-Oriented Culture

All countries were unanimous in emphasizing that a prerequisite to successful development and sustainability of an outcome-oriented approach is the creation of a culture that values an orientation to outcomes. In this context, people focus on outcomes not because it is mandated, but because they see the value in it themselves, often because they cannot conceive of doing things any differently. The *thinking* process is critical. The values and beliefs inherent in an outcome orientation are internalized and acted upon as a matter of course. Conversely, participants gave examples of how, without an actual commitment to the process, the result is just going through the motions, resulting in a paper exercise rather than actual change in approach.

Mainstream human resources and management thinking recognizes that effective leaders work not by ordering people what to do but by instilling a desire in them. Particularly with knowledge workers, a command-and-control style of management or narrow application of a principal-agent approach can have the opposite effect from that intended. This was acknowledged during discussions at the Roundtable. Leaders work at the basic human level by guiding, by providing stimulation and motivation, and by transmitting a vision that people *want* to buy into. Thinking in outcome terms cannot be mandated—but conditions can be set in place where this can germinate and develop.

There is no simple means of creating culture change. Following are some strategies in this direction that different countries have used:

Developing an approach that is seen as relevant and useful to programs. Participants underlined the importance of an outcome approach being

"You need to convince managers that the system is for them, to aid them in their own decision making, a tool to aid them. But it takes time to change the culture. You need to convince people rather than to force them, otherwise the information will not be used."

— Roundtable participant

"The system is less important than the behaviors that follow."

— Roundtable participant

---

applicable, and being recognized as such, at the grassroots level. Otherwise, staff will see little point in investing the considerable time and effort into implementing an approach that does not have any value to them in their work. Conversely, they are most likely to buy into the process when they can see its benefits.

Fostering bottom-up participation and ownership. The evidence is overwhelming, from the experiences of the countries represented at the Roundtable as well as from many other sources: Buy-in and support arises through the active involvement of all staff. People are inclined to reject an approach imposed upon them. But if they are actively involved in its development, then it becomes their own. Nevertheless, an outcome-oriented approach is more likely to be relevant and to be perceived as useful when there is sufficient flexibility such that the staff in each program area can develop an approach meaningful for their own context and situation and that they feel is relevant to them.

It is quite appropriate, indeed essential, that line ministries and programs be required to adopt an outcome-oriented approach. It is appropriate to provide guidelines for what this means and must include. Yet it is also necessary to recognize that one size does not fit all among the wide variety of different types of programs and initiatives across any government.

Many of the countries identified another good,indeed essential, reason why program staff—preferably in conjunction with communities, civil society, and beneficiaries—rather than senior government figures should determine the most appropriate outcomes at their level. This is because they are closer to the people and may be better placed to determine what is needed. For example, the Chile background paper observed that "agencies need to work closer to people," and the United Kingdom paper spoke of the advantages of its approach of "devolving decision making." As some of the Roundtable participants observed, the alternative is to return to the central planning model, where a central unit imposes targets and conditions, which we know from numerous failed attempts around the world does not work.

"During the Roundtable, the experience of one country was shared where a new minister, Harvard Business School–trained but with no previous public sector experience, came in and said: 'Government is broken, I don't think it's very efficient, it has to change, and I have all kinds of ideas.'

"A new outcome focus, along with many other changes, was imposed, requiring changes in basic program structures and procedures, as well as extensive reporting in an impossible time frame. The result? Compliance but with passive resistance, along with confusion and, at best, considerable cynicism to an approach that, if handled differently, might have met with approval and support within a system that already supported at least the idea of outcomes."

— Roundtable participant

Providing feedback. As the Discussion Note indicated, one of the major complaints of staff within government, as well as within external agencies, is that they are required to report to government, but they do not always hear back on what happens with the information. They sometimes have no idea how their submissions are used, if at all. Without at least some form of feedback, people start to question if there is any value to the work they are required to do on performance measurement. This can be very demotivating and breed cynicism.

Providing training, assistance, and support. Taking an outcome approach can represent a fundamentally different way of thinking and managing, and requires expertise and skills that few managers start out with. The experience of many different jurisdictions is that technical assistance and guidance is required over a period of time.

Training, assistance, and support have been provided in a variety of different ways. Examples of approaches that have been used include training courses and seminars; identification of selective managers to attend intensive, university-based programs resulting in some form of certificate or diploma; availability of outside consultants to advise and to assist; an internal advisory service within government (either centrally

"At the level of someone who lives in a village or far from the center of government, they say, 'Well, what are you going to do about our own problems? And no one is hearing us.' Should we be leaving the president to set these goals? Doesn't it have to be bottom up?"

— Roundtable participant

"Ireland, as well as some other countries in both the north and south, has been emphasizing extended training and development of up-and-coming middle managers. Over a period of time, as these individuals receive promotions, this leads to increased understanding of an outcome orientation."

— Participant from Ireland

or based within line ministries) that can provide advice and assistance; mentors and secondments of experienced staff and managers to help out in other areas; and informal and formal networks to provide for sharing of experiences.

Appropriate use of incentives. One way that has been used to promote an outcome-oriented approach is through appropriate use of recognition, rewards, and punishments. Both positive and negative incentives can be effective, at a minimum indicating what types of approaches are considered appropriate or not. As suggested earlier, mere acknowledgment and feedback of what has been done can be an important first step. Various countries have found that recognition of exemplary efforts can be motivating for those involved and illustrate to others what is expected. This can also give an important message that an outcome orientation *is* considered important and that positive efforts will be recognized.

It is equally important to take care not to punish those who try, even if the initial efforts are not perfect. In particular, it was acknowledged that there are few perfect programs. One of the major uses of outcome evaluation that was identified is to identify weaknesses and areas where changes or improvements can be made. An example of this is by rewarding rather than punishing managers who undertake honest evaluations, identifying the limitations as well as strengths of their programs, as long as they can indicate how they are addressing any identified deficiencies. Otherwise, managers will believe, perhaps justifiably, that evaluation is something best avoided, which can cast a negative pallor over the entire outcome perspective and lead to self-serving evaluations in the future. While the right incentives have been helpful in creating support for an outcome approach, there was also recognition of a real danger of the wrong incentives, perhaps unintentionally, reinforcing undesired behaviors.

"Reward the ones who try.... The perceived threat of 'eager fault finders' may lead to quite substantial defensive mechanisms."

— Netherlands background paper

A Strategic Approach That Provides for a Long-Term Vision and Attention to Appropriate Medium-Term Outcomes

The Importance of a Long-Term Vision

As the previous section indicated, most reform efforts represent significant efforts to bring about fundamental change in the very nature and focus of government, such as in Egypt, Mexico, Spain, and other countries. Many goals are very ambitious, such as the intent in Uganda and Tanzania to eradicate poverty.

Goals such as these are strategic and long term in nature. They require a multitude of strategies and interventions, with intermediate outcomes over a period of time. An outcome orientation represents a fundamentally different way for the management and organizational culture of the public sector. This can include significant changes in structure, responsibilities, means of decision making and operating, and liaising with civil society and others outside of government.

Perhaps most importantly of all, moving from a focus on inputs and outputs to one on outcomes requires a different way of thinking. Organizational change of this nature and magnitude can never be achieved quickly. As it became clear throughout the discussion of the experiences in the different countries, a sure way to sabotage an outcome approach is to try to rush it. A key challenge and prerequisite to success is to manage expectations—while ensuring that the process does not get bogged down or abandoned when it encounters the inevitable setbacks.

A clear strategic focus, such as has been discussed, is essential. Otherwise, the reform effort will not be relevant and will become just a technical exercise with no meaningful consequences.

What time frame is appropriate? Mexico has developed a 25-year plan! This reflects the reality that outcomes are long term in nature, and a desire to avoid the typical short-term political cycle. This is similar in nature to many other ambitious change initiatives (for example, the Millennium Development Goals, as described in the sidebar). Spain acknowledged that

---

"A long-term orientation is critical. Outcomes don't happen quickly, and there is a limited time frame of elected officials."

— Roundtable participant

Mexico created a "national development plan with the vision of 2025. We had each objective at different levels connected to indicators and to goals."

— Participant from Mexico

Millennium Development Goals

"The Millennium Development Goals (MDGs) are among the most ambitious of global initiatives to adopt a results-based approach towards poverty reduction and improvement in living standards. The eight comprehensive MDGs were adopted by 189 UN member countries and numerous international organizations in 2000. They consist of a series of goals for the international community—involving both developed and developing nations—to achieve by the year 2015."[2]

it would take a number of years to change many decades of thinking. Egypt recognized from the beginning that it would take at least two years to see the very first fruits of its outcome approach, and longer for fundamental change to set it.

The Nature of Outcomes, Taking into Account the Entire Results Chain

Roundtable participants highlighted the importance of considering the place of outcomes in the results chain. This has significant implications for planning and management, and in establishing realistic expectations for what can be expected to be achieved when, and what forms of monitoring and evaluation would be most appropriate.

As the discussion highlighted, outcomes are long term in nature. This is particularly the case for higher-level outcomes, such as major policy objectives. They are typically several steps along the results chain, so that outcomes generally arise only indirectly as a result of program interventions. And unlike outputs, outcomes are influenced not just by the action of the program but by other factors as well, such as other interventions, actions of other programs and players within and outside of government, as well as by social, economic, and environmental factors. Context can be critically important. These factors would apply to most public sector initiatives of any significance. In addition, most major government initiatives have more than one expected key outcome, with different pathways and intermediate outcomes for each.

The participants were well versed in the concept of the results chain (or logic model), and discussed a number of the implications—and perhaps limitations—of this for successful and meaningful implementation of an outcome orientation.

Government Interventions, by Their Very Nature, Are Complex

Country presentations highlighted that interventions to achieve major government goals are of necessity multi-dimensional. Major outcomes rarely come about as a result of a single action. For example, strategies for

"Governing is a very complex thing to do, so governments need to care about both outputs and outcomes, as well as inputs and everything."

— Roundtable participant

poverty reduction require action along many different fronts and by many different government departments—education and training, health, macro-economic policy, and trade, just to name a few. Similarly, health promotion efforts to reduce the incidence of smoking typically require actions going well beyond those of just the Health Ministry—for example, various forms of communications, educational activities in the schools and at the workplace, changes in taxation and pricing policies, legal changes regarding availability of tobacco products, actions by customs officials, and legislation restricting smoking in public (and perhaps private) places.

It may be appropriate to hold a program and a program manager accountable for outputs. But outcomes are further down the line in time and space from what a program does, and thus can be difficult to identify and quantify. And in particular, they rarely result from just a single intervention, but rather through the interaction of multiple interventions and a variety of other factors. While it might be possible to speak of a specific intervention *contributing* to an outcome, it is rarely possible to say that it *caused* it.

As the example in the sidebar "Looking at Indirect Outcomes in the Netherlands" suggests, government interventions are complex and indirect

---

Looking at Indirect Outcomes in the Netherlands

"In the case of the Ministry of Foreign Affairs in the Netherlands, I think at least one third of our activities are toward helping others to achieve goals. For example, coordinating in the case of the European Union. The Ministry of Foreign Affairs is supposed to allow the line ministries to be effective in Brussels. The ones who are achieving the results in these regards are the line ministries, whereas the Ministry of Foreign Affairs is taking care of the enabling environment for them to do this, getting them at the right moment in Brussels to be at the critical moment in the negotiations and so on, and for them to be aware of what is happening and so on.

"This kind of indirect involvement in the results chain has to be recognized. If the results-based management is just simply thought through as a linear process, you are going from A to B, then you are not recognizing the complexities of some of the things that we are doing in government. So this is a lesson also from the pragmatic side. We have to take that into account in setting up results-based systems."

in nature. Many interventions cannot be expected on their own to *cause* the desired outcomes, but rather to put in place the necessary conditions so that others can do this. For example, more and more multilateral and bilateral donors are focusing on capacity building, so that countries and communities themselves can address their needs on their own. The impact of such activities, by design, is indirect and long term in nature. But this is true of many other government interventions, such as when a central government removes barriers to the development of infrastructure by the private sector that in turn can enable increased development at the local levels.

Thus, it was acknowledged that it is not always appropriate to hold programs and program managers accountable for the actual achievement of higher-level outcomes. Nevertheless, many countries still expect managers to be accountable for taking a results *orientation*, thinking through the results chain and identifying how their own initiatives are contributing to the desired outcomes, taking into account the activities of others as well as external factors.

For these and other reasons, Roundtable participants noted that outcome information tends to have somewhat different characteristics from input or output data. Unintended and unexpected consequences also can be as important to identify as stated objectives. Indeed, any significant policy initiative is almost certain to have a number of unintended effects that can be positive or negative. Outcome information, by its very nature, often is "messy" in nature, involving qualitative as much as quantitative data, and frequently is more approximate than exact.

Consideration of the Right Level of Outcome at the Appropriate Point in Time
Given the nature of outcomes, a long-term approach of some form invariably is required. Measuring a long-term outcome or blaming a program

---

"It is essential to consider the entire results chain when working with and reporting on outcomes.... There is a danger of outcome measures that are cast too high."

— Roundtable participant

"If you pass the test of are you trying to measure a result that really matters to your population, then it doesn't matter whether you've really got a final outcome or whether you've got an intermediate outcome or whether you have an output. If that's the thing that your population and your political leadership think is important, then I think that's all that matters."

— Roundtable participant

Developing/Developed Country Perspectives

To an observer, perhaps one of the most remarkable aspects emerging from the Roundtable discussion was the overall commonality of issues, questions, and concerns across developed and developing countries. Yet despite this, some differences did emerge.

For example, there often seemed to be more fervor to the reforms coming from the developing countries than from those in the north. There appears to be a simple reason for this: Reforms in the developing countries tend to be dealing with more fundamental issues, such as the eradication of extreme poverty or establishing appropriate govern-ment structures in relatively new democracies that still have sometimes archaic public sector systems. Indeed, an outcome approach, demonstrating responsiveness of the government to what it has promised to do in response to what people feel is important, is seen as basic to democracy. Outcomes for developing countries, such as establishing very basic education or health services, may be even more important than for some Western countries whose citizens take these for granted and are more concerned about waiting times, for example. Perhaps for these reasons, the outcome orientation often seems to be more closely connected to top-level political agendas and is attracting attention and support right from the president or equivalent.

Developing countries also are influenced more by the support and demands of the international donor community. There were many examples of how this direction and guidance—for example, from the World Bank—has acted as a catalyst for change that has been found to be extremely helpful in enabling outcome reforms to take place and continue, and in developing capacity that can lead to sustainability of the efforts in the future. But sometimes demands of different donors can be highly intensive and conflicting ("the new conditionality"), and may be more closely aligned to the accountability requirements of the donor agency or country itself than to what may be most appropriate for the recipient country.

By design, the developing countries represented are among the leaders in the area of outcomes. All have democratic structures of some form, along with a functioning public sector. In this respect, they may not be typical of some other developing countries that are not so advanced. There was some discussion, but no clear resolution, about at which stage it is appropriate to begin work on an outcome approach. For example, should this happen at the very beginning of democratic and bureaucratic reforms, or is a prerequisite that a basic government structure, with at least minimal budgetary controls, be in place first?

An independent review of poverty monitoring systems in Tanzania, carried out on behalf of two donors, observed "international pressures towards outcome and impact measures and away from monitoring changes in performance and outputs over shorter time periods."

It recommended a shift "towards a more systematic monitoring of the intermediate levels of the results chain between inputs and final policy objectives."[3]

or intervention for lack of impact prematurely makes no sense, can be demoralizing, and can defeat the point of an outcome approach.

But, as some participants noted woefully, the above considerations are often forgotten. Too often, there is a tendency for central agencies, legislative bodies, and donors to demand high-level outcome information that may be premature or not relevant and that gives no consideration to how these can be achieved or not.

A number of participants suggested that there should be more attention to intermediate objectives and targets that may be achievable in a given period of time and can indicate if the intervention is on the right path toward the desired overall outcomes or impact. Some participants noted that outputs themselves can be useful, and that the primary focus at a given point in time should be on "what matters to people," whatever it may be called.

Using Results Information to Demonstrate Understanding

There is little value in identifying whether or not outcomes have occurred without being able to say *why* this was the case, what this means, what should be done to address identified problems or to increase the impact that has taken place. For this, information about intermediate outcomes is of particular importance. A number of examples of this were mentioned at the Roundtable.

Integrated 'Whole of Government' Approach

Background documents and discussion made it clear that significant outcomes such as poverty reduction, economic development, employment creation, or crime reduction rarely arise from initiatives in just one program area or department. There is increasing recognition that solutions to horizontal issues such as these that governments need to address require action, and coordinated action, from across multiple program areas.

An outcome orientation potentially can aid in taking a crosscutting approach to issues that transcend program or departmental boundaries.

Indeed, it was noted that an outcome approach potentially could serve as a unifying framework for interdepartmental collaboration. Nevertheless, experience across numerous jurisdictions indicates that it can be challenging to instill an all-of-government approach, with true coordination across departmental and program boundaries. While there was discussion about ways to do this, no simple and easy solution emerged.

One means that has been used in some jurisdictions as a way of addressing horizontal approaches is to identify a lead department or agency so somebody takes responsibility for ensuring that the results information is identified in one of the budget documents. Others, however, observed that there is a mixed record with respect to the lead agency approach. In some cases, it has worked well, such as with the Treasury Board of Canada and regarding research and development in the United States (see the sidebar "Successful Lead Agency Approaches in the U.S. and Canada" below for more information). But in other

Successful Lead Agency Approaches in the U.S. and Canada

"Cross-program coordination is very difficult to do. We are really struggling because if you miss out on some of these sectors in terms of their contribution, you are clearly disadvantaging your final outcome. And it's very difficult to correct those mistakes once they have been made. So you really have to keep a very, very tight check on all of them to make sure that they are moving together."

"In terms of committees and councils, our best example is with regard to research and development. That's coordinated in a loose and collaborative fashion by an adviser to the president and it actually works reasonably well, putting attention on issues like nanotechnology or climate change and other big crosscutting issues. And the agencies over time have grown accustomed to working together and setting priorities and executing these big-science issues together. And that's on a fairly loose and collaborative basis."

"To the extent that there is a more coercive and powerful degree of control, the less effective the arrangement turns out to be." "It's necessary that they as persons feel comfortable with each, because when one agency is too important or too big or the person feels that he doesn't need anybody else, he's not included and the program doesn't work."

"But where it's a joint responsibility, two or three ministries have equal responsibility. No matter what the balance is between the different ministries who have to deliver the outcome, they have equal responsibility both in terms of public reporting, reporting to Parliament, and also accountability to the center."

cases, "the participating agencies get offended and see the lead agency as the owner and they kind of walk away and say if it's your party, fine, you take care of it, but I'm just not contributing, and have a nice day."

The *importance of the process* and the creation of joint ownership emerged as vital to the success of joint coordination of crosscutting considerations. At an organizational as well as at a personal level, it is apparent that if one party feels dominated or marginalized by others, they will have a lack of commitment to the process—and to the outcome. Neglect, or even sabotage of some form, is a potential outcome in such situations.

Also, most organizations in both the public and private sectors likely have vertical structures, budgets, and reward systems. The wrong approach to measurement and rewards, including decisions on promotions, can reinforce "silo" thinking and action and act as a barrier to a cross-functional approach. Managers typically get recognized and rewarded for doing their own jobs and meeting their own targets, not for helping other people do their work. Counter-balancing horizontal mechanisms, along with rewards for cross-functional work, may be required to avoid this situation and give people—and organizational units—a reason and appropriate incentives to work together.

Making It Happen: Approaches to Facilitating Implementation

The Use of Carrots, Sticks, Sermons—and Capacity[4]

Countries that have been implementing an outcome focus have found that a multi-faceted approach is required to bring this about. A combination of different policy instruments, including carrots (incentives), sticks (requirements and sanctions), and sermons (information) is needed, along with various forms of assistance—particularly with respect to the development of capacity and the necessary resources that are required.

For example, experiences to date indicate the need for understanding and commitment to an outcome focus across *all* levels of government, from the highest political levels to the grassroots public officials and other workers in remote villages. In particular, a prerequisite to any outcome approach becoming a real rather than a procedural sleight of hand is commitment and buy-in at the middle-management level. Development and support of an outcome-oriented culture is essential.

One of the identified challenges in moving to an outcome focus is the need for development of the necessary expertise, or capacity. There is a need for increased capacity at all levels—for example, among managers in

---

"The scope for achieving results is highly constrained by the limited public sector capacities in the critical skills like planning and budgeting, monitoring and evaluation, accounting and value for money auditing."

— Uganda background report

---

results-oriented thinking and managing—as well as expertise in more special-ized tasks, in particular with respect to monitoring and evaluation.

Lack of capacity was identified as a particular challenge in many of the developing countries, such as suggested in the quote above from the Uganda background report. But it was also recognized as a problem in some devel-oped countries as well. For example, both Canada and the United States, countries with many years of experience with program evaluation and with extensive evaluation training programs of various forms, surprisingly indicated that it nevertheless frequently is difficult to find the expertise for high-quality, robust evaluations.

Following are some of the ways in which capacity is being developed and expanded:

- **Formal training sessions, provided internally or externally to government.** For example, Egypt identified the training provided to many of the manag-ers involved in its pilot projects by the World Bank as a major asset.
- **Learning through experience.** This represents a traditional—and still the most common and often the most effective—way in which managers and professionals learn. Nevertheless, the management literature indi-cates that learning on the job can only occur when certain conditions are met. These include being exposed to new and challenging situations in which opportunities for learning are provided—that is, where managers are given an opportunity to make mistakes and preferably where there are structured settings in which learnings arising from these experiences can be identified. Pilot projects were identified as one example in which learning opportunities can take place. Other examples can include work-ing with others with more or different experience and expertise, from within the same government or sometimes in other settings.
- **Higher-level education for middle managers.** The sidebar "Education for Senior Managers in Ireland" briefly summarizes Ireland's approach to this, which helped to create greater understanding and support for outcome approaches throughout government. Similar approaches have been used elsewhere—for example, in Malaysia, where selected middle managers were given specialized training in evaluation in Malaysia and in Australia, leading to a university certificate. This helped to create expertise and com-mitment to a results orientation, which again permeated the system as these individuals were promoted into more senior positions.

Education for Senior Managers in Ireland

"One thing we did quite well in the Irish case was at the senior management level, the investment that was put into educational initiatives for senior managers, the next level down from the top level in terms of a high, prestigious master's degree in public service management. The idea was that you would expose those senior managers to good practice examples internationally, new thinking, academic literature; so that as they then moved on into the top positions, they would be a critical mass of supporters for change initiatives, including more of a focus on outcomes.

"And that was quite a bold and a wise decision in the Irish government because obviously with that kind of investment, you're talking about a three-, four-year lead time before you actually see any outcomes from that event itself. But when you look back, you can see the difference that has made; it has created the 25 percent [of the early adopters and enthusiasts]. And because this program is continually running, you're maintaining, renewing, and developing that 25 percent over time. That's one lesson we could pass on."

- **Combining international with local consultants to assist in the development of local expertise.** This was suggested as one way of getting the best out of expensive international consultants, so that they could pass on their expertise to researchers and consultants living and working within the country.

Nevertheless, despite these ideas and examples, capacity development remained a "hanging issue," important to all countries in both the north and the south, to which there still does not appear to be a clear and simple answer.

A Progressive Approach to the Development of an Outcome Approach

The consistent experience of all countries is that implementation of an outcome orientation has proved to be much harder than was anticipated. Participants were perhaps most passionate in emphasizing that one should not expect perfection initially, as well as underscoring the importance of patience and the need to allow for—indeed to encourage—mistakes. This is consistent with the experiences in other countries that have also attempted to implement a results-oriented approach, such as discussed at an OECD expert meeting discussing challenges to a results-focused orientation.[5]

Numerous participants emphasized that moving to an outcome focus represents a fundamentally different way of thinking and managing. A major organizational change of this nature is rarely easy. Participants pleaded not

"This is extremely important because I don't want anyone in my country to have to face a sudden shift from what they are accustomed to over almost half a century, or close to a century, to something else that they would like to try. So a transition period is extremely important so that we will not fail."

— Roundtable participant

to underestimate the challenge of moving toward an outcome orientation. Proper management of expectations—by the political leadership as well as within government—can be very important to the ultimate development and success of an outcome-oriented approach.

A key finding, emphasized in various background papers and in the discussion, was the importance of providing for some form of phased or transition period, an opportunity for trial and error, where failures are not punished. Different countries have followed various strategies. There was no clear answer about which approach is best, because it can depend upon the circumstances.

However, there is considerable interest in using a pilot-project approach to introduce an outcome orientation. Egypt and the United States represent countries with sophisticated approaches to piloting.

Egypt's approach was driven by the need to improve the effectiveness of its budget expenditures and to reduce the gap between expenditures and revenues. Part of this strategy required a move from an input-based budget to one that is performance-based, focusing on outcomes. The strategy involved a set of 10 "performance pilots" among interested parts of the government, including such diverse areas as the Post Office, the Ministry of Planning, the Ministry of Industry, the Ministry of Health, and the Ministry of Education. All pilots met biweekly with the minister of finance to discuss progress.

This led to some significant results, documented by a World Bank mission. It also led to a sense of pride and accomplishment in the pilot areas—and to some degree of jealousy and interest in other areas in being able to do something similar themselves.

The United States took a multi-year, progressive approach in developing its results-oriented approach, now in its 11th year. The first three to four years started with a small number of pilots that were subsequently expanded. The next six or seven years involved operational experience, but with no connection to the budget. Linkages to budgetary information have been applied progressively, 20 percent at a time, with a set of consequences that have been modest, at best.

This strategy provided opportunities to develop and test out approaches developmentally, since initially there were no major consequences attached to the findings. In the experience of the United States, this transition period was absolutely essential. It was particularly important to give breathing

"The process has to be gradual."

— Roundtable participant

"An overly critical approach can kill it [implementation of an outcome approach]."

— Roundtable participant

"Risk avoidance and the fear of exposing failure have been blocking the way to further improvements."

— Roundtable participant

space, so that new approaches could be tried without risking an overly critical reaction.

Another developmental strategy is to require everyone to initiate action of *some* form in the direction of a results orientation. But perfection is not expected initially, and managers are allowed to put in a lot of "to be determined" in their interim reports.

The alternative is a "big bang" approach, where one attempts to move to an outcome orientation all at once, across all of government. While this may seem appealing, the reality has been that this represents such a fundamental change as to be nearly impossible to bring about. Such an approach is certain to encounter resistance and cynicism. It is unlikely to be perceived as useful to the program areas themselves.

A mandatory big-bang approach perhaps may result in the *appearance* of compliance, with the production of all required numbers and detailed reports. But it rarely results in a change in thinking or in management, or a change in what actually happens on the ground. Indeed, it can result in cynicism about the value of a results-oriented approach. The experience of the World Bank is that big-bang approaches rarely are effective in changing the orientation of government, nor are they sustainable.

It was clear from the country experiences that there can be strengths, as well as limitations and dangers, to all possible approaches. There is no clear answer about which approach is best, since it can depend upon the particular

"We really haven't done pilots, but what we have done is we have said, look, this is what we want everyone to do, but you're allowed to put in a lot of 'to be determined.' So as long as you're stating in there that you are working on doing it, it's okay. So it's a different approach, but with the expectation that, in time, it will come right."

— Roundtable participant

"What we're getting in the bureaucracy is passive resistance. If we have to do
this, we will do this, so we're all doing it. I've got outcomes like you wouldn't
believe, but it's not going to help me. It's not going to help me get the kind
of change I want.... What would be more helpful is if I keep the outcomes at
the very high level for my activity, make linkages to any other kind of strategy,
such as reforming government, improving operations, but do that qualitatively
and not quantitatively. But it's much more helpful for me to have more output-oriented measures for my sub-activities. And for me to manage my own
organization, I'm going to have to create those and I'm going to have to tell a
story which is not going to be a measurement story on the other things that
I'm being asked to produce."

— Roundtable participant

circumstances. For example, there was some concern about a pilot approach
being used to sideline the debate and to marginalize the process rather than
to lead to widespread adoption. It was apparent that this would depend very
much upon how the pilot approach was managed. In this respect, important
contributing factors to the success of pilots included an emphasis on learning,
on providing support and encouragement, on publicizing successes across
government, and in particular on avoiding punishment for "failure."

Similarly, it was observed that not all countries are at the same stage
of development. In situations with very fixed bureaucracies, voluntary
approaches may be difficult to bring about and it may be necessary to force
at least some change.

Provision of Flexibility

Experiences in different countries demonstrated both the importance
of being clear that, over time, an outcome orientation *will* form the basis of
government management, and at the same time allowing considerable flexibility in how this can be approached.

As suggested earlier, implementing an outcome orientation has proven
to be challenging almost everywhere. Things are unlikely to proceed exactly
as planned. Country representatives emphasized that expectations of perfection can be the kiss of death for changing to a fundamentally different
way of thinking and doing business. The approach to implementation should
allow room for flexibility, including changes in approaches and strategies to
get around the inevitable bumps that will be encountered.

One important factor that has led to buy-in and commitment to a
results orientation and successful implementation is when programs and

managers view the approach as relevant and useful to themselves, and not just a bureaucratic requirement. This means that programs should be free to develop an approach suitable for their own situation and context that can provide *them* with useful information that they can use *themselves* for reviewing the impact of what they are doing and identifying how this information can aid them in their own planning and practice. This, however, has a challenging corollary. It recognizes that one size does not fit all types of programs and initiatives across an entire government system. Each program needs some flexibility in order to adapt the overall approach to make it most useful to its own situation and information needs.

A Diffusion of Innovation Approach

It was noted that there typically is a common pattern in how populations adopt a wide variety of new innovations, such as use of new technologies (computers, mobile telephones), cultural changes (patterns of dress, new management practices), or innovations in other domains. At the early stages of an innovation or new development, just a minority of the population—perhaps the 15 or 20 or 25 percent "early adopters" or enthusiasts—are willing to give it a try. But once a critical mass have done so, interest spreads or "diffuses" and most others will follow along. What is left is a minority, perhaps 20 or 25 percent, the hard-core resisters or holdouts who will adopt the new practice only much later, if at all, and usually very reluctantly so, fighting it to the end. This is commonly referred to as "diffusion of innovation."

This has implications for implementation of an outcome approach within a public service. As the discussion in the previous section indicated, a big-bang approach, where one expects immediate compliance and full implementation, is rarely realistic or advisable.

Instead, during the *initial* stage of implementation, just a minority of managers can be expected to express interest. But this can be used as a strength. To facilitate initial participation, it should be as easy as possible for those who require little persuading to get involved, such as the innovators, those who already are aware of the benefits of an outcome approach, or others who are interested enough to give it a try. This, for example, could involve the provision of incentives, training, and support. Above all, as was emphasized, one should avoid punishing the innovators, even if problems arise or things do not work out quite as expected. That would give a negative message to other potential innovators or even followers.

A pilot approach, such as discussed earlier, is compatible with a diffusion of innovation strategy. As the Egyptian experience illustrates (see the sidebar "Pilots in Egypt" on page 138), none of the pilots received special funding to participate. Recognition for their efforts served an important incentive.

Pilots in Egypt

"None of the pilots secured extra funds....It was public recognition and competition inside."

"I am not at all interested in reducing your annual budget, but I am interested in seeing results so that I can defend the increase in your annual budget. So this was one of the Incentives."

"For the first year and second year, no one was listening, as if I am telling a story that has no impact whatsoever on anybody. But when results became successful, I [minister of finance] cited the results— I never quoted anything in the Ministry of Finance; I was quoting results in the Ministry of Electricity, in the Ministry of Industry—and the ministers were very proud that I was citing them as performing very well in the area of results. So everyone started to ask what is going on in the ministry of this or that.... So it started to arouse their interest to know more and to join the program."

"It became sort of a jealousy—why these ministers started these efforts, and they are now getting some results, and there are some improvements...."

Once information about the benefits of the new outcome approach started to "diffuse," others became interested. In Egypt's case, many other middle managers asked if they could become pilots as well. This is typical of how innovations become mainstream. Others will follow along the footsteps of the pioneers because they now can see the benefits—or at least recognize that everyone will be moving in this direction and that they will be out of step if they do not join in. It will start to become apparent that this is normal, expected behavior of an effective manager.

One can stimulate the diffusion process, such as using a variety of approaches to disseminate information about the new approach—and how the pioneers have benefited from it themselves. As discussed further in the next section, promoting and supporting natural champions who will use their own informal networks to spread the word is another means of facilitating the diffusion process.

Typically, this leaves perhaps 20 or at most 25 percent of managers who still resist what is no longer an innovation. It will eventually become clear that they represent a backward minority. Some may reluctantly follow along, just as there are still some managers who refuse to use a computer, and others will resist to the bitter end. One can deal with the hard-core recalcitrants later on, when it is clear that they are in the minority and out of step with current thinking.

"The most classic example of failure is when you give over the agenda to the bottom 25 percent and say, we won't move forward until we have consensus."

— Roundtable participant

Roundtable participants advised against wasting too much time and effort with the resisters. As the Pareto principle (frequently referred to as the "80-20 rule") suggests, it is too easy—and all too common—to spend 80 percent of one's efforts on the 20 percent of the most difficult cases. Rather than expecting everyone to come on board and wasting attention on those most resistant, one will have more success by starting initially with those who are most open.

Champions at All Levels

Substantial evidence exists that major organizational and culture change and innovations frequently succeed through the efforts of champions. Champions typically are passionate about their cause, never giving up and doing their best to overcome hurdles and to win others over. Passion and enthusiasm can be at least as important as rational argument and hard evidence.

Champions can be at any level within an organization. Just as there is a need for both top-down and bottom-up support for an outcome approach, discussion at the Roundtable highlighted the need for champions at two levels:

- With connections to the top decision-making levels
- At the grass-roots level within the government hierarchy

Advocates or champions with connections close to the center of policy making are needed to obtain high-level commitment to an outcome orientation. This includes making sure that priority to an outcome approach is maintained, in spite of the inevitable ups and downs, and to defend it against attacks from those who have not yet bought into the process.

"You made sure you had in each of those pilot ministries somebody whom you could view as a champion or a person who is specifically there because of their expertise and training they received, and they are there to help accomplish this change. But if you just give it to the ministries and say: 'Do this,' everybody in the ministry already has a job. They are all busy. This is just an added burden."

— Roundtable participant

A high-level champion can be a senior official or even a politician. The personal dedication and dogged determination of a senior executive officer to a cause can go a long way toward setting the tone across the entire organization. For example, in Egypt, the outcome orientation was led very directly and personally by the minister of finance. In other situations, an official with close connections to key decision makers can help ensure that commitment to an outcome approach does not fall off the agenda.

But frequently champions can be hidden within isolated "pockets" or program areas ("islands of excellence"). They may not be known at the central agency level. In many cases, especially in the early stages of an innovation, champions work semi-fugitively, using informal networks rather than formal structures, finding allies, generating small successes, and gradually winning over others to their cause. Champions can also be located at middle levels—for example, in units specifically devoted to supporting an outcome-based approach.

Thus, innovation and buy-in to an outcome focus can come from inspiration from the top, as well as the diffusion of innovations from champions at various locations throughout a governmental hierarchy. Personal commitment and enthusiasm is key to an effective champion, and this cannot be mandated. Sometimes the best way of supporting champions is to get out of their way. But often they can be supported—for example, by providing networking opportunities for them to spread the word and generate support, and by providing recognition of their efforts.

Sustainability of Outcome-Oriented Approaches

Implementing an outcome orientation is one thing. Sustaining it is something else again. As was noted, there are numerous examples of well-intended past efforts that led nowhere. Unless the outcome focus can be sustained, there will be limited benefit from the investment of the considerable effort required to establish it in the first place.

Outcome-Oriented Thinking Embedded Within the Bureaucracy and Culture

It was noted that there could be a danger of continuity to an outcome approach if the political leadership changes and if the main driving force is top-down pressure. Roundtable participants were very clear about how to avoid this danger. It is necessary to use the political leadership as a springboard, but also to embed a commitment within the civil service, with outcome-oriented thinking and with support for a results orientation down the line.

The importance of bottom-up as well as top-down support was emphasized, once again, with the former considered even more important to keep the process going. Once a critical mass of support has been created, with outcome thinking part and parcel of thinking throughout, it will be nearly unstoppable.

"The key aspect of leadership is that it usually tends to institutionalize good practices, such as in the case of Colombia. In our case [Chile], I believe that leadership such as this, which focuses on results, can really set standards that other governments are going to use because the people get used to obtaining information from governments regarding results."

— Participant from Chile

"This process of introducing a focus on results may reflect on institutions, norms, and things like that, such as in the Colombia case. But the more difficult and the most important thing to do to make these efforts sustainable is to see that they really, really permeate the daily practices of public servants and politicians."

— Roundtable participant

Much of what is required for sustainability has already been discussed, and is just touched upon again briefly below.

The experiences of countries implementing reforms indicate that the most important way of providing for sustainability is to embed outcome thinking within the culture. In this way, it can become internalized. People will want to carry on with this approach because they believe in it, because they see it as valuable to their own work. One knows from social and organizational psychology that when motivation is extrinsic, when it comes from the outside, the desired behavior will persist only while the external pressures are present. With intrinsic motivation, however, it will continue on its own.

Availability of Necessary Supports

Supports can include various forms of capacity building as discussed earlier, such as training, and guides. But it can also include organizational supports to make it as easy as possible for managers and staff to implement and to make the best use of outcome information. This can include tangible supports, such as the availability of external expertise and funding assistance. But it can also include other forms of organizational support, including appropriate recognition and rewards, so that an outcome orientation is recognized as a basic component of good management rather than as an add-on.

Acknowledging the Role of Champions

As discussed earlier, champions, especially those at the program level, can play an important role in providing informal support and encouragement to their co-workers.

Making the Best Use of External Pressures for a Results Approach

Sources external to government can aid in leading to the development of an outcome-oriented approach, supporting both its credibility and often its sustainability. As noted earlier, one of the driving forces behind the implementation of results-oriented approaches in some countries has been pressure from donors, such as the World Bank and the European Union. For example, the World Bank has been credited for assisting with reform efforts in Egypt, Uganda, and Colombia.

Pressures such as these have a lot in common with top-down support, as discussed earlier. The countries involved, however, say that this has been invaluable as a catalyst. But unless this results in an understanding and commitment at lower levels within government, the result will be tenuous compliance rather than enduring commitment that is likely to continue. Some donors, such as the World Bank, have attempted to address this issue by providing training and other forms of ongoing support and capacity building, and making available other tools and assistance over an extended period of time.

In some countries, the media has been identified as a source of support for a results orientation and as an aid to transparency. In other countries, however, the media has been identified as a negative, especially when its interest is in selectively searching for findings that can be used to embarrass the government. This can result in difficulties for officials whose mistake may have been being too honest about situations needing attention or who may be caught in the middle. Unless those officials who genuinely try to do their best are protected, this can act as a deterrent to the openness that should characterize outcome-oriented thinking and lead to a defensive mentality.

Involvement of Civil Society

Perhaps one of the surprises from the presentations of numerous countries was the significance and importance placed on civil society to the success of an outcome approach. This was particularly pronounced in presentations from the developing countries.

Civil society was identified as being able to play three important roles in the development and sustainability of an outcome approach:

- **Providing legitimacy to the government's goals and strategies.** Civil society involvement has helped to demonstrate that government is responding to what citizens feel is important to them. Indeed, this represents democracy. Without at least some involvement from civil society, an outcome-oriented approach risks becoming, or at least to be viewed as, an internal bureaucratic exercise detached from what the citizenry views as important—or worse.

- **Adding support—and pressure—for results.** Civil society has been identified as a major supporter and ally of a results approach by demanding that government focus on results that matter to citizens and

"It was very, very important to introduce channels to disseminate those efforts [at results] and try to include civil society organizations in the analysis and validation of the information the government was generating, because we didn't want to have a government propaganda instrument. We wanted to have a system that was really able to make the government more accountable, to have effective accountability.... So we have been trying to establish alliances with civil society organizations in order for them to be the ones who analyze and validate information that the government was producing."

— Participant from Colombia

"[The] democratic process has increasingly embraced open government and an expectation of popular consultation before major policy changes."[6]

— OECD

"Civil society is keen to track what is happening to the budget and to speak out very openly on what might be going wrong....This leads to more attention by ministers."

— Roundtable participant

document what is actually being delivered. Civil society frequently may be more concerned about what outcomes are produced than the officials who deliver services. This form of support from outside government can help to reinforce the importance of a results orientation, emphasize its raison d'être, and, as a result, help to provide for its sustainability.

- **Providing validation and credibility.** Involvement of civil society organizations has been identified as an important means of providing for validation of results information produced by government. This plays an important role in ensuring that results information is credible and meaningful and is seen as such.

The Role of Monitoring and Evaluation in Making an Outcome Approach Possible

Countries have found that being able to document what actually happens is absolutely critical to an outcome orientation. Without good information on what has happened, a focus on results is impossible. And for good

> *"If you want to have a focus on results, you have to have information. If you don't have good information, you cannot have a good focus on results.... Management by results schemes can only be successful with adequate and timely information."*
>
> — Colombia background paper

information, all countries recognize that one requires *both* monitoring and evaluation. It is not, however, always clear what types of information are most appropriate in given situations, or how this information could be put to best use. Almost all the countries identified lack of sufficient expertise and capacity in monitoring and evaluation as a barrier.

A Forward-Looking, Strategic Approach to Assessment

Many of the Roundtable participants emphasized the need for more strategically oriented evaluations that could provide guidance for future policy directions. Participants noted that even in the developed countries, it sometimes has been difficult to generate interest in policy-oriented (as opposed to project-level or operational) evaluations.

This raises a paradox. Most information is about what happened in the past. Yet all decisions are about what needs to take place in the future. There was agreement that monitoring and evaluation are most useful when they are future oriented, concentrating on providing information that is most likely to be of strategic use, even if this means information that is "softer" in nature than the "hard" information that can be provided about past accomplishments.

This paradox was noted by at least some of the participants, for example: "I was struck by the remark on the dynamics of policy evaluation and the static nature of performance indicators."

Monitoring

The primary purpose of monitoring is to determine if what is taking place is as planned. The results approach in most of the countries represented at the Roundtable tends to be based, to a greater or lesser extent, upon setting indicators or targets in advance and then assessing the extent to which they have been reached or not. While indicators can be qualitative, they most frequently are quantitative in nature, as this facilitates ease of measurement.

Non-Traditional Indicators of Performance

A challenge to the monitoring of performance in the public sector that has been identified is:

"The need to consider dimensions of performance beyond the traditional ones of economy, efficiency, and effectiveness. With an increasingly diverse, inter-dependent, and uncertain public sector environment, for some stakeholders meeting objectives fixed some time ago may not be as important as the capacity to adapt to current and future change."[7]

"Management and boards of directors [in the private sector] focus far too much on financial results that represent lagging indicators of past performance. We believe they should pay far more attention to non-financial factors such as customer satisfaction, product and service quality, operational performance, and employee commitment—leading indicators of future performance."[8]

There was considerable discussion at the Roundtable about the appropriate use of indicators, with no clear consensus. For example, as the background papers make clear, the outcome approach in the United Kingdom is heavily based on the use of explicit targets. In contrast, Ireland is concerned that "an overly target-driven focus on outcomes may lead to goal displacement, misplaced incentives, etc." Other countries were at various points on this spectrum.

How Many Indicators Are Appropriate?

Some countries have been using a huge number of indicators, into the thousands in some cases. What is noteworthy is that as these systems started to mature, the numbers of indicators tended to be reduced. The general view arising from the discussion is that too many indicators can confuse rather than help.

Yet there is no clear answer to the question of how many indicators are enough. As was noted, this should be based, at least in part, on the capacity

---

"Far better an approximate answer to the right question than an exact answer to the wrong question, which can always be made precise."

– attributed to noted scientist John Tukey

"If we only look for quantitative indicators, we'll never be able to achieve anything."

— Roundtable participant

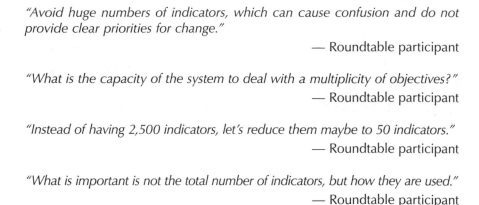

"Avoid huge numbers of indicators, which can cause confusion and do not provide clear priorities for change."
— Roundtable participant

"What is the capacity of the system to deal with a multiplicity of objectives?"
— Roundtable participant

"Instead of having 2,500 indicators, let's reduce them maybe to 50 indicators."
— Roundtable participant

"What is important is not the total number of indicators, but how they are used."
— Roundtable participant

to manage all the information that will be produced and, even more importantly, on how this information will be used. For example, indicators can be used at many different levels within a government hierarchy. Program staff may be able to use indicators that are more specific in nature than may be required by the President's Office, for example. Different stakeholders may be interested in just their own small subset of indicators.

Characteristics of Indicators and Important Factors to Bear in Mind
The nature of indicators. Two very different types of indicators were touched upon in the discussion:
- Indicators that are used or translated into mandatory targets, or minimum standards. These indicators are expected to be met, one way or another.
- Indicators indicating direction, such as "steering by the stars." These types of indicators are highly ambitious in nature, suggesting what one should strive toward and in what direction one needs to move. They can be very useful as a management tool—for example, in helping to create a consensus about important issues that need to be addressed and motivating staff to go all out in this direction. But because they can be very ambitious in nature, they do not necessarily represent achievable targets.

"Indicators such as the Holy Grail, indicating direction, have driven people to dream."
— Roundtable participant

"What gets measured gets done."

— Roundtable participant

"You mentioned this idea that we have to measure everything. That scares me. In a way, I understand you have to try to do that. But you know that what you measure is what you do, and you don't do anything that is not measured. So to what extent can this represent a problem?... From my perspective, you are trying to measure and control everything, not to measure and manage, trying to use your apparatus, your instruments, your software, etc., in trying to control in a very rational way. I think this is an aim that we all search for, but I think there is no space then for management."

— Roundtable participant

"There is a lot of debate about targets and the nature of the targets and how perverse target setting can be."

— Roundtable participant

There can be a danger of confusing the two types of indicators,[9] which can result in undesirable consequences, such as rewarding those who are just interested in "meeting the numbers" and looking good, and punishing those who are ambitious, innovative, and responsive. The same indicator can be interpreted in very different ways by different people.

For example, some ambitious managers think big and strive toward outcomes that it is unlikely they will attain, at least in the short term. Nevertheless, this can help energize those involved, and may result in accomplishments that would not have occurred with a narrower perspective. Other managers, however, may want to be sure that they reach their target, and thus set them more narrowly. Yet even if both managers accomplish exactly the same thing, the first one could be labeled a failure and the second a success.

Dangers of the misuse of indicators. Participants noted that there could be a real danger of focusing just on what is easiest to measure rather than on what is most important. This danger is most prominent when indicators need to be quantitative. This was identified as a common mistake that can sabotage the process.

For example, it often is easier to monitor inputs, activities, and outputs than outcomes. Thus, there is a tendency to fall back to monitoring performance at these levels. While it is quite important, indeed essential, to monitor outputs as well, this should be done consciously and not at the expense of thinking about outcomes.

The danger of perverse, unintended consequences resulting from the misuse of indicators was also discussed. For example, too much pressure to achieve predetermined targets can lead to goal displacement (that is, working to the indicator rather than to the actual program goal) and even manipulation or distortion of the data. These dangers are particularly strong when incentives and punishments are attached to target achievement. There is an increasing body of literature that discusses some of the potential dangers of the misuse of performance indicators.

Making indicators as appropriate and useful as possible. There was some discussion about how to develop indicators so that they can be as appropriate as possible. These points are closely related to those previously discussed with respect to making the outcome approach itself relevant. For example, buy-in and commitment to indicators will be greater when those responsible for delivering the performance improvements, and those who will need to collect the data, are involved in establishing indicators that are meaningful to them. If indicators are viewed mainly as a tool for control rather than for management, this will make it harder to obtain commitment to the process, and can even lead to perverse effects such as previously touched upon.

Also, participants emphasized that developing meaningful indicators is not easy. It cannot be done in a single setting. First attempts are rarely perfect. This suggests a dynamic approach, so that indicators and targets are reviewed periodically and revised as necessary. But in some cases this may not be so easy. For example, it was noted that the political leadership may fear that revising targets once set, particularly if this is done downward, may be interpreted by the public and interest groups as the government backing down on its commitments.

In summary, the overall view was that monitoring of some form is essential to track progress. Indicators of some form are required. But they need to be used appropriately, and it is necessary to bear in mind the potential for inappropriate or perverse use or misuse of indicators.

Evaluation

All countries acknowledged that there has been considerably more attention to monitoring than to evaluation. It was also observed that many of the indicators that are being used are more activity- and output-oriented than focused on outcomes. Participants nevertheless recognized the need for evaluation as a complement to monitoring. For example:

> It has been important to make the distinction between monitoring and evaluation. We have had a relatively long tradition of monitoring since the system was born 10 years ago, but we didn't really have evaluation practices. With monitoring, you use one tool to follow up on indicators that you have set up. With evaluation, you are trying to see the causality between an intervention, a public policy, and its results. This has major implications for policy making, both for budgeting and for defining programs and policies.

Indeed, while the need for more efforts along these lines was highlighted, at least some evaluation appears to be taking place in all the participating countries, given its importance to effective management and to the policy process. Countries are using evaluation for purposes such as the following:[10]

- **Assessing the appropriateness of programs, policies, and strategies for the present and the future.** Unlike monitoring, which largely takes existing objectives and indicators as givens, evaluation can consider the rationale of a strategy or policy and its continued relevance, as well as the strengths and limitations of alternative approaches.

"There was considerable discussion a year ago if these types of evaluations were too expensive and if the government should or [should] not use them as an instrument. But the majority of the social programs and other sector programs have never been evaluated seriously. So you have had programs that have been running for 20 to 40 years, and you have allocated an incredible amount of resources year by year, and you don't know now if those programs really reach the objectives they were formulated for.... So when compared in those terms, the cost of impact evaluation really becomes low."

— Roundtable participant

- **Identifying the continued appropriateness of objectives, indicators, and targets used for monitoring.** As discussed, there is potential for the misuse of performance indicators and targets. Evaluation can help identify when this may be occurring or is in danger of occurring, and suggest how these problems can be avoided, and how objectives and indicators can be kept up to date and focused on what is really important.
- **Providing "why" and "how" information that is needed for an understanding of how and in what circumstances a program approach "works" or not.** Frequently evaluation can take off where monitoring data leaves off. For example, just knowing that a program has failed to meet its performance targets provides limited guidance about what to do about it, unless the reasons for the given performance are identified.
- **Explaining the factors behind positive impacts.** This information could potentially help inform good practice in other contexts or settings. In addition, evaluation can demonstrate linkages across the results chain and can play an essential role in demonstrating if various outputs and intermediate outcomes are likely to lead to the desired impact.
- **Identifying unintended or unexpected consequences.** Evaluation can look at outcomes and impacts, including those that were planned or not. The latter often can be at least as important as stated objectives.
- **Demonstrating causality or attribution—the linkage between inputs and activities and results.** Evaluation is needed to determine if the program intervention was indeed responsible for any documented results, or if these results would have occurred in any case. It is impossible to make informed decisions without understanding what results, if any, really came about in response to the program or policy. Given the complex linkages between activities, outputs, and outcomes that are typically influenced by a variety of factors and are long term in nature, evaluation that can document the nature of these linkages was identified as essential to an outcome orientation. Given these complexities and the indirect nature of many government interventions, qualitative as well as quantitative data usually are needed to explore these linkages, and it may be more appropriate to speak of the *contribution* of a program to outcomes, or of *plausible association* (or *reasonable attribution*), rather than of *cause*.

Technology as an Enabler

Technology emerged as an important enabler to an outcome approach. Some form of automated approach is necessary to keep track of all the data that are generated and to link them to the appropriate expenditure categories and to objectives.

There was some discussion, but no consensus, about the type of software that would be most appropriate. Opinion was also divided about the merits and limitations of a centralized information system. Mexico, for example, wants to be able to identify objectives and indicators at all three levels within its government structure and to track progress in accordance with its national development plan with the vision of 2025. It did not find any existing software suitable, so it developed its own web-based system with the help of an outside supplier and then started applying the system, first on a pilot basis with one department, and then gradually expanding across all other areas.

Similarly, Tanzania is in the process of developing software that will be able to identify all its poverty reduction strategy (PRS) targets and non-PRS targets and to link operational outcomes with sector strategies and with the budget.

There were, however, mixed views about the applicability of a centralized, all-of-government information system. As the sidebar "Decentralized IT in the UK" suggests, some of the participants felt that it is more appropriate to leave departments to decide which types of systems are more appropriate for them.

In conclusion, information systems and other forms of technology may be essential to the ability to monitor what is taking place. Technology, however, as with measurement in general, should not be viewed as an end in itself. There sometimes can be a danger of measurement and technology taking on a life of its own, which could inhibit outcome-oriented thinking and could be self-defeating.

Data Quality

As indicated at the beginning of this section, good information has been identified as essential for an outcome approach. Yet "good" information implies information that is based upon accurate, trustworthy, and relevant

---

Decentralized IT in the UK

"Mostly, in the UK we don't have a single information system, and as a Ministry of Finance we wouldn't prescribe one. We want departments to manage this performance and manage the planning for the outcomes. And it's up to them to decide what systems they use.

"Some of the most radical results in the UK haven't been a result of IT. It has been as a result of planning, of innovation, of people being motivated and of people actually focusing on outcomes and not necessarily being bound into particular outputs. And that's where the real value lies."

"Data quality is a very essential part of the whole process. You have to have from the beginning what will be considered as quality data. Otherwise, if you don't have the right data, you'll never be reaching anything really. You're just wasting your time and say, well, no, after all, the measures are excellent, but the data are garbage in, garbage out, as one says."

— Roundtable participant

"So I think we have to be very realistic in terms of what are we requiring of people, because the worst scenario is that you think you have good measures. You make judgments on them and they're not robust. This should not be the kind of information you make decisions on.... So I think that's a concern, and it may mean that you have to cope with it in other ways, like the suggestion of having evaluation done by a panel of experts. You'd rather have numbers, but if you can't have numbers, you need something else that is sufficiently robust."

— Roundtable participant

data. If the data are not accurate and valid, then they are worse than useless; they can lead to inappropriate decisions.

Participants indicated that there can be real questions about data quality—in developed as well as in developing countries. Much of the discussion about data quality at the Roundtable was focused upon the use of indicators. For example: "A lot of what has been behind the conversation over these two days in terms of data and data quality has been about the monitoring systems, as opposed to the evaluative data."

There are several aspects when considering the quality of indicators. First, are the indicators that are used appropriate reflections of what is really taking place? As discussed earlier, do they result in perverse effects (for example, "gaming" the system)? And are the data accurate?

While data quality was identified as a concern, there was no clear answer. To some extent, data quality can be linked to capacity and greater expertise in monitoring and evaluation, which all countries identified as a concern. Given that those responsible for setting indicators and for collecting the data can be found across all levels within government, all program staff have a need for a greater understanding of these considerations.

How Countries Are Reporting on Outcomes and Providing for Their Credibility

Countries have found that outcome information rarely speaks for itself, even with attention to quality data, as discussed in the previous section, unless attention is paid to how outcome information is viewed by citizens and what contributes to its credibility. Based upon the experiences in many countries, what was apparent is that government data, indicators, and reports will not be believed unless there is already strong support for the government.

For example, in the United Kingdom, where there is often a hostile press and trust in the government has been limited, people tend to have little confidence in the government's own reports and indicators, and question if indicators on healthcare, for example, truly reflect the experiences of the public. In Colombia, in contrast, where the president reportedly has 80 percent approval and where the president himself is always talking about results and people can see things happening that did not happen before, reports have considerable believability.

Roundtable participants shared many ideas, with good examples, about how to enhance credibility and believability in information about results.

An Emphasis on Transparency and Visibility

All countries have recognized the importance of transparency and visibility of results information as a prerequisite to credibility. If the information is largely hidden and government officials offer just selective bits when it fits their agenda, this is unlikely to result in confidence in either the information or in the government. Conversely, when results themselves are visible to ordinary people, this helps to generate trust in government.

"Indicators are not enough if people don't trust the government."

— Roundtable participant

"We have this focus on outcomes and lots of information that goes into the public domain, and a lot of it making very positive steps. The public doesn't believe it, no one believes it, probably because the media don't believe it and they don't report it."

— Roundtable participant

Representatives from new democracies in particular emphasized the importance of transparency. They said that demonstrating that the government is producing results that matter to people is as an essential part of the democratic process and accountability of political leaders.

As the quotes in the sidebar "Transparency" suggest, there are many ways that are being used to make information transparent. Perhaps surprisingly, many of the developing countries describe the Internet as an important means of dissemination, along with more traditional approaches. Political leaders, such as those in Colombia and Chile, who personally believe in a results approach and who are always talking about results, help to create visibility and also to increase the interest of the media and others, such as civil society, in reporting results information.

Transparency

"Civil society and the ordinary public have been sensitized in a way. There is a lot of material going out, and now people are more conversant with what is in the budget and what the budget means. Apart from the quarterly reports which are available, there are more user-friendly documents for transparency, which can even be read by an ordinary citizen, and the civil society is more keen to track what is happening and to speak out very openly."

— Participant from Uganda

"I think the issue on information is to make it public. I think we have to think more about how to make more public the information that the government produces. If you do that, that is the more powerful validator.... The first incentive and disincentive at the same time is visibility. It is visibility—information is available to the public all the time, through the media and through the web page of the government. We have a system where we have in real time the results on all these indicators. The system is very simple, and every citizen can access the system and see in the system how it is going regarding education and other programs. That visibility is very important."

— Participant from Colombia

"We can try to introduce quality standards and controls and verification means for the information that the government produces, and that's a good thing to do, but the best evaluator at the end is that the people know if a public work is being done or not—they do know it. So just put the information out and make sure that it goes to everyone."

— Participant from Chile

"We need independent institutions somehow to validate in front of the citizens and in front of the press, and probably we no longer can accept the traditional parliamentary way of informing or reporting to the public, which is not working well."

— Roundtable participant

This does, however, raise a potential paradox. As discussed elsewhere, too many indicators and too many long reports can serve to obscure rather than to inform.

The Use of Independent and External Bodies to Carry Out Evaluations and Analyses, and to Produce Reports

If information is prepared and presented by government itself, there can be a built-in conflict of interest that can lead to questions about the credibility of what is reported. One approach that a number of countries have adopted, in order to increase the believability of evaluations and other information about outcomes, is to make use of evaluators and others external to government to produce at least some assessments of progress.

External people who frequently are used for this purpose can come from a variety of places:

- Respected experts from academia
- Independent research institutes
- Independent consultants, from within or from outside the country
- Civil society

"The single-minded focus of inspectors general in the United States, an oversight group licensed to investigate, audit, and go after fraud, waste, and abuse, was on process and compliance. They ignored results.... One of my favorite examples is a study by the Department of Energy inspector general, who wrote a scathing report about the bicycle racks in front of the building. He wasn't paying much attention to energy and energy policy and anything having to do with the program; it was the condition of the bicycle racks in front of the building. That typified the focus on compliance and inputs and led to quite a bit of frustration."

— Roundtable participant

- Accounting or auditing bodies that are considered to be independent from the government administration

Provision of Some Form of External Oversight and Validation

This can be viewed as a variant of the previous approach. In this situation, external individuals or bodies do not carry out the evaluation or analysis of results information, but they serve to provide for independent confirmation of its validity. Providing for external oversight, again recognizes that it is not sufficient for the government just to say that it has been achieving results, unless this holds up to independent scrutiny.

The oversight role can be ongoing or after the fact. For example, external citizens or experts could be part of an ongoing advisory or review committee that meets on a regular basis to advise on the development of the results approach. Or oversight can consist of agreeing that final figures and reports are presented accurately.

All of the categories of experts listed above could also provide an oversight role. In addition, sometimes panels or committees of experts and/or citizens can take on this role. Sometimes this can also be done by an external body, such as the review of Egypt's pilots by the World Bank.

Civil society involvement was singled out as essential to provide for validation of results information produced by government. Indeed, countries from the developing world in particular see civil society involvement as essential to provide for the legitimacy of the entire outcome focus and to help ensure that government is focusing on the priorities of citizens.

Perhaps what was surprising was the limited mention at the Roundtable of the audit as a tool to enhance an outcome-oriented approach. Traditionally, the role of auditors has been to attest to the integrity of the financial accounts and expenditures. Increasingly, public sector auditors are engaging in performance or "value for money" audits that consider performance information. Increasingly, such as in Canada, supreme audit institutions are taking an active role in providing quality assurance for performance reports and, perhaps, for the integrity of the overall approach to performance management and the resulting performance data.

However, most mentions of audits depicted them as more of a problem rather than a support to the development and implementation of an outcome focus. Auditors were described as taking an overly process- and compliance-oriented rather than a results-oriented approach. Auditors typically carry out their reviews in the context of a top-down, principal-agent, command-and-control model. As we have seen, such an approach does not acknowledge the importance of a bottom-up approach that creates buy-in for a results orientation throughout the hierarchy, and that is essential for the sustainability of an outcome orientation and true outcome thinking and acting.

In addition, auditors were criticized for taking a short-term rather than a longer view of what is needed to bring about such a fundamental change in the approach to government as represented by an outcome orientation. They were criticized for a lack of recognition of the implications of a transition period, which were discussed earlier, such as the importance of encouraging experimentation where not everything will work right, at least at the beginning, sometimes resulting in a danger of punishing the innovators and placing a chill on the outcome orientation.

Despite this, it would seem that audit bodies still do and will continue to play a role in validating the integrity of results information produced by government. Perhaps this discussion has implications for redefining the role of auditors in the context of an outcome approach, recognizing that this represents a different management philosophy from what many auditors may have been trained in. To have the ability to carry out effective monitoring of outcome information, it is essential that audit bodies have the appropriate capacity and expertise. At a minimum, this would require auditors with backgrounds in evaluation, policy development, or in the social services rather than in accounting or economics.

Reporting That Is Meaningful

There is little point in collecting outcome information if nothing is done with it. This in turn implies the need for a variety of different forms of reports. Following are examples of the types of reporting that are taking place:

- Regular reports from programs and departments to the Center, indicating what has been achieved with respect to objectives and indicators, along with syntheses putting these data into context
- Reports of a more strategic nature, for example, discussing the impact of various interventions on a higher-level outcome.
- Reports to legislative bodies, and perhaps also to other oversight bodies such as auditors, external donors, etc.
- Reports for program managers indicating how their programs are doing and potential areas for improvement.
- Reports to stakeholders and to the public.

Reporting emerged as another area with some good ideas but also with a number of challenges for which there are no simple solutions. One challenge concerns the manner of reporting. A number of participants observed that some reports represent procedural compliance but do not provide useful information. An approach that is too common is the preparation of reports that provide lots of data but no real information.

"Too many reports, too long, with too many indicators result in no real information."

— Roundtable participant

"The outcome framework is largely 'a supply machine,' generating reports, representing procedural compliance but with no requirement or evidence that they are used."

— Roundtable participant

"There is this burgeoning number of measures and paper and almost malicious compliance that drowns it all."

— Roundtable participant

"We have a statutory requirement to produce three yearly strategy state-ments. And the legislation requires each department to produce an annual progress report on how they're proceeding against that strategy. But it has been very hard to shift departments away from an activity and output focus. And despite it being a statutory requirement, some departments have not produced reports every year and others have not produced any at all."

— Roundtable participant

As noted earlier, the results systems in some countries track hundreds or even thousands of indicators. Participants observed that reporting on so many indicators ("data dumps") could obscure what is really important. Indeed, some participants indicated that for reports to be meaningful, they need to focus on just a small number of strategically important core indicators. It is not always so clear-cut what level of detail in reporting is appropriate.

Related to this is the quality of reports. There was a feeling that too many reports are of poor quality, representing nominal or even "malicious" compliance at best. Many reports still focus more on activities or outputs rather than on outcomes. In some cases reports are not even produced at all, or at a very minimum level, in spite of statutory requirements.

Participants also proposed some suggestions for improved reporting. For example, reports in the Netherlands address the three key questions illus-trated in the box on page 159. Other participants found this approach very helpful. It was also noted that a simple framework such as this could also provide focus to the entire results approach, right from the beginning.

The Three Questions Used in the Netherlands

- What do we want to achieve (outcomes)?
- What will we do to be able to achieve it (outputs)?
- What will be the cost of our efforts?

There was also some discussion about the importance of keeping the audience in mind, of providing for the credibility of reports, and of considering alternative means of providing information. It was noted that reporting to the public in some fashion is necessary to provide for the transparency and accountability that is also basic to democracy. For example, Canada publishes a summary of key results information entitled *Results for Canadians*. Ireland does something similar, but it uses the central statistics office, an independent, well-respected body, to publish its report *(Measuring Ireland's Progress)*. Working in partnership with civil society to identify progress toward outcomes was identified as another way of providing results information in a credible way.

There are also alternative means of reporting to formal written reports. For example, some countries such as Chile make extensive use of the Internet. And the presidents of Colombia and Chile, who talk frequently of results and accomplishments when meeting with the media and in public speeches and gatherings, represent another form of reporting.

A Developmental Approach, with Regular Review, Evaluation, and Revision of the Outcome Approach

The experience of all countries attempting an outcome approach is that this is never easy, and that it is never right the first time. Implementation rarely is equally successful across all areas. This suggests that an outcome reform effort should itself, just as with other government initiatives, be subject to regular review, evaluation, and revision. This can provide an opportunity to identify what is and is not working well, what are the barriers, and what might be modified to make the approach more effective. As with other forms of

"You have to walk the talk.... Until the policies are truly used and reviewed, departments will not fully believe in the government's commitment to results-based management."

— Roundtable participant

evaluation, needed modifications could range from minor fine-tuning to more significant changes to the approach and how it is implemented.

In essence, as suggested in the Discussion Note, this means taking a developmental approach to the outcome-oriented approach, with regular review and revision based upon the evidence of what is working well or not. This can represent one way of demonstrating commitment to outcome evaluation, which by itself can assist in establishing credibility for a focus on outcomes across all areas of government.

To what extent has the outcome approach achieved its own intended outcomes? Are there unintended consequences, and are these positive or negative? How can the approach be improved or modified? Evaluation of reform efforts can be helpful in identifying any potential problems in the early stages of the process while they can still be addressed. This can also be a way of identifying learnings and good practices that can be shared with other areas. Documenting the benefits of the approach can help in establishing its credibility and in generating additional support.

Participants acknowledged the need to take a developmental approach to the development and implementation of outcome approaches. Nevertheless, there have been few systematic evaluations to date of outcome-focused reform initiatives.

Using Outcome Information Meaningfully

The Purpose of an Outcome Approach: To Be Used

As is apparent from the country experiences, there is little point in engaging in a major reform effort such as shifting an entire government toward an outcome focus unless it is going to be used in some way. Furthermore, if staff do not see how the outcome approach can be used—for example, with limited feedback on their own reports and little appreciation of how their work fits into the strategic direction of the overall organization—this is likely to result in cynicism that can make further efforts to apply outcomes more difficult.

Use (or "utilization") is sometimes viewed as something to start thinking about after the data have been produced. But considerations about use need to start at the beginning of the process and guide *all* aspects of the outcome approach, including the form of the strategy and how it is implemented, who is involved, which data will be collected and analyzed, and how these will be reported. In fact, many of these considerations were raised throughout the Roundtable and have already been referred to in this report.

"What is important is not so much to have a strategy and a set of outcomes fixed in a document, but the continuous debate, updating both as learning and contextual changes take place."

— Roundtable participant

"In Colombia, everyone is talking about results."

— Participant from Colombia

A New Way of Thinking and Managing

Use is often thought of as a very direct, short-term application of information. There is considerable evidence, however, that outcome information most often is used conceptually rather than instrumentally. The nature of use in this way may be diffuse, but its effects potentially can be most profound.

All countries have emphasized that an outcome focus represents a fundamental change in the approach to thinking and managing within government. Indeed, it represents a shift in the entire orientation of public services—away from a primary preoccupation on inputs and activities to a focus on the benefits and results of these activities. This form of use may be intangible, but arguably it may represent the greatest benefit of an outcome approach.

This is one reason why participants emphasized the importance of instilling a results-oriented culture, and why it is so absolutely critical to the success of an outcome approach to generate buy-in and commitment at all levels of a government hierarchy. This can result in change that can represent the most enduring—and the most significant—form of use.

As is apparent from many of the country experiences, a results orientation means that information about impact informs the policy debate and helps to determine the agenda. In this way, questions about outcomes, and what forms of approaches are likely to be effective or not, may be taken into consideration in the design of policy. One of the important values of an outcome approach is providing vision, which acts as a frame of reference for everything including planning, setting priorities, organizing government services, allocating resources, assessing the appropriateness of what was done, and thinking about future needs and the types of strategies that will be needed.

Actual data about what works or not and in what contexts can help inform the development of new policies, strategies, and programs. This can only increase the potential for the relevance and effectiveness of new policy directions and interventions.

A move to an outcome orientation thus results in a change of mentality—away from keeping busy and thinking about what one needs to do, to identifying what needs to be accomplished. This in turn leads to related questions and steps, in particular:

- Asking how one would know what has been accomplished, and identifying what information will be needed through monitoring and for evaluation and in order to be able to assess results and to identify implications for future actions.
- Challenging current assumptions and thinking about different ways of addressing the identified needs and producing results that are important to people.

An outcome orientation can be useful at the highest strategic level of government. Indeed, its primary benefit is often thought of in this way, and much of the discussion in the background papers and at the Roundtable was about use at this level. But participants also identified the role that an outcome approach can play in program improvement.

Program delivery typically involves work by staff in the lower levels of a government hierarchy. Work at this level is often given little recognition, and may be nearly invisible to those at the Center. It may not appear in high-level objectives or indicators. But many of the countries emphasized that it is often those at the grassroots level who have the most contact with the citizenry, and that outcomes or even outputs at this level may be more visible and viewed as more important to citizens than macro-level initiatives.

Demonstration of Value to the Citizenry

One of the major reasons given for moving to an outcome orientation is to enable governments to demonstrate how public services are addressing the needs of their citizens. As noted earlier, political leaders in countries such as Mexico, Colombia, Chile, and the United Kingdom are using outcome objectives and results as a way of demonstrating what they have accomplished. Countries are emphasizing transparency and using a variety of means to make results information available to all. For example, some countries, such as Chile, make results information available on a real-time basis on a public website.

In this respect, an outcome approach represents an important form of accountability. It differs, however, from some traditional approaches

---

"Focusing on results is also a powerful tool to increase the credibility of political institutions."

— Roundtable participant

to accountability by placing less emphasis on procedures and use of resources (although that clearly is important as well), and instead attempting to show the benefits that people gain from government interventions and programs. Publications such as *Results for Canadians* and *Measuring Ireland's Progress* serve as examples in which outcome information is used to demonstrate accountability.

Linking Outcome Information Appropriately with the Budgeting Process

One of the major rationales for an outcome-oriented approach is to provide for more rationality to the resource allocation process, so that funds are allocated where they are most likely to maximize the achievement of outcomes. At a minimum, linking outcomes to budgeting can illustrate what benefits arise from expenditures.

Nevertheless, countries indicated that a mechanistic link between outcomes and budget allocations is neither possible nor desirable. Resource allocations do not appear to have been influenced significantly to date in any jurisdiction. Nonetheless, (information about) outcomes can play a very significant role in the overall budgeting *process*.

As the statements in the sidebar "Budgets" suggest, the budgetary decision-making process is complex. There are many other factors besides technical information based upon "rational" analysis that must be taken into account in making decisions about future directions. These can include political priorities, competing priorities and alternatives, value judgments of stakeholders, administrative and economic considerations, and many other issues that need to form part of the government decision-making process. Information about results is used most appropriately as one input into the budgetary process.

There are other reasons why a mechanistic link between performance and budget can be problematic. As various participants emphasized, one can only

---

Budgets

"The budgetary process is a very complex process that implies political restrictions, legal restrictions, administrative restrictions, economic restrictions."
— Roundtable participant

"Priorities and politics and other matters will continue to trump budgetary decisions, as they should in an open and democratic fashion. Performance information just makes that debate richer."
— Roundtable participant

"Results are always tied to money."

— Roundtable participant

"In Chile, the budget office plays a crucial role in making sure that the right incentives are being allocated through the budget."

— Participant from Chile

budget to outputs and not to outcomes, as managers only have direct control over the former. Nevertheless, as one participant put it: "If you have your theory of change right, this should lead to outcomes."

It also is necessary to understand *why* given outcomes have been achieved or not in order to be able to make informed decisions. For example, poor performance potentially could be a result of poor management, insufficient funding, inappropriate staffing, factors beyond anyone's control (for example, an environmental disaster), or a host of other possible variables. If the need is still there, it may be appropriate to even increase funding and/or to make management changes.

There is also increasing evidence from both the private and public sectors about unintended consequences that can result when there is a mechanistic link between funding or compensation with results attainment. This can result in goal displacement, in working toward the target rather than to the *raison d'être* of the program, as well as to outright distortions of performance data.

Nevertheless, participants identified the importance of highlighting the relationship between resource allocations and outcomes. At a minimum, this helps provide a *frame of reference* for assessing the overall strategy. It provides an important context for assessing the alignment between strategic priorities and resource allocation. It can serve as a framework for identifying areas where there should be greater (or fewer) resources allocated. Thus, results information can play an important role in *informing* the budgetary process.

As the sidebar "Linking Budgets and Outcomes in Tanzania" on page 166 suggests, Tanzania is using its outcome approach to bring more coordination and linking of the budget with the broad areas of outcomes that it has defined in the national strategy for growth and poverty reduction. In this way, outcome information may be able to play a significant role in helping to focus expenditures on those areas that are most likely to result in the reduction of poverty. Similarly, Mexico is moving toward showing how all goals and indicators are linked to its strategic plan and to the budget. Parliament in particular has asked for more information demonstrating how the budget is aligned to the strategic plan.

"The consequence in the United States has not been rigid or mathematical, which is to say that if you perform well, you get more money, or if you perform poorly, you get less. In fact, just the opposite occurs in many cases. What it has done, though, is enriched the debate in the policy process about which programs ought to proceed and at what pace and with what management style, and which need to be redesigned."

— Participant from the U.S.

"In the UK system there is absolutely no mechanistic link between the results and the outcomes that people achieve and the resources that they receive. But by setting an expectation of outcomes alongside the spending review, when it comes to the next allocation of resources, there's a very clear statement there of what the currency of that discussion is going to be. People know what they were expected to deliver. They know what they were expected to show progress against, and that then forms a basis for the resource allocation."

— Participant from the UK

"A less fundamentalist approach will tell you that a results-based budget might be a very good additional tool to improve the budget process, which means that you will have more elements. You, the people who program the budgets, formulate the budget, will have more elements to allocate better."

— Participant from Colombia

Participants noted that a results-oriented budget is very different from traditional approaches. They emphasized that a progressive approach is required to develop buy-in and support (for example, budgetary officers often view this as a challenge rather than as a support to their own roles), and also to be able to develop the proper technology and to present the information appropriately. For example, both Tanzania and Mexico indicated that they are currently involved in major efforts to be able to demonstrate the links between objectives and results and areas of expenditure.

The country experiences regarding linkages between performance information and budget are reinforced by the literature. For example, an Organization for Economic Cooperation and Development (OECD) report specifically dealing with this issue[11] discusses the implications of technical limitations in both performance and financial data, and suggests that integration could be appropriate only for certain types of programs, in particular those involving the delivery of tangible, standardized activities providing recurring products or services. The report also observes that given the outcomes of many public

"Performance data inform, but do not drive, budgetary decision making."
— Melkers and Willoughby (see endnote 12)

sector activities can only be achieved some time in the future, they thus are not on the same time scale as budgetary cycles.

The IBM Center for The Business of Government has supported two studies dealing with this topic.[12] The findings and recommendations in these reports, again, are consistent with the experiences and perspectives of countries that have undertaken outcome reforms.

In summary, outcome information rarely can be applied directly or mechanistically in making budgetary decisions. It *can*, however, play an important role in informing the budgeting process.

Linking Budgets and Outcomes in Tanzania

"Various initiatives within the poverty reduction strategy are coordinated by different institutions within government. The instrument that is used to link the reforms or the results that we are anticipating with the budget is the strategic plan. And the strategic plan is coordinated by the public service management team that is reforming the public sector.

"What we plan to do is link the budget with operational outcomes, which are then linked with the sector strategies. We hope that in this way, over time, the non-PRS targets will continue to be reduced so that the ministries, departments, and agencies link their strategic plans with the poverty reduction strategy, which is defining the broad outcomes that we are expecting."

Acknowledgments

The author would like to acknowledge the support of the following:

- Ray C. Rist, Operations Evaluation Department, and R. Pablo Guerrero O., Operations Policy and Country Services Vice-Presidency, both of the World Bank, and Jonathan D. Breul, IBM Center for The Business of Government, who were responsible for the organization and implementation of the Roundtable—including the idea that it should take place. All three contributed valuable editorial support to the preparation of this report. Special thanks also goes to Ray Rist, who so ably chaired the session.
- Carol Reed, World Bank, for her invaluable assistance with all administrative aspects of the event.
- The IBM Center for The Business of Government, the Netherlands Ministry of Foreign Affairs, and the World Bank for their financial support.
- The participants at the Roundtable—for their thoughtful and highly informative observations and ideas, and for their candor, good humor, and enthusiasm. The information in this report is based largely upon their insights, presented in short background papers prepared by each of the participants and particularly during the discussion at the Roundtable proper, and would be impossible without their contributions.

Endnotes

1. Robert D. Behn. "Performance Leadership: 11 Better Practices That Can Ratchet Up Performance." IBM Center for The Business of Government. May 2004. Available at: http://www.businessofgovernment.org/pdfs/Behn_Report.pdf.

2. Jody Zall Kusek and Ray C. Rist. *Ten Steps to a Results-Based Monitoring and Evaluation System.* The World Bank, 2004.

3. David Booth. *Poverty monitoring systems: An analysis of institutional arrangements in Tanzania.* Overseas Development Institute (ODI), Report prepared for (British) Department for International Development (DfID) and the World Bank. 2004.

4. For example, see Marie-Louise Bemelmens-Videc, Ray C. Rist, and Evert Vedung (eds.). *Carrots, Sticks, and Sermons: Policy Instruments and Their Evaluation.* Transaction Publishers, 1998.

5. Burt Perrin. *Implementing the Vision: Addressing Challenges to Results-Focused Management and Budgeting.* OECD, 2002. Available at:
http://www.oecd.org/dataoecd/4/10/2497163.pdf.

6. OECD. *Public Sector Modernisation. A Ten Year Perspective.* Background document for the 24th session of the Public Management Committee. Château de la Muette, Paris, 5–6 November 2001.

7. John Mayne and Eduardo Zapico-Goñi (eds.). *Monitoring Performance in the Public Sector: Future Directions from International Experience.* Transaction Publishers, 1997.

8. William Parrett. *The Economist.* 11 December 2004.

9. In fact, an indicator represents the quantitative or qualitative factor or variable that provides a simple and reliable means to measure achievement, and a target represents the specific level of the indicator that is aimed for (see Kusek and Rist, op. cit., for further discussion of the distinction between indicators and targets). In keeping with common practice, however, many of the country papers, as well as discussion at the Roundtable, have used "indicator" in a way that encompasses "targets" as well.

10. See Kusek and Rist, op. cit., for a further discussion on the types of information that can be provided from evaluation, and how this relates to and complements monitoring information.

11. Christopher Pollitt. *Integrating Financial Management and Performance Management.* OECD report: PUMA/SMO(99)4/FINAL, 1999. Also available at: http:www.oecd.org/puma/.

12. Philip G. Joyce. "Linking Performance and Budgeting: Opportunities in the Federal Budget Process." IBM Center for The Business of Government. May 2004. Julia Melkers and Katherine Willoughby. "Staying the Course: The Use of Performance Measurement in State Governments." IBM Center for The Business of Government. November 2004. Both reports available at: http://www.businessofgovernment.org/pdfs/.

CHAPTER FIVE

Performance Budgeting: How NASA and SBA Link Costs and Performance

Lloyd A. Blanchard
Assistant Professor
Department of Public Administration
and Senior Research Associate
Center for Policy Research
The Maxwell School of Citizenship and Public Affairs
Syracuse University

This report was originally published in February 2006.

Introduction

The President's Management Agenda (PMA) of the George W. Bush administration significantly advances the development of performance budgeting in the federal government through its Budget and Performance Integration (BPI) and Program Assessment Rating Tool (PART) initiatives. Faced with the extraordinary task of measuring government performance directly and consistently across thousands of programs, the Office of Management and Budget (OMB) developed PMA BPI standards for agencies and PART evaluation questions for programs with a focus on managerial practices thought to be used by high-performing organizations. The PMA BPI initiative established clear practice standards for intermediate and high levels of success toward aligning agency budgets more closely with mission, goals, and agency performance. PART asked program managers about program purpose and design, planning, and management, as well as results for the purpose of scoring and ranking the programs for budget formulation purposes. While most of these PMA BPI standards are focused on the development and general use of performance information, two are focused on performance costing—the full cost and efficiency criteria. This chapter highlights the requirements of these two performance costing criteria and demonstrates how two agencies, the National Aeronautics and Space Administration (NASA) and the Small Business Administration (SBA), met these criteria using different costing approaches.[1]

The notion that budget allocations should favor higher-performing programs is the defining principle of performance budgeting. Performance-based allocations are said to give incentives for agencies to improve program performance, providing a more rational basis for allocating tax-funded resources. The alternative to performance budgeting is continued reliance on traditional political forces that dominate budgetary allocations, revealed in two common patterns: "pork" and incremental spending. While performance budgeting reform initiatives are not new in the federal government, the performance focus was firmly established with the Government Performance and Results Act (GPRA) of 1993. The problem is not in the supply of performance information, which GPRA provided in abundance. The problem is the lack of use of performance information for budgetary and managerial decision making.

The PMA BPI initiative seeks to shift the government's performance focus to the use of such information. Through its criteria, it sets standards for using performance information, but it also recognizes that linking performance with full cost and efficiency information is central to successful use in the areas of both performance enhancement and budgetary decision making. To meet the PMA BPI standards of success, federal agencies must demonstrate success on each of the following criteria:

Performance Information
Criterion 1. Regular use of performance information by senior managers,

Criterion 2. Focus on a limited set of outcomes included in PART and the agency's strategic plan,

Criterion 3. Employee performance plans are linked to program and agency goals and effectively differentiate between low and high performers, and

Criterion 4. Demonstrate results on most programs and use PART findings in budget justifications and for management improvement.

Performance Costing
Criterion 5. Agencies report the full cost of their programs, are able to compute the marginal cost of performance changes, and

Criterion 6. Have an efficiency measure for all "PARTed" programs.

The first four of these requirements prescribe the development of performance information (criteria 2 and 3) and its general use (criteria 1 and 4). The last two of these requirements are *performance costing* requirements, and these provide decision makers with the ability to determine the relative *cost-effectiveness* of government programs. Performance costing is defined as the process of linking a program output or outcome with its associated costs into a single cost-based performance measure. Cost-effectiveness is defined as the full cost required to meet a program performance goal. Performance costing produces the full and marginal costs of a program output, and these together with a measure of efficiency are required to obtain a measure of cost-effectiveness. The section of this chapter "A Framework for Integrating Costs and Performance" (beginning on page 183) demonstrates how to develop a cost-effectiveness measure, both quantitatively and qualitatively. Output- and outcome-based performance measures often are not comparable across programs, but the associated costs are comparable, and when they are linked to performance, they provide decision makers with better information to make performance-based budget allocations. This chapter shows how to perform such performance costing generally and by highlighting the full costing approach used by NASA and activity-based costing approach used by the SBA.

The full cost of a program differs from the program's budget appropriations in that it captures all resources dedicated to delivering program output, and not just the directly appropriated resources. The importance of this distinction becomes clear when one considers the prospect of a small grant program consuming a much larger share of an agency's resources than the program appropriation would suggest. As in the SBA case study, it took the SBA's Activity-Based Costing (ABC) model to help identify the fact that it dedicated $9.5 million of agency personnel resources to deliver a $396,000 grant program. This example shows how program costs can be misinterpreted if all related costs are not considered, and how the ABC model helped the

Acronyms and Abbreviations

ABC	Activity-Based Costing
BIC	Business Information Center
BPI	Budget and Performance Integration
CFO Act	Chief Financial Officers Act
FASAB	Federal Accounting Standards Advisory Board
FFMIA	Federal Financial ManagementImprovement Act
FMS	Financial Management Service
FTE	Full-Time Equivalent
G&A	General and Administrative
GAAP	Generally Accepted Accounting Principles
GAO	Government Accountability Office
GMRA	Government Management Reform Act
GPRA	Government Performance and Results Act
JFMIP	Joint Financial Management Improvement Program
NACA	National Advisory Committee for Aeronautics
NASA	National Aeronautics and Space Administration
OMB	Office of Management and Budget
OSB	Office of Small Business
PART	Program Assessment Rating Tool
PMA	President's Management Agenda
PPBS	Planning-Programming-Budgeting System
RFC	Reconstruction Finance Corporation
SBA	Small Business Administration
SBDC	Small Business Development Center
SLA	Service Level Agreement
USSGL	United States Standard General Ledger
WFE	Workforce Equivalent

agency properly interpret the cost-effectiveness of the program. The NASA case study shows how that agency uses its full cost policy to reveal the corporate administrative costs (at headquarters and the centers) being included in programs' "fully loaded" budgets, creating an incentive for program managers to push back and question the indirect costs whose burden they now bear. This example shows how including indirect costs within a performance costing framework can create pressure to reduce administrative budgets and shift agency resources toward direct program needs. This chapter is aimed at not only helping federal managers better understand how to meet the requirements of the PMA BPI initiative, but also to show how to use these required measures to obtain a measure of program cost-effectiveness.

How Should Performance Information Be Used?

In Chapter Two, "Linking Performance and Budgeting: Opportunities in the Federal Budget Process," Professor Philip Joyce establishes a comprehensive framework for considering budget and performance information. He suggests a number of ways in which performance information can be used strategically within each of the major stages of the federal budget process—formulation, approval, execution, and audit/evaluation. He argues that the performance budgeting focus to date largely has been on the supply of performance information. Joyce, along with John Kamensky, Albert Morales, and Mark Abramson in "From 'Useful Measures' to 'Measures Used' " (2005), propose a shift in focus toward creating a demand for this performance information. It is argued here that, to some extent, the PMA has done this by requiring key cost information. As any economist will admit, good cost (as price) information must accompany good performance information if there is any hope to attract demand for and use of the latter.

A number of other related reports published by the IBM Center for The Business of Government focus on various aspects of performance budgeting. For example, Harry Hatry, Elaine Morley, Shelli Rossman, and Joseph Wholey's report, "How Federal Programs Use Outcome Information" (2004), offers advice toward, and federal government examples of, successful use of performance information. Howard Risher's "Pay for Performance: A Guide for Federal Managers" (2004) shows how to develop an effective employee performance reward system, while OMB publishes extensive guidance on the application of PART.[2] A cursory review of these requirements will reveal that leadership and experience are being called upon as much as costing proficiency. Accordingly, Robert Behn's "Performance Leadership: 11 Better Practices That Can Ratchet Up Performance" (2004) reviews leadership practices that can help agencies successfully address their deficiencies in PMA BPI status. This chapter complements these by examining the costing dimension of performance budgeting, which is largely contained in criteria 5 and 6 of the PMA BPI initiative.

As of June 30, 2005, only eight of the 25 agencies rated in the PMA (not including OMB) have reached the highest, or "green," standard in PMA BPI—a success rate of 32 percent. Twenty-one of these agencies have been deemed successful at focusing on a limited set of outcomes tied to their strategic plan (criterion 2), 17 were deemed to have effective employee performance plans (criterion 3), and 14 have demonstrated regular use of performance information by senior managers (criterion 1).[3] This last finding is surprising because this requirement would seem to be the easiest to implement. Could the fact that just over half the agencies are shown to demonstrate regular use of performance information illustrate the lack of demand for performance information by senior managers bemoaned by the scholars mentioned earlier? Senior managers may well obtain a wealth of performance information regularly or on demand, but without the attendant cost information, what can we expect of them in terms of direction and program improvement? For example, with performance information showing a 5 percent shortfall of the target, what should the senior manager do to ensure that the target is reached next month or next year? The shortfall could be the result of the program operating efficiently with inadequate resources, or from the program operating inefficiently with adequate resources.

To determine which explanation is correct requires a measure of efficiency (i.e., output per unit of input). Without such a measure, at best, a senior manager must rely upon program managers' ability to apply intuition and experience to determine whether additional resources are truly needed. A program manager might ask, "What's wrong with using intuition and experience?" Program managers may well possess detailed knowledge relevant to their program, but the level of precision called for in Congress' effort to improve financial management requires more than such skill can provide. It calls for measurable results.

One explanation for the lack of demand for performance information might be found in the lexicon of economics, which defines "demand" as the relationship between the price and quantity of goods and services. In the market, a lack of demand could result from the absence of key price information that consumers use to evaluate the quality of a good or service. This begs the question, "What is the analogue for price information in government operations?" It is argued here that the complete costs of program service delivery as well as the marginal costs associated with producing additional units of service are the price analogues for government. This chapter focuses on linking the government's price analogue, costs, to performance.

The two performance costing standards, criteria 5 and 6, essentially summarize the costing requirements for good performance budgeting, and without this information, senior managers and members of Congress are hard-pressed to make good resource allocation decisions based on performance information alone. They might see how effective programs are toward achieving their goals, but do not know what new resources are required to meet such goals. With a measure of program full cost, one can obtain the marginal, or additional, cost associated with a performance increment. With a measure of efficiency, one can begin to discern the potential reasons for performance shortfalls. Together, senior managers and members of Congress can better understand the "bang for the taxpayer buck" associated with government programs. Thus, the PMA BPI performance costing requirements are the linchpins that integrate, literally and figuratively, budgets and performance.

Preview of Chapter

This chapter addresses the performance costing requirements of the PMA BPI initiative by establishing the data requirements for the relevant cost measures, showing how to apply these data to produce full cost, marginal cost, efficiency, and cost-effectiveness measures, and telling the story of how two different agencies reached PMA BPI success using two different approaches to costing their programs.

This chapter draws on evidence from published reports and articles, as well as on the author's experience leading PMA reform efforts at NASA and SBA. While both costing methods are somewhat of hybrids between multiple approaches, NASA's Full Cost initiative relies more on a statistical-based approach to allocating indirect costs that cannot be directly attributed to program outputs. The second costing methodology is SBA's survey-based approach to allocating indirect costs using its Activity-Based Costing, or ABC, model. Indeed, long before the arrival of the PMA, both of these agencies were pioneers in the federal government in developing their respective costing methodologies, and two years after the PMA arrived, NASA became the first federal agency to achieve the "green" rating in PMA BPI. SBA was not far behind.

The remainder of this chapter proceeds as follows. "The Foundations of Costing Performance Budgets" section provides the reader with background on performance budgeting in the federal government, and a review of the conceptual foundations for costing performance budgets. The next section presents a framework for integrating costs and performance in budgeting, relating the conceptual definitions with the requirements of the PMA BPI initiative. Then a detailed case study of NASA's Full Cost initiative is presented, followed by a case study of SBA's ABC model. The chapter concludes with practical recommendations based on this discussion.

The Foundations of Costing Performance Budgets

While many attribute the advent of performance budgeting to GPRA, it has a much longer history in the federal government. Joyce's Chapter Two and the Government Accountability Office (GAO) (2005) provide brief reviews of this history, but the review here focuses on the foundations for developing costing requirements. The concepts identified with performance budgeting emerged with President Harry S Truman's establishment of the Commission on Organization of the Executive Branch of the Government in 1947 (known as the first Hoover Commission), which first recommended that budgets shift the focus away from the inputs of agency operations to its "functions, activities, costs, and accomplishments" (GAO, 2005). Following the commission's recommendations, Congress enacted the Budget and Accounting Procedures Act of 1950 that, among other things, required the president to present the "functions and activities" of the government in his budget submission to Congress, curiously avoiding the "cost and accomplishments" part of the commission's recommendations. It took a second Hoover Commission during the administration of President Dwight D. Eisenhower to observe that many programs did not have adequate cost information and suggest that the government synchronize "budget classification, organization, and accounting structures" (GAO, 2005).

Successful synchronization of budget and program performance data would prove critical to the success of later reform efforts, starting with the Defense Department's Planning-Programming-Budgeting System (PPBS) of the 1960s all the way up to the PMA of today.[4] One of the biggest and long-standing obstacles to integrating performance, cost, and budget information was the need for program and agency budget accounts to be restructured to align with their associated appropriation accounts. According to GAO (2005), the federal budget is organized into about 1,100 appropriations accounts, and most of these have subsidiary program activities that show budget authority for inputs funded by the account. This account structure may help satisfy congressional oversight objectives, but it does not always align well with agency performance goals. NASA and SBA paid particular attention to similar account structure issues that kept other federal agencies from replicating the Defense Department's success with PPBS 30-plus years ago.

Statutory Foundations of Cost Requirements

As summarized in the sidebar "Key Legislation," the modern statutory framework for costing performance budgets, as reviewed in GAO (1999), starts with the Chief Financial Officers (CFO) Act of 1990 and the Government Management Reform Act (GMRA) of 1994. While these laws

---

Key Legislation

Chief Financial Officers Act of 1990 (CFO Act)
Created the deputy director for management position and the Office of Federal Financial Management (with head as comptroller) at OMB, and established federal financial management and related system policies and requirements. Created agency CFO and deputy CFO in 24 agencies, and required them to develop and maintain integrated financial management systems; and direct, manage, and provide policy guidance and oversight of all agency financial management personnel and operations.

Government Performance and Results Act of 1993 (GPRA)
Required all agencies to set strategic goals, measure performance, and report on the degree to which goals were met. Required an annual performance plan that provides a direct linkage between the strategic goals and employees' daily activities. Required an annual report on program performance for the previous fiscal year, and in each report, the agency is to review and discuss its performance compared with the performance goals it established in its annual performance plan.

Government Management Reform Act of 1994 (GMRA)
Required all agencies covered by the CFO Act to have agency-wide audited financial statements, required a government-wide audited financial statement, allowed agencies to consolidate various financial and performance reporting requirements into a single report with a common reporting deadline, and extended the CFO Act to all agencies.

Federal Financial Management Improvement Act of 1996 (FFMIA)
Required agencies to implement and maintain financial management systems that comply substantially with federal financial management systems requirements, applicable accounting standards, and the United States Government Standard General Ledger at the transaction level.

Source: GAO (1998).

---

established the CFO function and position in federal agencies, the CFO Act calls for the "development and reporting of cost information" and instructs the CFO to regularly review "fees, royalties, rents, and other charges" for services provided and "make recommendations on revising those charges to reflect costs incurred."[5] Congress has long been concerned about the lack of sophisticated financial management practices in the federal government, stating the following as a rationale for the bill:

> Current financial reporting practices of the federal government do not accurately disclose the current and probable future cost of operating and

investment decisions, including the future need for cash or other resources, do not permit adequate comparison of actual costs among executive agencies, and do not provide the timely information required for efficient management of programs.[6]

Just before the passage of the CFO Act, but surely in response to the concern cited above, the secretary of the treasury, director of OMB, and the comptroller general (of GAO) established the Federal Accounting Standards Advisory Board (FASAB) for the purpose of establishing the financial accounting standards called for in the CFO Act.[7] The CFO Act requirement that is most relevant for the FASAB is the "integration of accounting and budgeting information." This means that the principles used in accounting for accruing, monitoring, and managing program costs should be consistent with those used in budgetary accounting. It is this requirement that creates the mandate for full cost accounting in the federal government, and it will be discussed in greater detail in the following section and, indeed, throughout this chapter.

The most significant law related to performance budgeting is clearly GPRA. Since there is a substantial literature addressing the merits of this legislation, which establishes federal requirements for strategic planning and performance accountability reporting, this chapter will not go into detail on GPRA's contributions.[8] While GPRA is largely responsible for the supply of performance information that we now observe in federal agency budget plans and accountability reports, it did not create specific requirements for costing the performance budgets it sought to create. This is true despite the requirement that performance plans describe how the agency will meet the newly required listing of goals and objectives, including a description of the operational processes and resources required.[9] This requirement suggests that Congress intended for the agency to show a clear link between program performance and the requested budgetary resources. However, this link has been missing from agency strategic and performance plans since the time they were first required (strategic plans for fiscal year 1998 and performance plans for fiscal year 1999).

In its first status report on GPRA, "Performance Budgeting: Initial Experiences Under the Results Act in Linking Plans With Budgets," GAO (1999) found that 30 of the 35 agencies whose performance plans were reviewed provided some discussion of the relationship between program activities and performance goals, but only 14 translated this relationship into budgetary terms showing how funding would be allocated to achieve performance goals. GAO (1999) found that agencies were more likely to have allocated funding to program activities if they (1) showed simple and clear relationships between activities and performance goals, (2) fully integrated their performance plans into congressional budget justifications, or

(3) changed their program activity structures to reflect their goal structures. GAO's (2005) update, "Performance Budgeting: Efforts to Restructure Budgets to Better Align Resources with Performance," shows that of the nine agencies it reviewed that had revised their budget and/or performance reporting structures, four have achieved green status in PMA BPI (NASA, SBA, and the Departments of Labor and Transportation). Since GAO (2005) summarizes the account structure changes made by NASA and SBA, this chapter will not repeat this component of their efforts. Naturally, both of these agencies also changed the structure of their congressional budget justifications to facilitate consistent reporting.

Finally, the Federal Financial Management Improvement Act (FFMIA) of 1996 required independent auditors to determine whether agencies comply substantially with financial management system requirements, applicable federal accounting standards, and the United States Standard General Ledger (USSGL) at the transaction level. The Joint Financial Management Improvement Project (JFMIP) established the financial management system requirements, FASAB established the accounting standards, and the Financial Management Service (FMS) of the Treasury provides guidance on posting to the USSGL.[10] The FFMIA cost requirements are largely embedded in the relevant accounting principles. For the purpose of performance budgeting, the relevant conceptual principles are enunciated in FASAB's Statement Number 4: "Managerial Cost Accounting Concepts and Standards for the Federal Government," which we review next.

GAO (1998) includes other legislation in its review, but these focus on reporting and acquisitions and are only tangentially related to the cost requirements that are relevant for this chapter.[11] Nevertheless, there is a very broad statutory foundation for performance budgeting, but this foundation does not create the demand for performance information that is critical to being used as intended by Congress. The legislation reviewed here—CFO Act, GPRA, and FFMIA—provide a solid foundation for the costing of performance budgets that are largely based on the Generally Accepted Accounting Principles, or GAAP, that govern private sector accounting. This is perhaps another explanation for why agencies have not adopted cost accounting for performance budgeting; the principles that guide budgetary costing are steeped in accounting principles. As budgeting is a prospective exercise and accounting a retrospective one, and because practitioners of the two are trained differently, there needs to be a set of clear guidelines that federal managers can use to align their budgetary accounting more closely with performance measurement. This chapter does not try to reconcile budgeting with accounting, but focuses on the key budgetary accounting tools required by the PMA BPI initiative and law.

Conceptual Foundations of Cost Requirements

The FASAB sets the budgetary and financial accounting standards on which the government bases budget and accounting policy. One of the defining characteristics of performance versus traditional budgeting is the focus on program *costs* rather than direct allocations. The FASAB defines cost in the following manner:

> "Cost" is the monetary value of resources used or sacrificed or liabilities incurred to achieve an objective, such as to acquire or produce a good or to perform an activity or service. Costs incurred may benefit current and future periods. In financial accounting and reporting, the costs that apply to an entity's operations for the current period are recognized as expenses of that period.[12]

FASAB's Statement #4: "Managerial Cost Accounting Concepts and Standards for the Federal Government" establishes five accounting standards most relevant to performance budgeting. These standards, shown in the sidebar "Key Components of FASAB Statement #4," set the overarching framework for managerial cost accounting in the federal government, and thus provide a framework for meeting the requirements of the PMA BPI initiative. It was argued earlier that one explanation for the lack of success toward meeting the first PMA BPI criterion (also the first standard listed in the sidebar) is that agencies have struggled with developing appropriate cost accounting systems. The problem could be in the quality of the data itself, which could well be related to account synchronization difficulties. Thus, accumulating and reporting costs are key system elements in producing good performance budgets.

The cost management function of financial management systems is where costs are matched with activities and outputs.[13] The level of sophistication of this function within the financial management system is dependent on the operational nature of the programs involved, but according to JFMIP, four basic functions must be present: cost recognition, cost accumulation, cost distribution, and a working capital fund.[14] Table 5.1 on page 182 summarizes these requirements. Once costs have been recognized as per the definition above, the financial system accumulates them in accordance with agency requirements.[15] The distribution function relates to the assignment of indirect costs to program cost objects, and the case studies will show how NASA and SBA perform this function, respectively.

Cost recognition is a fundamental aspect of the accounting process. It determines when expense transactions are to be posted in the financial management system and ensures that all similar financial events and transactions are accounted for consistently. Cost accumulation refers to the

Key Components of FASAB Statement #4:
Managerial Cost Accounting Concepts and Standards for the Federal Government

Five standards establish fundamental elements of managerial cost accounting:
1. Accumulating and reporting costs of activities on a regular basis for management information purposes.
2. Establishing responsibility segments to match costs with outputs.
3. Determining full costs of government goods and services.
4. Recognizing the costs of goods and services provided among federal entities.
5. Using appropriate costing methodologies to accumulate and assign costs to outputs.

Paragraph 35
Measuring costs is an integral part of measuring performance in terms of efficiency and cost-effectiveness. Efficiency is measured by relating outputs to inputs. It is often expressed by the cost per unit of output. While effectiveness in itself is measured by the outcome or the degree to which a predetermined objective is met, it is commonly combined with cost information to show "cost-effectiveness." Thus, the service efforts and accomplishments of a government entity can be evaluated with the following measures:
(1) Measures of service efforts which include the costs of resources used to provide the services and non-financial measures;
(2) Measures of accomplishments which are outputs (the quantity of services provided) and outcomes (the results of those services); and
(3) Measures that relate efforts to accomplishments, such as cost per unit of output or cost-effectiveness.

Source: FASAB Statement #4.

measurement of resources used in performing a service, providing a product, or carrying out an activity. FASAB Statement #4 requires that costs be accumulated by responsibility segments and classified by type of resource, such as costs of employees, materials, utilities, etc. Cost distribution is the process by which certain accumulated costs are assigned to responsibility segments that deliver strategic services. FASAB Statement #4 states that:

> ... the purpose of cost accounting by a responsibility segment is to measure the costs of its outputs. Thus, the final cost objects of a responsibility segment are its outputs: the services or products that the segment produces and delivers, the missions or tasks that the segment performs, or the customers or markets that the responsibility segment serves.

Table 5.1: JFMIP Requirements for Cost Management Function

Cost recognition	• Have the ability to post accruals to recognize the costs of goods and services used, consumed, given away, lost, or destroyed within the period of time the event occurred, regardless of when ordered, received, or paid for. Revenues must be recognized when earned. • Reduce asset balances as the assets are used and expensed. • Use the agency's accounting classification structure to identify fund, program, organization, project, activity, and cost center information to support the cost accumulation and assignment processes. • Provide the capability to measure and report the costs of each segment's outputs.
Cost accumulation	• Support the ability to capture, at lowest level, costs related to fees, royalties, rents, and other charges imposed by the agency for goods and services it provides. • Identify all costs incurred by the agency in support of activities of revolving funds, trust funds, or commercial functions. • Provide for a variety of information to support decision making, agency management, and external reporting, including cost reports, schedules and operating statements, and, among others, meaningful cost information needed to support performance measures.
Cost distribution	• Provide for identifying costs based on the accounting classification structure. • Identify and record direct costs incurred, including input on costs from feeder systems, such as inventory, travel, or payroll. • Assign indirect costs to interim and final cost objects using a method consistent with agency cost accounting standards. Indirect costs will be assigned on a basis that best provides for a causal/beneficial relationship between the costs being distributed and the cost object receiving the cost. Indirect cost assignment may be based on total cost incurred, direct labor hours used, square footage, metered usage, or any other reasonable basis. • Allow for multilevel assignment and reassignment. • Support the use of historical data to conduct variance analysis, adjustment of rates, and disposition of variance by performing periodic assignments to adjust cost based on estimated rates to the actual costs incurred for the period. • Assign costs to entities or cost centers regardless of how they have originally been posted to the system (e.g., for financial statement presentation). • Provide an audit trail that traces the transaction from the original cost pool to the final cost object.

Source: JFMIP, Core Financial System Requirements, February 1999.

It is up to the agency to define the basis for consistent assignment, or distribution, of costs. Agencies that have been successful toward integrating their performance and budget information have made this critical choice. The next section will present a comprehensive framework for integrating costs and performance, followed by examples of how NASA and SBA used full costing and Activity-Based Costing, respectively, to distribute indirect costs to their program-based responsibility segments.

A Framework for Integrating Costs and Performance

FASAB Statement #4 stipulates that the financial management system must assign costs to intermediate and final cost objects (for example, outputs) using either "a direct tracing, a cause-and-effect basis, or a prorated basis using a cost allocation methodology." This cost distribution function is the key to integrating costs and performance and is a necessary step toward meeting the full cost requirement of the PMA BPI initiative. Table 5.2 on page 184 summarizes how FASAB Statement #4 defines the three distinct methods of allocating indirect (non-program) costs to direct cost centers (programs).

The preferred method is through direct tracing, which implicates a financial management system with broad access to program accounts for direct posting of a wide range of costs. We will see that NASA implemented a system that facilitates direct tracing to a large extent. Assigning costs on a cause-and-effect basis is appropriate when an intermediate output serves as the link between indirect resource costs and program outputs. In this case, the resource cost of the intermediate output is determined, and then the program's use of the intermediate output determines the indirect costs allocated to the program. NASA uses the cause-and-effect approach to allocate its service pool costs, which are costs derived from homogenous groups of intermediate services charged to programs based on the consumption of such services. SBA uses the cause and effect approach (through its ABC model) to allocate its loan servicing and liquidation costs to the respective loan programs. These methods will be discussed further within the context of the NASA and SBA case studies. This section concentrates on describing the prorated allocation method, and how to integrate the result—program full cost—with performance to inform decision making.

Table 5.2: The Three Methods of Assigning or Distributing Costs

Direct tracing	Direct tracing relies on the observation, counting, and/or recording of the consumption of resource units, and directly assigning the associated costs to specific programs, to be linked to program outputs. It can be a relatively costly process, and should be applied only to items that account for a substantial portion of the cost of an output and only when it is economically feasible. For example, direct tracing the cost of office supplies to outputs may not be worth the increased accuracy in assigning such resources by such a method.
Cause and effect	For costs that are not directly traced to outputs, intermediate objects can be established as links between resource costs and outputs. Costs that have a similar cause-and-effect relationship to outputs can be grouped into cost pools. Activities or work elements that contribute to or support the production of outputs are commonly used as intermediate objects, based on the premise that, on the one hand, outputs require the performance of certain activities, and, on the other hand, the activities cause costs incurred by the program. Thus, an activity is considered a linkage between the cause and the effect.
Prorated allocation	Sometimes, it might not be economically feasible to directly trace or assign costs on a cause-and-effect basis. These may include general management and support costs, depreciation, rent, maintenance, security, and utilities associated with facilities that are commonly used by various segments. These supporting costs can be allocated to segments and outputs on a prorated basis. The cost allocations are usually based on a relevant common denominator such as the number of employees, square footage of office space, or the amount of direct costs incurred in segments.

Source: FASAB Statement #4.

The Prorated Allocation Method

Cost allocation on a prorated basis is a common, relatively low-cost approach to performing the cost distribution function critical to deriving the full cost of programs. The cause-and-effect approach is preferred by FASAB over the prorated allocation method, and it is used often when an intermediate output exists to provide a clear consumption basis. However, in lieu of such a clear consumption basis, the prorated allocation method uses one or a few "cost drivers" as intuitive proxies, which can be any number of quantifiable measures of "general and administrative" (G&A) services. A program's prorated share of the cost driver—say employees or square feet—determines the basis of allocation, and is thus multiplied by the total indirect costs to be allocated to determine the program's share of the indirect costs.

Cost drivers are those factors that explain the largest share of costs incurred by a program. With labor-intensive operations, the main cost driver is full-time equivalent, or FTE. With capital-intensive operations, material is the main cost driver. In terms of the allocation of indirect costs, cost drivers represent the factors that most influence G&A costs, and these factors depend on the management function. Procurement costs are usually incurred on behalf of programs, where much of the direct materials or service costs are directly traced to programs. However, the indirect procurement costs are driven mostly by the FTE performing the function. Allocating procurement personnel time to programs based on the time spent on the respective program procurements is possible, but a good proxy may be the program share of procurement actions (weighted or not by the size of the procurement). Allocating human resource management costs to programs clearly should be driven by the program's share of total employees, and facility management cost allocation might be driven by the respective program use of agency facilities, measured in square feet, floors, buildings, or whatever makes the best sense. Financial management costs are driven by the number of financial transactions and reporting requirements, and measures that capture the respective program share are good cost drivers for such a G&A service.

As shown in the case study, NASA's Full Cost initiative allocates its G&A costs to direct service delivery accounts based on key cost drivers using the prorated allocation method. NASA directly assigns as much costs as feasible to program accounts, and allocates the service pool costs on a cause-and-effect basis. The prorated basis of allocation has an advantage over the other methods due to its being relatively easy to implement. As shown in the second case study, SBA implemented an ABC model to collect detailed data used in the application of each method. SBA directly traces most personnel support costs, uses cause-and-effect methods for allocating certain support costs, and uses the prorated allocation basis for all other indirect costs.

What can we do with full cost information? The following section shows how full cost information can be integrated with performance information to create intuitive measures to aid decision making.

Integrating Performance and Costing for Decision Making

The sidebar on page 181 restates paragraph 35 of FASAB Statement #4, which emphasizes three performance terms relevant to using performance for budget decision making: effectiveness, efficiency, and cost-effectiveness. The PMA BPI's full and marginal cost requirements in criterion 5 allow a senior manager to discern the relative cost-effectiveness of programs, with the ability, for example, to project the cost requirements associated with planned performance increments. The PMA BPI's efficiency requirement in criterion 6 provides the senior manager with information that helps her to determine the source of ineffectiveness (or performance shortfall). If an ineffective program operates efficiently, the ineffectiveness may be due to inadequate resources. If the program is operating inefficiently, however, then operational changes alone can lead to greater effectiveness. This section shows how having cost, effectiveness, and efficiency measures can significantly improve the use of performance information. Next, the cost and performance measures are defined carefully, and then we show how they can be integrated with performance output or outcome measures to create measures of efficiency and cost-effectiveness—both cost-based performance indicators.

Full Costs

To measure the full cost of government programs, and satisfy part of the requirement for PMA BPI criterion 5, one of the methods described earlier (and detailed in Table 5.2) must be applied to assign indirect costs to program outputs. The full cost of a program is the sum of all direct and indirect costs associated with the delivery of a program output. It allows senior managers to see the extent to which the various components of agency costs are (1) uniquely and directly related to the services provided, (2) pooled and shared by other programs, and (3) centrally based administrative functions. The full cost of a program's output takes into account all three of these costs. Most people think about cost distinctions in terms of fixed and variable costs, or direct and indirect costs, but these are helpful only for the most basic understanding of costs. The first of these three are direct costs, which may be fixed or variable, but most likely variable, and are directly traceable to the services provided. The second of these are the costs of shared or support services that can be directly attributed to programs based on program use or consumption. The third are G&A costs, which are fixed in the short run and variable in the long run, and most decidedly indirect. Since these indirect costs are substantial in the federal bureaucracy, it makes sense to find a reasonable method to assign these indirect costs to programs. Budget allocations across programs that do not consider the full costs of programs essentially treat non-programmatic services strategically, like programs. If non-programmatic services are not supporting programs, they are not necessary. Computing the full cost of programs by linking indirect to direct costs creates an incentive for program managers to scrutinize the potentially unnecessary indirect costs, and helps senior managers better understand the relationship between the two.

Marginal Costs

A reasonable question to ask in performance budgeting is, "How much does a performance increment cost?" The answer to this question requires a measure of marginal costs, which are the additional costs associated with a program producing one more unit of output or outcome. If federal agencies provided Congress with this kind of information together with their capacity to produce a given level of performance, Congress would make more efficient budget allocations simply because it would have a much better understanding of the budget and performance link than it did before.

The marginal cost of performance increments is perhaps the most difficult requirement of the PMA BPI, but knowing it is crucial to allocating resources efficiently. For economists, resource allocation efficiency in the market requires the unit price of services to equal the marginal costs of producing that additional unit. Linking performance increments with their marginal costs allows Congress to "value shop" in ways that consumers do in the market. Equation 1 defines marginal cost, which satisfies part of the requirement in PMA BPI criterion 5.

Fixed costs are not relevant to computing marginal costs. If program costs were all variable, and non-program costs were all fixed, then a full costing exercise would not be necessary, as the marginal cost of a performance increment is the variable cost. However, fixed and variable costs comprise program and non-program costs, so a full cost measure is necessary to obtain an accurate measure of the cost changes associated with performance increments. Indeed, non-program support service personnel—say employees in the human resources office—would argue that they face additional work when one program or another staffs up. Thus, the costs of support services can vary with program activity and should be linked to the programs impacting them.

Effectiveness

Paragraph 35 of FASAB Statement #4 (see sidebar on page 181) defines program effectiveness as "the degree to which a predetermined objective is met," and suggests that it can be measured in a number of ways. A common challenge in performance measurement is using outcome measures for measures of effectiveness. FASAB Statement #4 defines an output as the quantity of services provided, and outcomes as the results of these services. Another way to look at this distinction is to think of outputs as that which the program produces, and outcomes as the impact these outputs have on citizens' lives. Clearly, the program manager has some control over the output, but much less so over the outcome, largely due to the environment in which the program services are being delivered, which is beyond the control of the

EQUATION 1: MARGINAL COST		
Marginal cost of performance increment	**=**	**Change in full cost**
		Change in output or outcome

program manager.[16] For this reason, program performance, or effectiveness, in government has been measured largely in terms of outputs.

This is adequate if one wants to understand the operational effectiveness of a program, but not if one wants to understand its service effectiveness. The author defines the former as the extent to which a program reaches its operational goals, which are output focused and completely under the control of the program manager. The author defines the latter as the extent to which the program achieves its outcome-based service goals, which are the true impacts sought by policy and legislation initiating the programs in the first place. Unfortunately, the program manager has less control over outcomes. To understand how to achieve the latter, a manager must know how much the environment mitigates the translation of operational outputs to service outcomes, a topic beyond the scope of this chapter.

Efficiency

FASAB Statement #4 defines efficiency as a measure relating outputs to inputs, and since inputs can be expressed in terms of the financial resources used to purchase them, efficiency is often expressed by the cost per unit of output. Given our distinction above on outputs as measures of operational effectiveness and outcomes as measures of service effectiveness, we can expand the efficiency definition to be expressed in outcome terms as well. Thus, operational efficiency is measured by the cost per unit of output, and service efficiency is measured by the cost per unit of outcome. Since outcomes are often difficult to quantify, programs rely on outputs, focusing on operational efficiency—again, factors completely under the control of the program manager.

Let's return to the senior manager faced with a performance shortfall in one of her programs. How would she know whether the program was efficient and thus requires more resources, or whether the program squandered the resources provided? She needs a measure of efficiency to judge how well or poorly the program used the resources provided. This means that she needs cost information linked with the performance indicators. To the extent that the cost information is comprehensive, she can make a better judgment on the resource shifts required. However, if costs are expressed only in terms of direct appropriations, senior and program managers will misjudge the additional resources required, as we will learn with some NASA and SBA experiences.

If a program manager has quantitative output- or outcome-based performance measures, he can use one of two equations. First, he can divide the performance measure by the number of the most important input (usually FTE) to get a basic efficiency measure, as shown in Equation 2. The disadvantage of this basic version is that it is limited to a single input. However, if the single input is a dominant one, then it facilitates a more comprehensive measure of efficiency, and if the input is FTE, it is also a measure of labor productivity.

EQUATION 2: EFFICIENCY I		
Efficiency	**=**	**Output or outcome**
		Relevant input

Because this basic approach does not capture all inputs relevant to producing program outputs or outcomes, a second approach is commonly used, which divides the total costs of the inputs by the performance measure to obtain a measure of efficiency expressed in cost terms. To obtain this, simply invert Equation 2 and replace the single input measure with the program's full costs. With no inversion, the efficiency interpretation is in "output per dollar" terms, but since dollar amounts often exceed output unit amounts, the interpretation in fractional terms is awkward and unintuitive. For example, dividing 10,000 output units by $250 million produces an efficiency measure of .00004 output units per dollar. With the inverted version shown in Equation 3, the interpretation is in "cost per unit of output" terms—$25,000 per output unit in this case. And although efficiency increases with smaller values, it is a more intuitive and useful efficiency measure, and satisfies criterion 6 of the PMA BPI initiative.

Equation 3 represents an intuitive way to integrate costs and performance information. The average citizen, senior manager, and member of Congress can make more reasonable judgments about the relative value of programs when such integration takes place. The trade-off between the benefits derived from five shuttle launches versus 26,000 business loans is placed in stark relief when one also considers the relative costs—$4.5 billion for the former (at $900 million per launch), and $22 million for the latter (at $950 per loan), according to NASA's and SBA's FY 2006 budget submissions respectively (both in full cost terms). These are measures of efficiency for NASA's and SBA's main programs, and they are examples of intuitive, cost-based performance measures that can enhance the quality of budgetary decision making.

What if the program manager has a performance measure that is not quantitative? Qualitatively measured outputs or outcomes can also help accomplish the performance budgeting goals of GPRA and the PMA. One can create categorical measures for just about any output or outcome simply

EQUATION 3: EFFICIENCY II		
Efficiency	**=**	**Total costs**
		Output or outcome

by delineating "above average," "average," and "below average" performance, or by making finer distinctions. Developing a cost measure can be done in a similar fashion. Table 5.3 shows how efficiency can be captured in categorical terms, relating categorical performance and cost measures. Of course, the categorical terms can be defined however the user chooses; those used in Table 5.3 are illustrative.

Let's say that average performance at average costs is the baseline target for efficiency (the center cell in Table 5.3). If performance improves or is deemed better than average (moving left from the center cell), or if total costs decline or are deemed lower than average (moving up from the center cell), then efficiency is said to have improved to say a "good" level. If both happen (moving diagonally up and to left), then we might say that efficiency is "excellent." On the other hand, if total costs increase to the above average range with average performance (moving down from center cell), or if performance declines to below average range on average costs (moving right from center cell), efficiency will have declined to "poor" levels, leading to inefficiency. Negative movements on both dimensions could be deemed "unacceptable," while a positive movement on one dimension and a negative movement on the other might produce a "fair" efficiency result. The point here is to provide a way to measure program efficiency using an easy-to-implement qualitative framework.

Cost-Effectiveness

Paragraph 35 of FASAB Statement #4 defines cost-effectiveness as the integration of cost and performance information. While the efficiency measure in Equation 3 integrates cost and performance by showing the average cost of production, cost-effectiveness is distinguished by its focus on the performance goal. Thus, cost-effectiveness measures the costs associated with achieving a performance goal (i.e., the costs of being effective), which is different from actual performance. Equation 3 measures the costs of actual performance, but

Table 5.3: Measuring Efficiency Using Categorical Measures

		Performance output or outcome		
		Above average	Average	Below average
Costs	Below average	Excellent	Good	Fair
	Average	Good	Baseline	Poor
	Above average	Fair	Poor	Unacceptable

EQUATION 4: COST EFFECTIVENESS

$$\text{Cost-Effectiveness} \quad = \quad \frac{\text{Total costs required}}{\text{Output or outcome expected}}$$

cost-effectiveness measures the costs of expected performance. As with the efficiency measure in Equation 3, the lower the value the better.

The denominator in Equation 4, the expected performance level, is the policy parameter. Decision makers set this number, and then analysts determine the costs of obtaining it. The numerator, the required costs to reach this goal, can be estimated using two methods. The first method takes the full cost of present program performance level and adds the product of the marginal cost of a performance increment and the difference between actual and expected performance. The second method substitutes average costs (i.e., full costs divided by output, or efficiency) for marginal costs, as shown in Equation 5.

The difference between the two methods depends on whether the program faces increasing, decreasing, or constant returns to scale in service production. Increasing returns to scale means that as the program produces more output, its average output costs decline (improving efficiency). Constant returns to scale imply no efficiency gains from producing more output. If program production faces increasing or decreasing returns to scale, the marginal cost method would be the most appropriate. However, marginal cost would have to be measured at each level of output to be precise. Assuming average cost per output is constant at all levels of output (i.e., cost environment displays constant returns to scale), the average cost method is appropriate. Nevertheless, as the costs decline, the program becomes more cost-effective, and Equations 4 and 5 demonstrate how program cost effectiveness can be derived from the measures required in criteria 5 and 6 of the PMA BPI initiative.

The full cost requirement in PMA BPI's criterion 5 is the main requirement for costing performance budgets, but good performance measures are important, too. However, "good" need not mean "quantitative" in a continuous manner. Thoughtful performance measures can be

EQUATION 5: TOTAL COSTS

Total costs required =
Full cost + marginal or average cost
x
(expected output – actual output)

characterized in categorical terms. And while marginal cost calculations need continuous measures, one can still strive to measure a reasonable marginal cost proxy by calculating the costs from changing from "below average" to "average" performance, and from "average" to "above average" performance, which could differ based on the cost environments. The PMA BPI's criterion 6 is the efficiency requirement that is rather straightforward, but requires some clarity on the type of efficiency measured. Again, this means one must have good performance measures to have good measures of efficiency. Nevertheless, allocating indirect costs is at the heart of costing performance budgets, so the next sections focus on how NASA and SBA allocated their indirect costs, concluding with recommendations on how agencies can adopt certain practices that will help them "get to green."

Case Study of NASA: How Full Cost Supports Performance Budgeting

The National Aeronautics and Space Administration (NASA) is one of the world's premier research and development organizations focused on aeronautics and space. Its mission is "to understand and protect our home planet, explore the universe and search for life, and inspire the next generation of explorers … as only NASA can." Clearly, the agency faces extraordinary challenges as a matter of course. Originally established as the National Advisory Committee for Aeronautics (NACA) in 1915, Congress transformed NACA into NASA with the National Aeronautics and Space Act of 1958.[17] For the first time since President John F. Kennedy committed the nation to achieving the goal of landing a man on the moon, President George W. Bush, on January 14, 2004, significantly expanded NASA's mission by announcing his new vision for space exploration, which seeks to return humans to the moon as a stepping-stone for human exploration on Mars.

These challenges impose unimaginable pressure on NASA, and its organizational structure reflects the complexity of its missions. With a civil service workforce of over 19,000 supplemented with 40,000 contracted employees, spread across its headquarters in Washington, D.C., and 10 research centers across the nation, NASA's programmatic divisions are represented by five mission directorates: Science, Exploration Systems, Space Operations, Aeronautics Research, and Education. These directorates comprise 12 programmatic themes, which provide the organizational basis for NASA's strategic and budgetary planning, management, and reporting. Table 5.4 summarizes the relationship between the mission directorates, the programmatic themes, and the research and flight centers.[18] Within each of the themes are the many related programs and projects (not shown), and NASA's strategic plan shows how these themes map to 10 strategic goals—seven science and research goals, and three "enabling" goals.[19]

NASA's budget has remained relatively stable over the past decade, ranging from $13.7 billion in FY 1994 to $14.6 billion in FY 2004. However, considered in 2004 constant dollar terms, NASA faced a slight but steady decline in real resources from FY 1991 to FY 2001, only for this to increase the past four fiscal years, with most significant increases coming between fiscal years 2004 and 2005, when the budget increased by 12 percent to $16.3 billion to accommodate the new exploration vision.[20] For NASA, restructuring its budget to align more closely with its mission and programs was a necessary step to clarifying its complex responsibilities and improving internal management and programmatic costing. This is where its Full Cost initiative comes into the picture.

Table 5.4: NASA's Mission Directorates, Program Themes, and Centers

Mission Directorate	Program Theme	Centers (State)
Science	• Solar System Exploration • The Universe • Earth-Sun System	• Ames (California) • Goddard (Maryland) • Jet Propulsion Laboratory (California)
Exploration Systems	• Constellation Systems • Exploration Systems, Research, and Technology • Nuclear Systems and Technology • Human Systems Research and Technology	• Headquarters (Washington, D.C.)
Space Operations	• International Space Station • Space Shuttle • Space and Flight Support	• Johnson (Texas) • Kennedy (Florida) • Marshall (Alabama) • Stennis (Mississippi)
Aeronautics Research	• Aeronautics Technology	• Dryden (California) • Glenn (Ohio) • Langley (Virginia)
Education	• Education Programs	• Headquarters (Washington, D.C.)

Full Cost Is More Than Budget Realignment

The complexity of NASA's organizational structure made it very difficult to manage its resources in a consistent fashion, partly because the budget, accounting, and management structures were not in alignment. Prior to the realignment, budgetary resources would come in a form that had little relation to the strategic plan, and resources for mission support were funded in a separate appropriation account from the programs being supported, with no clear relationship between the two. This disconnection was the result of a traditional budgetary framework that emphasized line-item amounts and incremental funding on object classes (for example, salaries, rent, and tele-communications). While tracking object-class spending across the agency is important, it does not allow the interested, taxpaying citizen to read the budget and clearly understand how much of the budget is dedicated to a given object class for every program. Moreover, there was no incentive for program managers to create efficiencies, because they were allocated resources that were essentially "free." That is, the program manager could have been assigned additional staff without having to worry about paying for or being held accountable for these additional resources.

To NASA's credit, the agency could have simply reformatted the budget to show more clearly how specific resources, mission-based and support, were connected to specific programs. Under the leadership of former NASA Administrator Sean O'Keefe, the agency chose to use the Full Cost initiative to align its budget, accounting, and management structures. Not only did it re-format its budget submission and justifications, it sought help from Congress to realign its appropriation structure and create flexibilities to give managers the "freedom to manage." And it implemented an agency-wide integrated financial management system that would consolidate all separate center-specific accounting systems into a single one. While the implementation of the integrated system has had its challenges, this effort demonstrated NASA's commitment to build the infrastructure necessary to support the best practices in financial management called for in the legislation reviewed earlier and the PMA.[21]

However, the most important component of NASA's full cost policy was the effort to link changes in management practices with the budgetary and accounting structure changes. NASA changed the allotment process at the beginning of the fiscal year and began allotting appropriated funds "directly" to program managers (through theme-based overseers in the mission directorates), who were then given greater flexibility to choose how to allocate their resources to accomplish their specific part of the theme-based mission. Previously, program and project managers had control over their contractor and non-personnel budgets only; they didn't have control over their civil service employee budgets. Prior to the full cost policy, program managers had no incentive to simply say, "I only need 15 FTE, not 25, for the new project." This statement should produce a chuckle in some knowing readers, as it reflects a violation of one of the sacred truisms in the federal bureaucracy: More is always better! NASA's full cost policy sought to create the incentive reflected in this hypothetical statement. How did NASA do this? This section will provide a detailed account.

What Is Full Cost?

"Full cost" is the term used by NASA to describe a comprehensive financial management policy that links all agency resources to its strategic programs in a meaningful way. For the reform to be meaningful, incentives had to be created to allow program managers to become more efficient on their own initiative, rather than on command. To accomplish this, NASA took the following coordinated actions:

- **Budgeting:** The FY03 budget was re-formatted in full cost terms, while budget formulation in full cost terms took place for headquarters in FY04 and for the programs in FY05. Appropriation accounts were changed to align with programs instead of with the centers.[22]
- **Accounting:** To execute the FY04 budget, NASA reconfigured its core financial management module to accommodate full cost alignments reflected in the budgetary changes.
- **Management:** To execute the FY04 budget, NASA allotted budget resources flexibly to program managers and allowed them to decide the number of civil service employees they could afford to pay for and still accomplish their mission.

These budgeting and accounting changes were made to support effective management practices, and the changes in all three together are what allowed for meaningful change to take place. According to NASA officials, it was not enough to make budgeting and accounting format changes, as these wouldn't have changed the behavior of program managers. The key was to allow these changes to support the managerial incentives that would arise from giving program managers greater discretion over the use of budgetary resources. For example, prior to full cost, all civil service employees were assigned to a mission or support program and funded out of a separate line item not linked to these areas. After full cost, a new budgetary category was developed called "Workforce in Transition" to denote the salary costs of those employees who had not been chosen to work in a mission or support program.[23] In other words, the full cost management changes created the incentive for program managers to reveal their true need for civil service employees, leaving some in this "limbo" status. These personnel would still be paid, but through center-based general and administrative cost pools (Center G&A), which in turn imposed costs on these resource managers, who face incentives to keep their G&A rates down (discussed in detail below). This new policy ultimately forces a decision on what to do with these unassigned civil service employees—either find managers willing to pay their salaries or consider the application of other (dreaded) personnel actions, like buyouts or reductions in force.

With NASA's traditional budget structure, program and project budgets included only the direct research and development costs, which consist of contract and supporting costs. These program and project budgets did not cover the costs for civil service employees or travel, nor did they cover the institutional and infrastructure costs, such as the business management functions and basic center operations. The full cost budget structure allocates the entire agency budget among programs, using upgraded reporting systems to directly assign related costs to the programs where feasible, and straightforward statistical methods to allocate indirect and other costs where direct assignment was not feasible. Before describing the elements of full cost, we review definitions of the key cost concepts used by NASA.[24]

The Mechanics of Full Cost

Full cost provides for the allocation or assignment of costs to NASA's programs. The sidebar "NASA Full Cost Concepts" on page 199 defines some of these costs, like direct costs, as those that are directly traced to a given program or project account. Other costs, like service pool costs, are assigned using the cause-and-effect method, relying on the program consumption of the respective pool's services. General and administrative, or G&A, costs are not very easily assigned, and therefore the prorated allocation method is used to accomplish this task.

The costs of each program can be broken down into direct, service pool, and indirect costs. While service pool costs contain both direct and indirect components, one can think of indirect costs as the costs of being in business, and the direct costs as the costs of performing the business activities themselves. Another way to think about this distinction is that direct costs are those that are "pay as you go" costs, and indirect costs are assessed against the program budgets based on a determined basis of allocation. The direct cost elements for a program include the associated civil service labor costs (including salaries and fringe benefits), procurements, and travel costs. The service pool cost elements derive from the production of specific intermediate services on behalf of the programs, and include both direct and indirect cost elements. The indirect cost elements include mainly G&A costs based at headquarters and at the centers. Thus, the full cost of a program is given by Equation 6.

Clearly, the assessment and allocation process that assigns service pool and G&A costs to the programs is at the heart of the full cost policy, allowing

EQUATION 6: FULL COSTS
Full costs =
Direct costs + Service pool costs + G&A costs

one to determine the full cost of programs called for in GPRA, FASAB Statement #4, and the PMA BPI initiative. How is this accomplished? Let's start
with the G&A costs.

Corporate G&A

Corporate G&A costs include agency-wide (non-program specific)
management and operations (whether at headquarters or at a center on
behalf of headquarters), independent verification and validation activities,
construction and demolition of facilities, security, and safety and assurance activities. Corporate G&A, expected to total $882 million in FY 2006,
include the costs associated with the offices of the chief financial officer,
chief information officer, chief engineer, space architect, and others, as
shown in Table 5.5 on page 198. The assessment of Corporate G&A costs
occurs on a monthly basis, and these costs are assigned to programs based
on their share of total program budget authority. That is, Corporate G&A
costs are allocated by the program's share of the agency-wide sum of new
budget authority for all direct and service pool cost elements. Corporate and
Center G&A are not included in this calculation. Thus, the Corporate G&A
rate is computed by Equation 7, and represents the agency-level overhead
rate, which is 5.4 percent of the total agency budget of $16.3 billion.

This process begins with an assessment cycle that assesses accrued
Corporate G&A costs to the programs based on this rate. For example, if a
program had a total budget authority of $20 million, then of the $73.5 million
worth of accrued Corporate G&A costs agency-wide for the first month ($882
million divided by 12 months), this program would be assessed $90,000 ($20
million divided by 12 months times 5.4 percent) for the first month, which
represents the project's share of the Corporate G&A costs incurred to date.[25]
Once the budget allotment process assigns all budget resources to the programs, the programs must pay for the headquarters-based overhead costs,

EQUATION 7: CORPORATE G&A RATE		
Corporate G&A rate	=	Headquarters G&A costs
		Total program budget authority

Table 5.5: NASA's Corporate G&A costs

Corporate G&A item	FY 2006 amount ($ millions)
Headquarters corporate activities	373
Engineering and Safety Center	79
Integrated Financial Management Program	77
Chief information officer	70
Environmental compliance and regulation	69
Chief engineer	53
Safety and mission assurance	52
Agency operations	27
Independent verification and validation facility	27
Advanced planning and integration	20
Center-based Corporate G&A	11
Corporate construction of facilities	10
Security management	9
Chief health and medical officer	5
Total Corporate G&A	**882**

Source: NASA FY 2006 Budget Request.

and this is accomplished in the assessment process just described. So, each month, this program would face a $90,000 reduction in their budget amount available for obligations to cover accrued Corporate G&A. Since the program manager knows this, he will set aside $1.08 million ($90,000 monthly assessment times 12 months) of his annual budget to cover these cost assessments.

Center G&A

At the same time the Corporate G&A pool manager begins assessing costs against programs, the Center G&A pool managers do the same thing. Center G&A costs, which total $1.5 billion in FY 2006, include costs associated with the center director and his or her immediate staff, center management and operations, and systems management. These costs, shown in Table 5.6 on page 200 for nine of the 10 centers, are the costs required to operate and maintain each center, largely independent of the programs being carried out at the center.[26] Center G&A costs are allocated to programs

NASA Full Cost Concepts

Costs: The monetary value of resources used or sacrificed, or liabilities incurred to achieve an objective, such as to acquire or produce a good or to perform an activity or service. Costs incurred may benefit current and future periods.

Direct costs: The costs that are obviously or physically related to a project at the time they are incurred and are subject to the influence of the project manager. Examples include contractor-supplied hardware/software and project labor, whether provided by civil service or contractor employees.

Indirect costs: Costs that cannot be specifically or immediately identified to a project, but can subsequently be traced or linked to a project and are assigned based on usage or consumption. For NASA, this includes general, administrative, and service pool costs.

General and Administrative (G&A) costs: The support costs that cannot be directly related or traced to a specific project in an economical manner, but benefit all activities. Such costs are allocated to a project based on a reasonable and consistent basis. Examples of G&A costs include costs associated with financial management, procurement, security, and legal activities.

Corporate G&A: The indirect costs of headquarters personnel and activities such as the administrator and his immediate staff, mission directorate management, headquarters operations, and functional management are managed through a pool and allocated to individual projects, including activities implemented and managed by the centers on behalf of the agency.

Center G&A: The indirect costs of center-based personnel and activities such as the center directors and their immediate staff, center management, center operations, and systems management are managed through center-based pools and allocated to individual projects based on on-site workforce.

Service pools: The accumulation of similar costs and cost types that are distributed to projects by an assignment or allocation methodology that best represents the types of costs in the pools. Service pool costs are those that cannot be specifically and immediately identified to a project, but can be subsequently traced or linked to a project and assigned based on usage or consumption. These costs are charged or assigned to a project based on project-controlled use of the service. Examples include information technology and fabrication services.

Source: *NASA Financial Management Requirements, Volume 7.*

Table 5.6: NASA's Center G&A Costs*

Centers	FY 2006 G&A ($ millions)
Kennedy Space Center (Florida)	232
Marshall Space Flight Center (Alabama)	226
Goddard Space Flight Center (Maryland)	214
Johnson Space Center (Texas)	207
Langley Research Center (Virginia)	195
Ames Research Center (California)	191
Glenn Research Center (Ohio)	161
Dryden Flight Research Center (California)	40
Stennis Space Center (Mississippi)	39
Total Center G&A	**1,505**

These costs do not include Jet Propulsion Lab costs.
Source: *NASA FY 2006 Budget Request.*

based on the on-site workforce, which NASA calls Workforce Equivalents (WFEs). The on-site workforce includes civil service and contract employees. Center G&A is funded through budget transfers from the programs like that described for Corporate G&A. Thus, the Center G&A rate for a given center is computed by Equation 8, and represents the center-level overhead rate, which in FY 2006 is estimated at $1.505 billion, or 9.1 percent of the total agency budget.

The Center G&A rate is expressed as an average cost per employee (regardless of civil service or contract status), and the monthly assessment at this level is based on this rate. For example, if a center had annual G&A costs of $200 million, 1,000 full-time civil service employees, and 3,000 full-time contract employees, then the Center G&A rate would be $50,000 per WFE ($200 million divided by 4,000 WFEs). Accrued G&A costs for this center in the first month would be $16.7 million ($50,000 rate divided by

EQUATION 8: CENTER G&A RATE	
Center G&A rate $=$	$$\dfrac{\text{Center G\&A costs}}{\substack{\text{Total Center} \\ \text{Workforce Equivalents (WFEs)}}}$$

12 months times 4,000 WFEs). If 300 of these WFEs were assigned to a given program, this program would be assessed $1.25 million in the first month for Center G&A costs (300 WFEs times $50,000 rate divided by 12 months). Again, since the budget allotment process assigns all budget resources to the programs, the programs pay for the center-based overhead costs through the assessment process. In this scenario, the program manager would set aside $15 million ($1.25 million monthly assessment times 12 months) for the year's Center G&A costs at this one center, and he would have to complete the same calculations for each center containing civil service or contract employees assigned to his program.

One might say that in this full costing framework, the programs are being "taxed" for the G&A services being provided by headquarters and the relevant centers. This implies an involuntary transfer of resources, but this is precisely how NASA wants the program managers to feel. NASA intends to create a managerial environment where program managers question the costs on which these assessments are based, effectively holding the providers of G&A services (for example, human resources and general counsel) accountable for the costs they impose on the programs. One can argue, as some have at NASA, that a lower cost alternative is to allocate these funds directly to the G&A pools, but this wouldn't give the program manager a sense of how much they draw upon these services or any incentive to reduce their reliance on these services. We will return to this debate below.

Service Pool Costs

Corporate G&A costs are allocated on the basis of a program's share of total program budget authority, and Center G&A costs are allocated on the basis of the on-site workforce. In addition to these, NASA uses "service pools" to allocate a hybrid class of costs (some direct, some indirect) to programs. As defined in the sidebar "NASA Full Cost Concepts" (see page 199), service pools are mechanisms by which NASA accumulates the costs of similar services that cut across programs (like indirect G&A costs), but are more readily attributable to a program based on its usage or consumption of the service (like program direct costs). NASA has established seven standard service pools at each of the 10 centers, and they are listed in Table 5.7 on page 202 along with their respective bases of consumption (allocation).[27]

During budget formulation, service pool managers must estimate the amount of services they expect to provide to their program customers. This service level then allows them to establish a per unit rate that covers the costs of delivering the service provided by the pool. For a given program customer within the agency, their budget transfer to the pool would equal this per unit rate multiplied by the units of the relevant service. However, this budget transfer does not account for all costs associated with the service activity, but only those costs incurred by the service pool entity in delivering the service.

Table 5.7: NASA's Service Pools and Bases of Consumption

Service Pool	Basis of Consumption
1. Facilities and Related Services	Square footage
2. Information Technology (IT) Services	
Desktop	Seats
Computing	Central processing units
Telecommunications	Lines
Other IT services	Direct labor hours
3. Science and Engineering Services	Direct labor hours
4. Fabrication Services	Direct labor hours
5. Test Services	Direct labor hours
6. Wind Tunnel Services	Operating shifts
7. Independent Technical Authority/Safety and Mission Assurance Office	Direct labor hours

Source: NASA Financial Management Requirements, Volume 7.

A good way to think about the operation of service pools is to think about how you are billed when you take your car to the auto shop for repairs. Some of the costs of the repair work appear on your bill as itemized charges, such as for parts or fluids. The remaining portion of the repair costs are rolled into an hourly rate multiplied by the number of hours it took to perform the repairs. This hourly rate encompasses primarily the labor costs of the mechanic, but the rate likely includes an allowance to cover some of the auto shop's overhead costs. NASA service pools operate in a similar manner.

Consider the IT service pool for computing. A program customer tells the IT service pool manager that he needs 20 additional laptop computers. The pool manager purchases these computers based on the specifications provided by the program, and directly posts the direct costs to the program budget account. The IT service pool manager then assesses a charge to the program equal to the pre-determined pool rate for that year multiplied by the number of computers it ordered (the basis of consumption). This assessment covers setup, maintenance, and a share of the overhead costs of providing and maintaining properly configured computers. Total IT service pool costs, then, are computed using the two-part formula in Equation 9.

EQUATION 9: SERVICE POOL CHARGE

Service pool charge =
Direct itemized costs
+
(Pool rate x Number of units of pool service)

The difference here from the auto shop example is that the auto shop does not have access to your checking account to extract the two-part payment. The realigned budget and accounting structures at NASA allow the service pool manager to access program accounts for posting costs against the program's unobligated budget. Thus, in the parlance of FASAB Statement #4, itemized charges in a NASA service pool are directly traced, while the pool's overhead costs are assigned on a cause-and-effect basis.

The service pool rate is established during budget formulation, after the pool manager compiles all required annual Service Level Agreements (SLA) with the program managers. The SLA defines the amount of service to be provided in advance to allow the pool manager to plan and establish a fair and competitive rate. As mentioned above, where itemized charges can be directly billed to the program, the pool will do so, and this is determined in the SLA. Where this direct charging is not feasible, the costs are embedded into the rate, which for all pools cover the associated civil service employee salaries and travel (analogous to the auto shop mechanics). Also embedded in the pool rate are those costs unique to the work of the service pool. For the IT service pool for telecommunications, this might include use of network services, voice and messaging services, and other items not directly charged. For the test and fabrication service pools, the pool rate would include equipment and fluids used in their unique services. For some pools, contract labor costs might be embedded in the rate, but these are typically provided by contractors based on billable hours, so often are directly attributable to the program.

The bases of consumption shown in Table 5.7 are essentially cost drivers for the service pool rate. If the managerial incentives work as they should, the cause-and-effect relationships inherent in the pool rate would be scrutinized by the program managers that ultimately bear the associated service pool costs. Thus, the managerial incentives provide an added mechanism for continued improvement on the choice of such pool-based cost drivers.

Clearly, NASA has made a substantial effort to assign direct costs where possible, and this will expand as it implements other planned modules within its integrated financial management system. However, this case study of NASA's full cost policy shows that when costs cannot be directly traced, they can be allocated by establishing cause-and-effect relationships, as with the service pools, and, in the last instance, by the prorated allocation method, as NASA does with Corporate and Center G&A costs.

Case Study of SBA: Activity-Based Costing Improves Performance Budgeting

The Small Business Administration (SBA) is another federal agency charged with a mission that seems to exceed its resource base. SBA's mission is to "maintain and strengthen the nation's economy by aiding, counseling, assisting, and protecting the interests of small businesses and by helping families and businesses recover from national disasters." The genesis of this mission began largely in response to the Great Depression, when President Herbert Hoover created the Reconstruction Finance Corporation (RFC) in 1932 to address the attendant financial crisis by lending money to businesses hurt by the Depression. Another agency, the Office of Small Business (OSB) within the Department of Commerce, provided services that were primarily educational, providing counseling to entrepreneurs, and other small agencies still provided unique services in response largely to the economic challenges of war. In 1952, President Dwight D. Eisenhower proposed to merge these disparate functions within a single independent agency, and in 1953, Congress passed the Small Business Act, which created the SBA.

The SBA has over 3,000 civil service employees, but also coordinates with a large number of lenders and grantees to deliver its services. SBA has undergone many changes in its history, largely due to the changing way it delivers its services and the controversial nature of its minority business assistance programs that are a major component of the affirmative action policy regime of the federal government.[28] According to GAO (2001b), the largest change to SBA's service delivery occurred in its lending programs, where the agency went from making loans directly to guaranteeing loans made by commercial lenders. This change occurred in 1995, likely because of incentives created by the Federal Credit Reform Act of 1990, which changed the budgetary accounting for government-guaranteed lending programs from requiring appropriations for the total amount of lending to requiring appropriations only for the expected defaults on guaranteed loans.

While lending tends to dominate the services identified with the SBA, the agency also delivers technical assistance and government contracting services, along with the advocacy function discussed above. To coordinate the delivery of its programs, the agency has 70 district offices organized within 10 regions throughout the nation. The SBA organizes its disaster response function separately within four area offices in New York, Georgia, Texas, and California. Table 5.8 summarizes the major program offices and programs of the SBA, which share a recently dwindling base of budgetary resources that have gone from $798 million in FY 1995, up to a peak of $1 billion in FY 2001, and down to $786 million in FY 2004, a fall from the peak of 27 percent.[29] Despite the swings in budget authority, which largely

Table 5.8: SBA's Major Program Offices and Programs

Major Program Offices	Programs
Office of Capital Access	• 7(a), 504, and Microloan programs • Investment programs • International trade programs • Surety and technical assistance programs
Office of Entrepreneurial Development	• Small Business Development Centers • Women's Business Ownership programs • SCORE (volunteer counseling) • Native American outreach • Small Business Training Network • Other business and entrepreneurial development programs
Office of Government Contracting and Business Development	• 8(a) and 7(j) business development programs • Prime contract program • HUBZones • Small Disadvantaged Business program • Procurement Matchmaking • Subcontracting and BusinessLINC programs
Office of Disaster Assistance	• Loan making • Loan servicing
Office of Advocacy	• Research and regulatory policy
Other advocacy programs	• National Women's Business Council • Ombudsman/Regulatory Fairness Board • Veterans Business Development Program

reflects the design of its credit programs, SBA's annual credit activity has almost doubled from $14.0 billion in loan guarantee commitments in FY 2001 to $21 billion in FY 2005.[30] Clearly, SBA has been forced to become more creative and efficient in the provision of its programs, and this is indicative in its PMA BPI success and being a pioneer in developing and implementing its ABC model, discussed next in greater detail.

Activity-Based Costing Illuminates True Program Costs

In 1997, SBA began using an Activity-Based Costing, or ABC, model to determine the full cost of its program outputs, as required by GPRA, and to produce unit-cost reports for internal operations and improvement. The agency continues to use this information in its annual Statement of Net

Costs and in the congressional budget justifications. In FY 2002, this package was enhanced to include a user-friendly, web-based Cost Allocation Survey (Survey) designed for SBA employees to log the allocation of their time to specific activities identified by the Office of the Chief Financial Officer, which manages the model. Compiled by interviews, reports, and the known details of the functional operations within the agency, the ABC model breaks the agency's functions down into three categories: agency level, field operations level, and program level. Most personnel costs, which constitute the vast majority of SBA's costs, are directly traced via the ABC model to one of the activity groups shown in Table 5.9. The reader will notice that these activities are grouped largely by the program office itself. Other agency-wide activities include eight agency management activities, seven activities related to the PMA, three field management activities, and five field programmatic activities. The five field programmatic activities are the counseling and training performed in the field on behalf of the major program offices.

Three types of indirect costs are allocated down to the district office level—field operations costs at headquarters, field-based management and administrative costs (including those at the regional offices), and field-based legal costs. The personnel and non-personnel costs of the Office of Field Operations (at headquarters) are allocated first to the 10 regional offices equally. These costs, together with the same at the regional offices, are allocated to the district offices based on the district's share of that region's sum of district budgets. Thus, field operations costs are allocated to district offices, a final cost object, by the prorated allocation method, and the agency-wide costs (agency management and the PMA) are similarly allocated to the headquarters-based program offices based on the share of total program budgets.

Before examining the process in detail, let's review some real examples of how the Survey and ABC model results can influence decision making. One of SBA's entrepreneurial development grant programs, the Business Information Centers (BICs), with an FY 2004 appropriation of $396 million, provides what amount to libraries in each of the 70 district offices. These BICs contain books, computers, and "how-to guides" for a wide range of small business opportunities. When entrepreneurs or prospective small business owners walk into one of these district offices, they are often directed to this resource as a starting point for targeting the customer's needs. The time spent by the SBA employee using or showing how to use this resource then gets allocated to the BIC program (the activity has not yet become a counseling and training activity). In the best case, without the ABC model, we would consider the costs of this program to be $396 million plus some estimated fixed percentage of overhead costs. However, with the ABC model, the SBA was able to learn that this program consumed

Table 5.9: SBA's Organization of Program Activities

Activity Group or Activity	Number of Activities
Capital Access	45
Government Contracting and Business Development (GCBD)	28
Entrepreneurial Development	11
Disaster Loan Making and Servicing	5
Advocacy Programs	
Office of Advocacy	1
National Women's Business Council	1
Ombudsman/Regulatory Fairness Board	1
Veterans Business Development Program	1
Regional & District Offices and Office of Field Operations	
Office of Field Operations	1
Field Offices—Management and Administration	1
Field Offices—Legal Services	1
Field Offices—Counseling and Training	5
Agency Management	8
President's Management Agenda	7
Total official agency activities	**116**

Source: *Office of the Chief Financial Officer.*

a large, disproportionate share of the field personnel's time. The FY 2004 Survey allocated $9.5 million in field costs to the BIC program, bringing the program's full cost to nearly $10 million.

In contrast, the Small Business Development Centers (SBDCs) comprise over 1,000 centers located at colleges and universities around the nation that provide technical assistance and regularized training and counseling to small business owners. The largest grant program within the SBA by far, these centers were funded by direct grants totaling $89.1 million in FY 2004. The FY 2004 Survey reports that $14.4 million of agency indirect costs were added to this direct grant amount, bringing the total cost of this program to $103.5 million. If we compare the administrative overhead rate for these two grant programs, defined here as all non-direct grant costs divided by total costs (administrative costs plus the grant amounts), we would find that the SBDC administrative overhead rate was 13.8 percent, while this rate for the BIC program was 96.3 percent! It is likely for this reason that the BIC program was not proposed in the FY 2005 and FY 2006 budgets.

Comparisons of this kind would not be possible without something like the ABC model. A prorated allocation method that used FTE as the main cost driver may come closest to replicating this result, but it is the Survey that allows employees to allocate their time to the various program activities, thereby gaining a clearer picture of how the agency's main resource, its personnel, are being deployed. Some might argue that the comparison of grant programs may reflect differences in costs covered by the grants (i.e., some grants cover more administrative costs than others), but this should not matter, as all costs—grant-based or not—are considered in the ABC model calculation of full program costs. Nevertheless, let's apply a similar analysis to the loan programs.

Before comparing SBA loan programs, one must address the fact that loan costs come in two forms: loan subsidy costs and administrative costs. Loan subsidy costs are the estimated costs of future defaults on loans made in a given fiscal year, which is required by the Federal Credit Reform Act. Administrative costs are the costs we have been addressing in this chapter, constituting all other costs of delivering program services. In costing loan program budgets for performance, one must consider the various and separable stages of the loan process and in which stage the activity belongs. For example, the cost of liquidating a loan that has defaulted has nothing to do with the costs of originating new loans. SBA is careful to make these distinctions when it develops unit cost measures. For our purposes here, it will suffice to demonstrate the uses of the information in aggregate form.

In FY 2004, the SBA's main loan program, Section 7(a) Loan Guarantee, provided $12.7 billion in lending at a total cost of $189 million, a total overhead rate of 1.5 percent. The subsidy costs were $100.6 million (or a .79 percent subsidy rate) and the administrative costs were $88.4 million (an administrative overhead rate of .7 percent). Compare this program with SBA's Section 7(m) Microloan program, which provides short-term loans of up to $35,000 to small businesses and not-for-profit child-care centers. In FY 2004, it provided $22.8 million in lending at a total cost of $24.9 million, a total overhead rate of 109 percent. The subsidy costs for the 7(m) program were $2.2 million (a subsidy rate of 9.55 percent) and the administrative costs were a staggering $22.7 million (an administrative overhead rate of 99.5 percent)!

The former loan program relies heavily on traditional banks to make the loans the government guarantees, and the latter also guarantees loans but relies on lending "intermediaries," which are community-based non-profit lenders, to make loans with an average amount of $10,500. These intermediaries also may be required to provide technical assistance to the borrowers. Nevertheless, the Microloan program has a subsidy cost 12 times that of SBA's main loan program, due to the higher expected defaults, but the administrative costs are 143 times the main loan program's costs. The information provided by the ABC model revealed these cost differences, providing agency senior managers with the kind of operational information they need to make improved trade-offs in resource allocation. Let's turn to how the model works.

How Does the ABC Model Work?

Two initial tasks must be accomplished before the ABC model performs its work. First, the activities of the agency must be defined and associated with a program. Table 5.9 lists the activity groups in which 116 defined activities fall. These activities include those supporting the PMA (five government-wide initiatives plus erroneous payments and SBA's unique component of e-government—the Business Gateway), and eight activities that make up the Agency Management group. These eight include activities such as general planning and management; information technology management (with six subcomponents); and procurement, contracting services, and other Office of Administration Services. Second, the Survey must be implemented using the activities defined to obtain the data that is then fed into the ABC model. Prior to implementing the Survey over a two-week window in April covering the first three quarters of the fiscal year, the CFO office obtains a payroll list from the human capital office and uses this as the basis for implementing the Survey. The FY 2004 Survey was completed by 96 percent of the agency's employees. SBA's resource base is dominated by personnel costs, which amount to 81 percent of the total operating costs of the agency. Figure 5.1 on page 210 depicts graphically how the ABC model works, which consists of three modules, one each for resources, activities, and cost objects.

Resources Module

Expenditure and obligation data for the resources module are derived from the general ledger accounts, which are organized by organization (major program office), program, and budget object class. These cost data fall into two categories: direct costs and agency-wide (indirect) costs. Direct costs include the compensation, benefits, training, supplies, equipment, contracted services, interest, penalties, and grant costs associated with a specific organizational unit. Within ABC, these costs are accounted for at the budget object class level separately for expenditures and obligations.

Figure 5.1: SBA's ABC Model and Flow of Costs

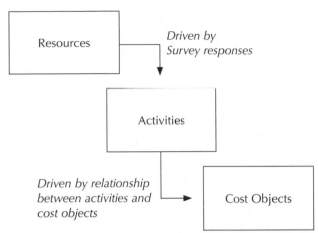

Agency-wide costs include rent, telecommunications, worker's and unemployment compensation, postage, and other indirect costs that are allocated within the ABC resources module based on the associated cost drivers listed in Table 5.10.

For its large field operations, SBA distinguishes these costs by the core programmatic activity of field employees (Field Offices—Counseling and Training) from those related to management and administration (Regional & District Offices and Office of Field Operations). There are two layers of indirect costs that must be allocated down to the district office level—field operations costs at headquarters and field-based administrative costs (at district and regional offices). At this point, district-level costs are fully loaded in the ABC resources module and ready to be linked to specific activities.

Activities Module

Within the resource module, cost drivers control the allocation of costs from agency-wide resource accounts to direct program accounts. This is where the ABC model relies on the prorated allocation method identified in the section "A Framework for Integrating Costs and Performance," and illustrated with the NASA case study. The activities module simply organizes the Survey responses on activities into the relevant organizational unit. In completing the Survey, employees determine the percentage of their time dedicated to various activities listed in the Survey. It is within these organizational units that cost objectives are found.

Once the activities have been defined and the Survey completed, the CFO office allocates the costs of each employee's salaries and benefits based on how that employee allocated his or her time to the activities. This is depicted in Figure 5.1 by the arrow from the Resources module to the Activities module. At this point, all costs have been linked to all activities, including headquarters overhead costs that are assigned to one of the PMA activities or agency management activities.

Cost Objects Module

Now the activities need to be linked to the cost objects (the arrow from Activities to Cost Objects in Figure 5.1). The cost objects are the programs across which all costs are divided and presented in SBA's congressional budget submission. Since SBA's activities are defined often no lower than the program organizational level, it is rather straightforward to directly link activity costs to the cost objects that are the program outputs. It is in this module that the final step is taken to allow SBA to link cost figures with the program's output, producing the integrated budget called for by the PMA. This cost-based performance information appears in the congressional budget justification and the Statement of Net Costs.

For example, from the FY 2006 congressional budget justification, we learn that in FY 2004, $189 million for the 7(a) loan program is related to SBA guaranteeing 20,631 loans, bringing the total unit cost to $9,161 per loan. However, these costs include loan making, servicing, liquidation, and other services related to the activities of the program office. So it is important to ensure that the unit costs are tied to the relevant activities

Table 5.10: SBA's Allocation Bases of Agency-Wide Costs

Allocated to HQ offices based on FTE
• Centralized training • Overnight shipping • Headquarters postage • Headquarters telecommunications • Printing
Allocated to all organizational units based on FTE
• FECA (Federal Employees' Compensation Act) liability • Performance awards • Reasonable accommodations • Unemployment compensation • Worker's compensation
Allocated to HQ offices based on square feet
• Rent
Included in overhead
• Credit cards • Interest charges • Database system
Allocated to loan-making activities based on dollars
• Credit reports
Charged back to cost source based on usage
• Relocation • Transit subsidy

Note: *Expenditure items allocated by cost driver in bold.*

Source: *Office of the Chief Financial Officer.*

in the Cost Objects module, and, in this case, the cost of guaranteeing new loans in a given fiscal year. Thus, we subtract from the $189 million program cost those costs related to loan servicing (because these relate to existing, not new loans), liquidations (these are the high costs of recovering assets on defaulted loans), and lender oversight (focused on lenders, not loans). The adjusted cost is reported as being $62.2 million, bringing us to a more accurate reflection of SBA's costs of guaranteeing a new 7(a) loan—$3,014 per loan.

The same is true for the grant programs. In FY 2006 congressional budget justification, SBA reports that the SBDCs trained 271,995 persons in 1,166,595 hours (or 4.29 hours per trainee) and counseled 170,742 in 898,174 hours (or 5.26 hours per person counseled). While the costs would have to be broken down by training versus counseling in the Cost Objects module to give a more accurate cost picture of each, in lieu of this SBA combines the trained and counseled into 442,737 "clients served," which translates into the average cost of $234 per client served. This number could serve as an efficiency benchmark against which to compare the costs of other entrepreneurial training programs. Another way to benchmark these services would be by hours, which totaled 2,064,769 hours (or 993 SBDC employees training and counseling every working day of the year) for an average cost of $50.15 per hour.

The ABC model provides SBA's senior managers with a powerful tool to better understand the costs of its operations and programs. It also provides the agency with the ability to measure a program's full and marginal costs, as well as efficiency, the costing requirements that led SBA to reach the highest standard in PMA BPI. While SBA's ABC model deploys both direct tracing and prorated allocation methods, it performs the key functions required in costing performance budgets. The following and final section offers recommendations based on the experiences and challenges found in the NASA and SBA experiences.

Recommendations

In the NASA and SBA case studies, the reader likely noticed some deviation from the conceptual approach presented in the section "A Framework for Integrating Costs and Performance." Deviations are expected as organizations must design cost accounting systems that fit their needs, organizational complexity, and budgets. This often requires using a variety or hybrid of techniques to trace costs to program outputs. This chapter showed how NASA incorporated elements of all three approaches suggested in FASAB Statement #4, and how SBA integrated the direct tracing and prorated allocation method. OMB will accept reasonable, practical approaches tailored to the agency's particular situation, but the conditions and capacities of the agency in question should be important considerations in which approach should be selected to accomplish these goals.

This chapter argues that the prorated allocation method is a low-cost way to meet the full costing requirements of FASAB Statement #4 and the PMA BPI initiative. While it is not the most accurate method of estimating costs, its accuracy is based on the agency's ability to select the most relevant cost drivers on which to base cost allocations. A disadvantage to using the prorated allocation method is that the accuracy may rely on assumptions that do not withstand scrutiny. For example, NASA allocates headquarters-based G&A costs to programs based on relative program share of the total agency budget. A relatively capital-intensive program, like the space shuttle program, would be allocated more indirect costs than a direct tracing or cause-and-effect approach would allocate. If G&A costs are driven more by the program share of agency employees than the budget share, then a more accurate allocation basis (i.e., cost driver) of G&A costs would be FTEs, as NASA does with its field-center-based G&A costs.

On the other hand, direct tracing often requires more employee involvement in the cost assignment function, and this could present problems that could do more harm than the potential bias in using weak cost drivers in a prorated allocation procedure. For example, SBA's Survey relies on self-reporting by employees across the agency about the allocation of their time to various activities. Even honest reporting might result in data irregularities that do not reflect accurately the allocation of personnel resources. An employee assigned to multiple program tasks could easily assess his time allocation erroneously, and the accumulation of this effect across employees could alter agency allocations in ways not considered or planned. Nevertheless, simple steps can be taken to validate employee responses, and, as one example, SBA has supervisors check the allocation of their employees' time. The point here is that direct tracing systems need to have the proper controls to ensure the validity of account access and postings, or using it can cause more harm than a less accurate prorated allocation.

The framework for integrating costs and performance presented here is an attempt to clarify the performance and cost components that constitute an "integrated" performance budget, and to show how to use such a framework when the performance measures are not quantifiable. To the extent that outcome-based performance measures are available, they can be used in this framework, and cost-performance integration is ideal. Reasonable people can disagree on the performance and cost distinctions made in this chapter, but they emanate directly from the FASAB Statement #4 definitions. This chapter should not be taken as the definitive treatment for the concepts raised, but taken as a guide on how to carefully construct usable (i.e., interpretable), cost-integrated performance measures called for in the PMA BPI initiative.

The recommendations listed below point to specific steps that agencies can take to improve their cost accounting policies and procedures. The hope is that they can help agencies successfully continue the long and persistent effort to manage government programs using cost and performance results as guides.

Recommendation 1: Align performance, costs, and accounts. Agencies should ensure alliance of program performance and goals with the guiding mission and overall agency strategy. To accomplish this, agencies must go through an exercise that carefully aligns, or maps, all program activities to one or more of the strategic goals of the agency. NASA accomplished this by organizing their programs into programmatic themes in their strategic plan, as well as aligning these more clearly within the mission directorates. SBA's strategic plan aligns agency activities with five strategic goals, one of which is specific to the PMA itself.

First, program performance measures must be synchronized with the mission and strategic goals. If these measures do not capture what is explicitly called for in the mission or strategic plan, then a logical narrative should be provided in the latter and annual performance plans to show the link between the two.

Next, program costs must be synchronized with the program performance measures above. Continuous or categorical measures can be used to develop this connection, but without this step, an agency will not be able to use the benefits of cost accounting.

Finally, agencies should follow examples from NASA and SBA in negotiating with their appropriations committees to better align the appropriation account structures to an agency budgetary structure that supports cost accounting and the efficiencies to be gained. Other agencies that have negotiated such changes include the Environmental Protection Agency, and the Departments of Justice, Labor, Transportation, and Veterans Affairs.

Recommendation 2: Build outcome-based measures for ideal cost-performance integration. Agencies should strive to develop the effectiveness, cost, and efficiency measures discussed above, because they are what allow senior and program managers to understand more precisely the relationship between budget costs and performance. To the extent that outcome measures can be quantified, the preferred measures of service effectiveness and service efficiency can be developed. These offer the best reflection of program performance, and the service efficiency measure, which is the full cost of producing a given outcome, can be used to evaluate the "bang for the buck" of various programs. Moreover, the computation of marginal costs, which is the cost associated with an increase in service impact, and the public sector price analogue, will allow the agency to scale its operation to an efficient level and understand the value of the services provided, and not just the budgeted amount.

If quantifiable outcome measures are not available, the agency could develop categorical outcome measures, as discussed above and shown in Table 5.3 (see page 190), or quantify reasonable output measures. When using output measures as proxies for outcomes, one should provide a logical narrative to clarify the relationship between the output being used and the service outcome desired, and that should be used but for lack of data. A logical narrative that holds up to scrutiny is a good indication that the output measure is a reasonable proxy. However, data on outcomes should still be pursued.

Recommendation 3: Develop a cost allocation method that fits the organizational design. Agencies should develop a cost allocation method that models downward cost flow, but is consistent with the organizational structure and how programs are situated within that structure. Even though NASA and SBA each have a substantial field presence, NASA's centers provide unique capabilities and operate programs and projects that in some cases cut across themes managed by mission directorates. Its Full Cost initiative recognized this complexity by focusing on directly attributing as much costs as feasible to the program home through its new integrated financial management system, regardless of center location, and then racked up indirect costs in terms of G&A costs (Corporate and Center) and service pool costs.

SBA's organizational structure is rather straightforward, and its programs are labor-intensive and delivered by district offices and other network partners that essentially do the same thing at each location across the nation. With just 3,500 employees and a small budget, SBA implemented a low-cost survey-based tool to collect information vital to understanding how the agency's resources are being used.

The structure of the cost allocation model should be dependent on the organizational structure. That is, take the organization chart for the agency, identify the programs that make up the agencies' service menu, and organize non-program activities into indirect cost categories that share the same cost drivers. G&A costs will exist at different levels in the organization chart, but unless they can be directly attributed to program activities, they should be lumped together in a helpful way. Human capital, procurement, and facilities management are the main examples of such indirect costs, and would likely make up separate categories given different likely cost drivers. The programs' share of these cost drivers agency-wide (for example, budget, personnel, and/or square feet) will then determine how these indirect costs will be allocated.

Recommendations

1. Align performance, costs, and accounts.

2. Build outcome-based measures for ideal cost-performance integration.

3. Develop a cost allocation method that fits the organizational design.

4. Supplement existing systems to support performance costing.

5. Create incentives to improve effectiveness and efficiency.

Recommendation 4: Supplement existing systems to support performance costing. Agencies should start modestly and improve budget-performance integration capacity over time. The biggest reason for such an approach is the cost of implementing new cost accounting systems to handle the tasks required for good cost management. Too many agencies have tried and failed to implement financial management systems, as the requirements for such systems are still developing for federal government use. The agency can, however, build modest subsidiary systems that are FFMIA compliant for the purpose of allocating indirect costs to direct cost centers. NASA and SBA took the two extremes. NASA is still implementing its state-of-the-art integrated financial management system, and the SBA only tweaks its very modest survey tool every year. Consult the JFMIP requirements for managerial cost accounting before signing on the dotted line.

Recommendation 5: Create incentives to improve effectiveness and efficiency. Agencies should create incentives for support and program managers to become more efficient on their own. Full cost at NASA now gives program managers authority over the use of a key resource: personnel. By making direct personnel costs the program's responsibility, and not a separate budgetary line item, NASA created an incentive for program managers to reveal their true need for personnel resources. By "taxing" the programs for the agency's indirect costs, NASA created an incentive for program managers to question support managers about the G&A and other costs being attributed to programs, but not controlled by the programs. In general, full cost at NASA creates the incentives for program and support managers to behave more as market-based producers, revealing their true need for certain resources, and paying for what used to be "free" from a budgetary standpoint.

A competitive marketplace works so efficiently because Adam Smith's "invisible hand" guides and sorts market transactions such that the price a consumer pays for a good or service is equal not only to the benefit gained from consuming it, but also to the marginal cost of producing the last unit. At SBA, full cost measures revealed an allocation of key personnel resources that could not be justified on mission-based or policy grounds. Developing them and using them in this simple way alone can help agencies better understand how resources are being used. Publishing the full costs of programs in the congressional submission and financial statements ensures that congressional and taxpayer choices are better informed, and this creates incentives for efficiency gains within the political process.

Development of the key effectiveness, cost, and efficiency measures will help manifest these incentives by providing the information needed to make better allocation decisions. In other words, these measures provide the best analogue to market prices available in the public sector. They allow senior managers, members of Congress, and taxpayers to effectively "value shop" the menu of government services. This chapter does not suggest that costing performance budgets will replace powerful political forces in the budget process. But with integrated cost-effectiveness measures in place, agencies will be in a better position to defend their budget submissions, to satisfy the PMA BPI criteria and "get to green," and to create the incentives for program and support managers to act more efficiently on their own.

Acknowledgments

This chapter would not have been possible without the help of a number of people within the subject agencies. In particular, I am grateful to CFO Gwendolyn Sykes at NASA, and former SBA Administrator Hector V. Barreto and SBA CFO Jennifer Main, for the access they provided me to do research for this chapter and for the leadership they exhibited in performance budgeting reform. I especially thank Mina Sumpter for her work developing SBA's ABC model, Tim Owen for his efforts to make the concepts of full cost workable at NASA, and both of them for helping me summarize their excellent work into this chapter.

Endnotes

1. See the sidebar on page 172 for a full list of acronyms and abbreviations used in this chapter.

2. See the PART guidance at http://www.whitehouse.gov/omb/part/index.html.

3. This information can be found at the White House website: http://www.whitehouse.gov/results/agenda/getting_to_green.html.

4. For a review of the Defense Department's PPBS reform, see Jones, L. R. and Jerry L. McCaffery, "Reform of the Planning, Programming, Budgeting System, and Management Control in the U.S. Department of Defense: Insights from Budget Theory," *Public Budgeting & Finance,* Vol. 25, No. 3 (September 2005).

5. The CFO Act established the CFO position in 23 major agencies, and GMRA expanded this requirement to all federal agencies. The CFO Act is Public Law (P.L.) 101-576. GMRA is P.L. 103-356.

6. The CFO Act.

7. The FASAB was established in October of 1990, and the CFO Act was signed into law by President George H. W. Bush on November 15, 1990.

8. For a review of GPRA, see McNab, Robert M. and Francois Melese, "Implementing the GPRA: Examining the Prospects for Performance Budgeting in the Federal Government," Public Budgeting & Finance, Vol. 23, No. 2 (June 2003).

9. GPRA of 1993, Public Law 103-62, Section 306(a)(3) and Section 115(a)(3).

10. For financial management standards, see JFMIP's Core Financial System Requirements at http://www.jfmip.gov/jfmip/fsio_systemrequirements.shtml. For accounting standards, see the Generally Accepted Accounting Principles (GAAP) at http://www.fasab.gov/accepted.html, as well as the FASAB statements at http://www.fasab.gov/pdffiles/vol1v4.pdf. For the USSGL, see http://www.fms.treas.gov/ussgl/index.html.

11. Other legislation reviewed in GAO (1998) are, chronologically: Inspector General Act (1978), Prompt Payment Act and Federal Manager's Financial Integrity Act (1982), Computer Security Act (1987), Federal Credit Reform Act (1990), Paperwork Reduction Act (1995), and Clinger-Cohen Act and Debt Collection Improvement Act (1996).

12. See FASAB's "Overview of Federal Accounting Concepts and Standards: Report #1" at http://www.fasab.gov/reports.html.

13. Other major functions include reporting and general ledger, payment, receipt, and funds management.

14. A working capital, or revolving, fund is relevant with enterprise-like business units that collect significant amounts of reimbursables and other revenue.

15. For the relevant financial management system requirements to support performance costing, see JFMIP's guidance at http://www.jfmip.gov/jfmip/download/systemreqs/mancostsysreq.pdf.

16. For the seminal treatment of the impact of public service cost environments, see Bradford, David F., Robert A. Malt, and Wallace E. Oates (1969), "The Rising Cost of Local Public Services: Some Evidence and Reflections," *National Tax Journal,* Vol. 22, June, pp. 185–202.

17. See Public Law 85-568. For a history of the agency, see Bilstein, Roger E., *Orders of Magnitude: A History of NACA and NASA, 1915–1990,* NASA History Series, Office of Management, Scientific, and Technical Information Division, Washington, D.C., 1989. This monograph is published online at http://www.hq.nasa.gov/office/pao/History/SP-4406/contents.html. For a history of space policy, see Lambright, W. Henry, ed. *Space Policy in the 21st Century.* Baltimore: Johns Hopkins University Press, 2003.

18. This organizational structure is based on the Fiscal Year 2006 budget submission, and has been changing recently due in part to organizational changes in response to the new exploration mission and the change in administration. The 18 themes in FY05 have now been condensed into 12 themes, with the Science Directorate combining eight themes into three; the Exploration Directorate combining five themes into four; and Space Operations, Aeronautics Research, and Education remaining the same, except that Education is no longer a directorate, and is listed as a function of the administrator's office.

19. NASA makes the following distinction between programs and projects. A program represents one or more projects that address a common theme or higher-level priority activity. A project is an element of a program that is separately managed, separately budgeted, uniquely identified within the budgeting and accounting system, and generally the lowest level at which a center will budget and account for its costs. For simplicity, this chapter uses "program" to represent both.

20. Budget figures are outlays from the FY 2005 Budget of the U.S. Government, Historical Tables, Table 4.1.

21. See GAO. 2003a. "Business Modernization: NASA Challenges in Managing Its Integrated Financial Management Program," GAO-04-255 (Washington, D.C.: Nov. 2003); and GAO. 2003b. "Business Modernization: NASA's Integrated Financial Management Program Does Not Fully Address Agency's External Reporting Issues." GAO-04-151 (Washington, D.C.: Nov. 2003) for a discussion of these challenges.

22. For a more detailed discussion of the appropriation account structure changes, see Appendix V in GAO (2005).

23. This category was first given the unofficial and oxymoronic name, "unfunded FTE," which reflected their unassigned status rather than whether they were being paid.

24. Definitions for these full cost concepts are taken from NASA's Financial Management Requirements (FMR), which is the primary financial management policy document. Volume 7 of this policy document covers costs, and Chapter 3 of this volume covers cost definitions.

25. This simplified example assumes that Corporate G&A costs are incurred on an even basis throughout the fiscal year. Thus, $73.5 million is 1/12 of the $882 million figure for FY 2005.

26. The Center G&A costs for the Jet Propulsion Lab are not provided, as it is technically a Federally Funded Research and Development Center. This means that its funds are treated as a grant, and therefore are not broken out in the same terms as the other traditional centers.

27. The Independent Technical Authority/Safety & Mission Assurance service pools are like G&A costs in that they are non-negotiable. These were developed in response to recommendations made by the Columbia Accident Investigation Board. Wind Tunnel service pools exist only at three of NASA's centers (Ames, Glenn, and Langley).

28. For discussions on SBA's service delivery and management challenges, see GAO. 2001b. "Small Business Administration: Current Structure Presents Challenges for Service Delivery." GAO-02-17. (Washington, D.C.: Oct. 2001); and GAO. 2001a. "Major Management Challenges and Program Risks: Small Business Administration." GAO-01-260 (Washington, D.C.: Jan. 2001).

29. Discretionary budget authority is presented here to avoid a presentation of outlays that swing substantially and therefore would be misleading. For example, outlays were disproportionately large in FY 2004 as a result of investment program losses, and outlays were negative in other years due to the nature of SBA's loan programs and the associated permanent indefinite budget authority.

30. These increases may seem counter intuitive given the agency's declining discretionary budget base. These are largely the result of improvements in forecasting the defaults on loan commitments and in loan program design over the last five years.

Bibliography

Behn, Robert D. 2004. "Performance Leadership: 11 Better Practices That Can Ratchet Up Performance." (Washington, D.C.: IBM Center for The Business of Government, May).

Bilstein, Roger E., *Orders of Magnitude: A History of NACA and NASA, 1915–1990*, NASA History Series, Office of Management, Scientific, and Technical Information Division, Washington, D.C., 1989.

Bradford, David F., Robert A. Malt, and Wallace E. Oates (1969), "The Rising Cost of Local Public Services: Some Evidence and Reflections," *National Tax Journal*, Vol. 22, June, pp. 185–202.

The Chief Financial Officers Act of 1990, Public Law 101-576.

The Federal Financial Management Improvement Act of 1996, Public Law 104-208.

GAO. 2005. *Performance Budgeting: Efforts to Restructure Budgets to Better Align Resources with Performance*. GAO-05-117SP.

GAO. 2003a. *Business Modernization: NASA Challenges in Managing Its Integrated Financial Management Program*. GAO-04-255.

GAO. 2003b. *Business Modernization: NASA's Integrated Financial Management Program Does Not Fully Address Agency's External Reporting Issues*. GAO-04-151.

GAO. 2001a. *Major Management Challenges and Program Risks: Small Business Administration*. GAO-01-260.

GAO. 2001b. *Small Business Administration: Current Structure Presents Challenges for Service Delivery*. GAO-02-17.

GAO. 1999. *Performance Budgeting: Initial Experiences Under the Results Act in Linking Plans With Budgets*. GAO/AIMD/GGD-99-67.

GAO. 1998. *Managing for Results: The Statutory Framework for Performance-Based Management and Accountability.* GAO/GGD/AIMD-98-52.

The Government Management Reform Act of 1994, Public Law 103-356.

The Government Performance and Results Act of 1993, Public Law 103-62.

Hatry, Harry P., Elaine Morley, Shelli B. Rossman, and Joseph S. Wholey. 2004. "How Federal Programs Use Outcome Information: Opportunities for Federal Managers" (Washington, D.C.: IBM Center for The Business of Government, February, 2nd edition).

Joint Financial Management Improvement Project. 2001. *Core Financial System Requirements*. JFMIP-SR-02-01.

Joint Financial Management Improvement Project. 1998. *System Requirements for Managerial Cost Accounting*. FFMSR-8.

Jones, L. R., and Jerry L. McCaffery, "Reform of the Planning, Programming, Budgeting System, and Management Control in the U.S. Department of Defense: Insights from Budget Theory," *Public Budgeting & Finance*, Vol. 25, No. 3 (September 2005).

Joyce, Philip G. 2003. "Linking Performance and Budgeting: Opportunities in the Federal Budget Process" (Washington, D.C.: IBM Center for The Business of Government, May).

Kamensky, John M., Albert Morales, and Mark A. Abramson. 2005. "From 'Useful Measures' to 'Measures Used.' " Chapter One in *Managing for Results 2005*, John M. Kamensky and Albert Morales, eds. (Lanham, Md.: Rowman & Littlefield).

Kelley, Joseph T. 1984. *Costing Government Services: A Guide for Decision Making*. Washington D.C.: Government Finance Officers Association.

Lambright, W. Henry, ed. *Space Policy in the 21st Century*. Baltimore: Johns Hopkins University Press, 2003.

McNab, Robert M., and Francois Melese, "Implementing the GPRA: Examining the Prospects for Performance Budgeting in the Federal Government," *Public Budgeting & Finance*, Vol. 23, No. 2 (June 2003).

The National Aeronautics and Space Act, Public Law 85-568.

Risher, Howard. 2004. "Pay for Performance: A Guide for Federal Managers" (Washington, D.C.: IBM Center for the Business of Government, November).

About the Contributors

Lloyd A. Blanchard is an Assistant Professor of Public Administration at the Maxwell School of Citizenship and Public Affairs at Syracuse University. His public sector experience includes serving as senior advisor for financial management at the National Aeronautics and Space Administration, chief operating officer of the Small Business Administration, and associate director for the Office of Management and Budget. Prior to his time in government, he served on the faculty of the Daniel J. Evans School of Public Affairs at the University of Washington, where he was named Teacher of the Year in 2000 and earned the Dean's Service Award for restructuring the school's budgeting curriculum.

Professor Blanchard's research interests are varied, ranging from government management to social policy issues. His research in performance budgeting is informed by his efforts leading NASA and SBA to become government-wide leaders in this area. His research in minority- and women-owned small business access to credit is motivated in part by his accomplishments at the SBA, which were honored by the Minority Business Professional Network in naming him one of the "Fifty Influential Minorities in Business in 2003."

His publications include a co-authored article, "Market-Based Reforms in Government: Toward a Social Subcontract?" in *Administration and Society*, and a co-authored chapter in the *Handbook on Taxation* entitled "Tax Policy and School Finance." His dissertation, *School Segregation, Social Capital, and Educational Costs*, examines the educational costs of performance accountability that take into account cultural, peer, and neighborhood influences that mediate disadvantaged children's cognitive development.

Professor Blanchard has a B.A. in economics from the University of Texas at Austin, and a B.A. in political science from the University of Texas at San Antonio. He earned his M.P.A. and Ph.D. in public administration from the Maxwell School of Citizenship and Public Affairs at Syracuse University.

Jonathan D. Breul is a Partner, IBM Global Business Services, and Senior Fellow, IBM Center for The Business of Government, where he provides consulting services and cutting-edge thought leadership to top political and career employees throughout the federal government. Formerly senior advisor to the deputy director for management in the Office of Management and Budget in the Executive Office of the President, Mr. Breul served as OMB's senior career executive with primary responsibility for government-wide general management policies. He helped develop the President's Management Agenda, was instrumental in establishing the President's Management Council, and championed efforts to integrate performance information with the budget process. He led the development and government-wide implementation of the Government Performance and Results Act. In addition to his OMB activities, he helped Senator John Glenn (D-Ohio) launch the Chief Financial Officers (CFO) Act. Mr. Breul is an elected fellow and member of the Board of Trustees of the National Academy of Public Administration and an adjunct professor at Georgetown University's Graduate Public Policy Institute.

Philip Joyce is Professor of Public Policy and Public Administration at The George Washington University. Professor Joyce's teaching and research interests include public budgeting, performance measurement, and intergovernmental relations. He is the co-author of *Government Performance: Why Management Matters* with Patricia Ingraham and Amy Kneedler Donahue (Johns Hopkins Press, 2003) and *Public Budgeting Systems*, 7th Edition, with Robert Lee and Ronald Johnson (Jones and Bartlett Publishers, 2004). The research on federal agencies published in the Johns Hopkins book was supported by a $1.2 million grant from The Pew Charitable Trusts. Dr. Joyce has also authored numerous articles and book chapters, appearing in outlets such as the *Public Administration Review, Public Budgeting and Finance, Administration and Society*, and the *Handbook of Government Budgeting*. His 1993 article "Using Performance Measures for Federal Budgeting: Proposals and Prospects" was reprinted in *Classics of Public Administration* (1997).

Professor Joyce is associate editor of *Public Budgeting and Finance*, is past president of the American Association for Budget and Program Analysis, and is immediate past chair of the American Society for Public Administration's Center on Accountability and Performance (CAP). He has taught in M.P.A. programs at the Maxwell School of Citizenship and Public Affairs at Syracuse University, the University of Kentucky, and American University. Dr. Joyce also has 12 years of public sector work experience, including four years with the Illinois Bureau of the Budget and five years with the United States Congressional Budget Office. He has consulted with several organizations, including the World Bank, the International Monetary Fund, and the Council for Excellence in Government. He has also testified before the Congress concerning budget process reform issues.

Dr. Joyce earned a B.A. in history from Thiel College, an M.P.A. from Penn State University, and a Ph.D. in public administration from Syracuse University.

Julia Melkers is Associate Professor of Public Administration in the College of Urban Planning and Public Affairs at the University of Illinois at Chicago. Dr. Melkers' work addresses the development and use of performance measurement and evaluation processes in public organizations. Her teaching and research interests are in the areas of performance measurement, public management, and science and technology-based economic development.

In conducting her research, Dr. Melkers has worked with public organizations at the local, state, and federal levels. She has conducted performance-measurement-related work for the National Research Council; the states of Georgia, Maine, Rhode Island, and Alaska; the City of Atlanta and the Atlanta Urban League; as well as the countries of Mexico and Latvia. Her funded research has included projects funded by the National Science Foundation ("Science and Technology-Based Economic Development Programs in the States: A Study of Evaluation Efforts"); the American Association for the Advancement of Science ("Research Competitiveness in EPSCoR States: Information Needs of Legislators and University Researchers"); and the Sloan Foundation ("Using Performance Measurement in State and Local Governments"). She is currently involved in a project with the Urban Institute and the Center for What Works to address common performance measures for the nonprofit sector.

Dr. Melkers has published extensively on the development and use of performance measures in state and local governments, as well as the legislative basis for performance measurement in the states. Her publications may be found in journals such as *Public Administration Review, Urban Studies Review, Policy Studies Journal, Public Budgeting and Finance, Journal of Public Administration Research and Theory, Journal of Technology Transfer,* and *Evaluation and Program Planning.*

Professor Melkers received a B.A. and an M.P.A. from the University of Wisconsin-Milwaukee, and a Ph.D. from The Maxwell School at Syracuse University.

Carl Moravitz is a Managing Consultant, IBM Global Business Services. He is a recognized expert in the federal budget process with over 30 years of experience in managing and directing budgets, including multiple and geographic financial plans for large and diverse organizations. He served as budget director for the Department of the Treasury and the Internal Revenue Service, and deputy director for resource management at the Voice of America. He was an integral player in the implementation of the President's

Management Agenda budget and performance integration initiative, leading systems and structural changes in resource allocation to better drive decision making. His leadership in performance budgeting includes the development of a prototype Results Act–compliant performance budget that has served as the model for the presentation of integrated budget and performance plans to OMB and Congress. While at the Treasury Department, he was a key player (and member) in the establishment of the department's corporate investment review board, overseeing investments across the department's 14 bureaus. He was a member of that board during his 20 months as acting deputy assistant secretary for strategy and budget.

Burt Perrin has over 30 years' practical experience internationally in evaluation, policy and program development, and strategic planning on behalf of governments at all levels, international organizations, non-governmental organizations (NGOs), and the private sector. Perrin, who is based in France, places strong emphasis on taking a practical approach, so that evaluation is most likely to result in action. He is particularly known for his ability to identify and synthesize information that cuts across topic areas, jurisdictions, and discrete program boundaries.

His clients include the European Commission, various national and local governments, United Nations agencies, the World Bank, the International Labour Organization, the Organization for Economic Cooperation and Development, NGOs, and private sector organizations. Perrin is recognized internationally as a leader in the evaluation field. He is frequently called upon to make presentations and present workshops around the world, and he provides editorial assistance to a number of academic journals. He is a member of the board of directors and secretary general of the European Evaluation Society, a founding member and fellow of the Canadian Evaluation Society, and a founding member of the Société française d'Evaluation, as well as actively involved with other organizations, such as the International Evaluation Research Group (INTEVAL).

Examples of recent publications include "How Evaluation Can Help Make Knowledge Management Real," "How to—and How Not to—Evaluate Innovation," "Making Yourself and Evaluation Useful," "Implementing the Vision: Addressing Challenges to Results-Focused Management and Budgeting," and "Effective Use and Misuse of Performance Measurement." Perrin is also co-editor of a forthcoming book examining how accountability mechanisms, including the roles of audit and evaluation, can support rather than inhibit innovation and effectiveness in modern, outcome-oriented public sector organizations.

Perrin earned an honors B.A. in psychology from Northwestern University and an M.A. in organizational and social psychology from York University.

Katherine G. Willoughby is Professor of Public Administration and Urban Studies at the Andrew Young School of Policy Studies at Georgia State University in Atlanta, Georgia. Her teaching and research focuses on budgeting, financial management, and public policy development in American governments. She has conducted extensive research on state and local government budgeting with specific attention to executive and legislative budget processes, the work of budget examiners, and state budget reform systems. Past research and applied projects include an assessment of the development of immunization registries in American state governments and their implications for individual privacy; analysis of performance-based budgeting reforms in the 50 states (research funded by the Alfred P. Sloan Foundation); and assistance with the development of an applied knowledge assessment tool for local government managers. She is currently an academic partner with the Government Performance Project—a research project funded by the Pew Charitable Trusts to support the advancement of management capacity and performance in U.S. state governments.

Professor Willoughby has conducted numerous training sessions for federal, provincial, and local budget and finance ministers from around the world. She is treasurer for the Association for Budgeting and Financial Management, a professional association for academics and practitioners of public budgeting and finance. She is the author of numerous articles, book chapters, and reports regarding public budgeting, financial management, public policy, and administration. Her book with Dr. Kurt Thurmaier of Iowa State University, *Policy and Politics in State Budgeting*, examines the relationship between budgeting and policy development as seen through the eyes of budget analysts employed in executive budget offices in 11 U.S. state governments in the South and Midwest.

Professor Willoughby received a bachelor of science degree in psychology from Duke University, her M.P.A. degree from North Carolina State University, and her doctoral degree in public administration from the University of Georgia.

About the IBM Center for
The Business of Government

Through research stipends and events, the IBM Center for The Business of Government stimulates research and facilitates discussion of new approaches to improving the effectiveness of government at the federal, state, local, and international levels.

The Center is one of the ways that IBM Global Business Services seeks to advance knowledge on how to improve public sector effectiveness. The IBM Center focuses on the future of the operation and management of the public sector.

Research stipends of $20,000 are awarded competitively to outstanding scholars in academic and nonprofit institutions across the United States. Each award winner is expected to produce a 30- to 40-page research report in one of the areas presented on pages 231–233. Reports will be published and disseminated by the Center.

Research Stipend Guidelines

Who is Eligible?
Individuals working in:
- Universities
- Nonprofit organizations
- Journalism

Description of Research Stipends
Individuals receiving research stipends will be responsible for producing a 30- to 40-page research report in one of the areas presented on pages 231–233.

The manuscript must be submitted no later than six months after the start of the project. Recipients will select the start and end dates of their research project. The reports should be written for government leaders and should provide practical knowledge and insights.

Size of Research Stipends
$20,000 for each research paper

Who Receives the Research Stipends?
Unless otherwise requested, individuals will receive the research stipends.

Application Process
Interested individuals should submit:
- A three-page description of the proposed research—please include a 100-word executive summary describing the following: (a) purpose, (b) methodology, and (c) result of the proposed project
- A résumé (no more than three pages)

Application Deadlines
There will be two funding cycles annually, with deadlines of:
- November 1
- March 1
  Applicants will be informed of a decision regarding their proposal no later than eight weeks after the deadlines. Applications must be received online or postmarked by the above dates.

Submitting Applications
Online:
businessofgovernment.org/apply
Hard copy—send to:
Mark A. Abramson
Executive Director
IBM Center for The Business of Government
1301 K Street, NW
Fourth Floor, West Tower
Washington, DC 20005

Research Areas: Crosscutting Management Issues

- **Collaboration, Transformation, and Leadership:** Areas of interest include the enhancing of public sector performance, service delivery improvement, profiles of outstanding government public sector leaders, collaboration between organizations, change management, and managerial flexibility. We are also interested in models for effective integration of organizations, processes, and techniques.
- **Competition, Choice, and Incentives:** Areas of interest include contracting out, competitive sourcing, outsourcing, shared services, privatization, public-private partnerships, government franchising, and contract management.
- **E-Government:** Areas of interest include government to business, government to citizen, government to employees, capital investment strategies, customer relationship management, enterprise architecture, supply chain management, and e-government on demand.
- **Financial Management:** Areas of interest include asset management, auditing, cost accounting, erroneous payment, financial and resource analysis, internal controls, risk management and modeling, systems modernization, and financial management on demand.
- **Human Capital Management:** Areas of interest include the alignment of human capital with organizational objectives; workforce planning and deployment; the recruitment, retraining, and retention of talent; pay for performance; leadership and knowledge management; e-learning; workforce development; workforce protection; and human capital on demand.
- **Managing for Performance and Results:** Areas of interest include strategic planning, performance measurement and evaluation, balanced scorecards and performance reporting, performance budgeting, and program delivery.

Topics of Special Interest 2006–2007

- **Innovation:** The IBM Center is interested in examining how to bring innovation to the operations and management of the public sector. Specifically, we are interested in the following types of innovation:
  1. *Business model innovation:* Innovation in the structure and/or financial model of programs, service delivery or support operations, such as the creation of the Department of Defense Business Transformation Agency;

2. *Operational innovation:* Innovation that improves the effectiveness and efficiency of core processes and functions, such as the application of Six Sigma; and

3. *Product and service innovation:* Innovation applied to programs or services or citizen-facing activities, such as the introduction of e-filing by the Internal Revenue Service.

- **Managing Change:** Organizations at all levels are increasingly operating in a volatile environment and strive for stability, whether that is good or bad for an organization. How can organizational tolerance for change be assessed and influenced? How much change is too much for an organization to effectively bear? Can "organizational anxiety" be reduced?

- **Networks—Organizing for Routine and Non-Routine Problems:** Traditional public institutions are organized in hierarchies. This has worked well in delivering routine services in stable environments. However, agencies increasingly face difficult, non-routine problems that demand networked solutions. Some public problems rely on distributed organizations (mixed hierarchical and networked approaches)—for example, homeland security, law enforcement, and public health. These increasingly important challenges require managers to weave strong hierarchies into effective networks. The complexity of this task presents difficult management challenges. We are interested in governance models for these networks that allow public sector organizations to effectively meet new and unforeseen challenges.

- **Shared Services—Beyond the Back Office:** The IBM Center is interested in organizations that have implemented enterprise-wide shared services that provide the basis for significant enterprise integration and transparency. What are the leading best practices and critical lessons learned in this area?

Research Areas: Program and Mission Issues

- **Defense Warfighter Operations:** The principles of network-centric operations are transforming warfighter operations. Providing interoperability within and between military forces is critical in today's world of asymmetric warfare and the increased focus on coalition operations. Areas of interest include command and control (C2), battlespace awareness, force application, force protection and focused logistics within the war theater, and the connection of back-office operations to the battlespace. Seamless integration of telecommunications and technologies, the application of service-oriented architectures, and open standards are critical to this transformation. How can improvements be made across operational stovepiped programs? How can collaboration and C2 effectively co-exist and complement each other within the warfighter domain?

- **Homeland Security:** The mission of the Department of Homeland Security (DHS) is to safeguard the U.S. homeland and critical infrastructures from terrorist threats of any nature. The interrelationships, dependencies, and missions of several diverse federal agencies are now being integrated to ensure effectiveness and efficiency under a single strategic umbrella, with the objective of winning the global war on terrorism. What models and innovations are required to win this war? In particular, what can be done to increase national preparedness for natural and man-made disasters, strengthen border security, improve maritime security, increase information sharing, or increase the efficiency of DHS operations?

  Topic of Special Interest—**Immigration:** Areas of interest include viability of a fee-based temporary worker program, examination of immigration programs worldwide, and efficient models for the detention and removal of illegal aliens.

- **Customs, Ports, and Borders:** Around the world, the threat of terrorism, illegal immigration, and challenges stemming from the globalization of commerce are reshaping the fundamental nature of national borders and how they are managed. What innovations are taking place in managing these challenges? Are there new technologies that can be applied? As border security increases, what models need to be developed for the detention and removal of illegal immigrants? How can different models of immigration reform be integrated with economic needs?

  Topic of Special Interest—**Disaster Response and Recovery:** What can federal and local disaster response organizations learn from the private sector about pre-positioning assets, managing assets, and leveraging the infrastructure of existing corporate or government supply chains?

- **Social Services:** Tightening budgets, demands for citizen-centric services, an increasing focus on accountability, collaborative delivery models, and a constantly changing legal and regulatory environment combine to create complex challenges for social service delivery organizations serving the needy and vulnerable. Are there new organizational models? Are there best practices in one field that can be adapted elsewhere? Are there new ways of delivering services?